What People Are Saying about

HOW NOW SHALL WE LIVE?

"A bracing challenge—just what the Christian church needs to hear in the new millennium. A very powerful book."—**The Honorable Jack Kemp**

"*How Now Shall We Live?* is truly inspiring for those who want to restore to our culture the values that made America great. It reminds us that we must not only defend what we believe, but also inspire others to give witness to the truth alongside us."—**The Honorable Tom DeLay**, Majority Whip, United States House of Representatives

"The singular pleasure that comes from it is its absolute—learned—refusal to give any quarter to the dogged materialists who deny any possibility that there was a creator around the corner. This is a substantial book, but the reader never tires, as one might from a catechistic marathon. The arguments are cogently and readably presented."—**William F. Buckley** in *National Review*

"The newest—and certainly the most important—of Charles Colson's books . . . the essence of this book is that the Christian faith is not just a theory, not just a system, not just a framework. It is an all-consuming way of life, robustly applicable to every minute of every day of the rest of your life."—*World*

"There is something wrong with the historical development of the evangelical mind, . . . a lopsidedness, a prodigious development of one divine gift coupled with the atrophy of another. . . . We know a great deal about saving grace, but next to nothing—though it is one of our doctrines—about common grace. The ambition of Charles Colson and Nancy Pearcey is to do something about this lopsidedness, to strike a blow against the scandal of the evangelical mind. . . . A highly intelligent book, it is not ashamed to speak to ordinary folk."—*First Things*

"*How Now Shall We Live?* is brilliantly lit by its in-depth and succinct diagnosis of the modern mentality . . . an intelligent and thoroughgoing critique from a Scriptural perspective, of the American/Western culture. . . . The book is a veritable mosaic of precious intellectual gems, artistically designed by Charles Colson and Nancy Pearcey. . . . This book is a virtual 'must' for the thinking Orthodox reader."—*DOXA*, a quarterly review serving the Orthodox Church

"A magnum opus in the best Schaefferian tradition. It is clearly intended to be . . . a handbook for today's Christian. . . . The authors presuppose that Christianity is more than just a religion of personal salvation: it involves a total world-and-life view."—*Christianity Today*

"A very good and much needed book. . . . Colson argues that Christianity isn't a private faith but a public worldview that, for believers, permeates politics, the arts, education, science and culture."—*Insight*

An "elegantly written tutorial on adopting a biblical worldview and the discipline of thinking Christianly."—*Good News*

"I'd like to recommend a book. It's *How Now Shall We Live?* by Charles Colson, the Watergate guy who got religion while in prison. . . . Now I don't agree with everything Colson says, but the importance of the book is that it raises a question every American ought to face and then answer to his or her own satisfaction: What is your world view?"—**Charley Reese,** nationally syndicated columnist

One of "Ten Books Every Preacher Should Read This Year."—*Preaching*

"Deeply troubled by the lack of biblical literacy within the American Church, this is Colson's heroic effort to enable believers to accept the importance of having a biblical worldview and devoting themselves to adopting such a life perspective. . . . This book provides a wealth of insight into how we may effectively challenge the post-Christian, post-modern culture in which we live."
—*The Barna Report*

"Colson and Pearcey aren't talking about influencing business, politics and culture—they want it transformed through a coherent Christian world view. Their book will challenge every Christian leader to make an honest assessment about his or her commitment to use leadership gifts in the new millennium to the cause of Christ."—*Christian Management Report*

"Colson and Pearcey challenge the church to stay on the front lines. Believing that America is on the verge of a great spiritual breakthrough, the authors want to equip readers to show the world that Christianity is a life system that *works* in every area—family relationships, education, science, and popular culture."—*Virtue*

"A radical challenge to all Christians to understand biblical faith as an entire world view, a perspective on all of life. Through inspiring teaching and true stories, Colson discusses how to expose the false views and values of modern culture, how to live more fulfilling and satisfying lives in line with the way God created us to live—and more."—*Youthworker*

[In developing and implementing an organizational learning strategy and integrating it with their organizational practices] "When it came to selecting materials, your *How Now Shall We Live?* was at the top of the list. To our minds this is now the best introduction to a Christian worldview and Christian cultural engagement available in English. At least in our organization, *How Now Shall We Live?* should become an indispensable resource."—*Christian Labour Association of Canada*

1999 Books of the Year—Award of Merit—*Christianity Today*

THE
CHRISTIAN
IN
TODAY'S
CULTURE

DEVELOPING
A CHRISTIAN
WORLDVIEW OF

THE
CHRISTIAN
IN
TODAY'S
CULTURE

CHARLES
COLSON

AND NANCY PEARCEY

Tyndale House Publishers, Inc.
Wheaton, Illinois

Library of Congress Cataloging-in-Publication Data

Colson, Charles W.
  The Christian in today's culture / Charles Colson and Nancy Pearcey.
    p. cm. — (Developing a Christian worldview)
  ISBN 0-8423-5587-1 (softcover)
  1. Christianity and culture. I. Pearcey, Nancy. II. Title.

BR115.C8 C545 2001
261—dc21   2001003075

Printed in the United States of America

07 06 05 04 03 02 01
7   6   5   4   3   2   1

CONTENTS

INTRODUCTION: WHAT IS A WORLDVIEW?

The way we see the world can change the world.

Our choices are shaped by what we believe is real and true, right and wrong, good and beautiful. Our choices are shaped by our worldview.

The term *worldview* may sound abstract or philosophical, a topic discussed by pipe-smoking, tweed-jacketed professors in academic settings. But actually a person's worldview is intensely practical. It is simply the sum total of our beliefs about the world, the "big picture" that directs our daily decisions and actions. And so understanding worldviews is extremely important to how we live—to know how to evaluate everything from the textbooks in our classrooms to the unspoken philosophy that shapes the message we hear on *Oprah*, from the stories and characters shown in contemporary movies to the lyrics in the music we listen to.

The basis for the Christian worldview, of course, is God's revelation in Scripture. Yet sadly, many believers fail to understand that Scripture is intended to be the basis for all of life. In the past centuries, the secular world asserted a dichotomy between science and religion, between fact and value, between objective knowledge and subjective feeling. As a result, Christians often think in terms of the same false dichotomy, allowing our belief system to be reduced to little more than private feelings and experience, divorced from objective facts.

Evangelicals have been particularly vulnerable to this narrow view because of our emphasis on personal commitment. On one hand, this has been the movement's greatest strength, bringing millions to a relationship with Christ. Somewhere in most of our spiritual journeys is a sawdust trail, as there certainly is in mine. I remember as vividly as if it were yesterday that sultry summer night in 1973, in the midst of the Watergate scandal, when I, a former marine captain—often called the "toughest of the Nixon tough guys," the "White House hatchet man"—broke down in tears and called out to God.[1] Apart from that encounter with Christ and assurances of his forgiveness, I would have suffocated in the stench of my own sin. My soul would never have found rest. But this emphasis on a personal relationship can also be evangelicalism's greatest weakness because it may prevent us from seeing God's plan for us beyond personal salvation. Genuine Christianity is more than a relationship with Jesus as expressed in personal piety, church attendance, Bible study, and works of charity. It is more than discipleship, more than believing a system of doctrines about God. Genuine Christianity is a way of seeing and comprehending *all* reality.

It is a worldview.

Understanding Christianity as a total life system is absolutely essential, for two reasons. First, it enables us to make sense of the world we live in and thus order our lives more rationally. Second, it enables us to understand forces hostile to our faith, equipping us to evangelize and to defend Christian truth as God's instruments for transforming culture.

MORAL ORDER

Because the world was created by an intelligent being rather than by chance, it has an intelligible order. As Abraham Kuyper, the great nineteenth-century theologian who served as prime minister of Holland, wrote, "All created life necessarily bears in itself a law for its existence, instituted by God Himself."[2] The only way to live a rational and healthy life is to ascertain the nature of these divine laws and ordinances and then to use them as the basis for how we should live. We tend to understand this principle very well when it comes to the physical order. We know that certain laws exist in the physical world and that if we defy those laws, we pay a steep price. Ignoring the law of gravity can have very unpleasant consequences if we happen to be walking off the edge of a cliff. To live in defiance of known physical laws is the height of folly.

But it is no different with the moral laws prescribing human behavior. Just as certain physical actions produce predictable reactions, so certain moral behavior produces predictable consequences. Hollywood may portray adultery as glamorous, but it invariably produces anger, jealousy, broken relationships, even violence. Defiance of moral laws may even lead to death, whether it is the speeding drunk who kills a mother on her way to the store or the drug addict who contracts and spreads AIDS. No transgression of moral law is without painful consequences.

If we want to live healthy, well-balanced lives, we had better know the laws and ordinances by which God has structured creation. And because these are the laws of our own inner nature, Kuyper notes, we will experience them not as oppressive external constraints but as "a guide through the desert," guaranteeing our safety.[3]

This understanding of life's laws is what Scripture calls wisdom. "Wisdom in Scripture is, broadly speaking, the knowledge of God's world and the knack of fitting oneself into it," says Cornelius Plantinga Jr., president of Calvin Theological Seminary.[4] A wise person is one who knows the boundaries and limits, the laws and rhythms and seasons of the created order, both in the physical and the social world. "To be wise is to know reality and then accommodate yourself to it."[5] By contrast, those who refuse to accommodate to the laws of life are not only immoral but also foolish, no matter how well educated they may be. They fail to recognize the structure of creation and are constantly at odds with reality: "Folly is a stubborn swimming against the stream of the universe . . . spitting into the wind . . . coloring outside the lines."[6]

Precisely. To deny God is to blind ourselves to reality, and the inevitable consequence is that we will bump up against reality in painful ways, just as a blindfolded driver will crash into other drivers or run off the road. We make the bold claim that serious Christians actually live happier, more fulfilled, more productive lives by almost every measure. (Studies are beginning to bear this out.) This simply makes sense. Someone who accepts the contours and limits of the physical and moral order doesn't engage in folly—whether stepping off a cliff or committing adultery or driving drunk.

THE REAL CULTURE WAR

Our calling is not only to order our own lives by divine principles but also to engage the world. We are to fulfill both the *great commission* and the *cultural commission*. We are commanded both to preach the Good News and to bring all things into submission to God's order, by defending and living out God's truth in the unique historical and cultural conditions of our age.

To engage the world, however, requires that we understand the great ideas that compete for people's minds and hearts. Philosopher Richard Weaver has it right in the title of his well-known book: *Ideas Have Consequences.*[7] It is the great ideas that inform the mind, fire the imagination, move the heart, and shape a culture. History is little more than the recording of the rise and fall of the great ideas—the worldviews—that form our values and move us to act.

A debilitating weakness in modern evangelicalism is that we've been fighting cultural skirmishes on all sides without knowing what the war itself is about. We have not identified the worldviews that lie at the root of cultural conflict—and this ignorance dooms our best efforts.

The culture war is not just about abortion, homosexual rights, or the decline of public education. These are only the skirmishes. The real war is a cosmic struggle between worldviews—between the Christian worldview and the various secular and spiritual worldviews arrayed against it. This is what we must understand if we are going to be effective both in evangelizing our world today and in transforming it to reflect the wisdom of the Creator.

WORLDVIEWS IN CONFLICT

The world is divided not so much by geographic boundaries as by religious and cultural traditions, by people's most deeply held beliefs—by worldviews. So argued the distinguished Harvard scholar Samuel Huntington in a celebrated article a few years ago.[8] And Christians would agree. Because we are religious creatures, our lives are defined by our ultimate beliefs more sharply than by any other factor. The drama of history is played out along the frontiers of great belief systems as they ebb and flow.

But if this is so, what does it tell us about the divisions in the world today? Where is the clash of civilizations most bitter?

Huntington predicted a clash between the worldviews of three major traditional civilizations: the Western world, the Islamic world, and the Confucian East. But one of his former students, political scientist James Kurth, took issue with him, contending that the most significant clash would be within Western civilization itself—between those who adhere to a Judeo-Christian framework and those who favor postmodernism and multiculturalism.[9]

I believe Kurth is right. And the reason this conflict within Western culture is so significant is that Western culture may soon dominate the globe. Information technology is rapidly crossing traditional barriers of geography and national boundaries. The fall of the Iron Curtain has opened a large area of the world to Western ideas. Asian and Islamic societies find they cannot insulate themselves from the influx of Western books, movies, and television programs. In Singapore, I met with a Christian cabinet minister who lamented that because Asians associate the West with Christianity, the flood of smut from the West is making his Christian witness difficult. Across the globe, people are complaining about what one French politician described as a "U.S. cultural invasion."[10]

As a result, people around the world are wrestling with the same questions that we face in the States. In Africa, one of the continent's most respected Christian leaders asked for permission to reprint transcripts of my radio program, *BreakPoint*. Though the program is targeted at an American audience, he found that the subjects are the same as those he is dealing with in Africa. Another African Christian leader told me that Western notions of multiculturalism are being used to justify tribalism, and the local church is baffled over how to counter the divisive force. As people in Pakistan get on-line with people in Pennsylvania, America's culture war is increasingly spilling over into other nations.

The sobering conclusion is that our own effectiveness in defending and contending for truth has repercussions across the entire globe. American Christians had better get serious about understanding biblical faith as a comprehensive worldview and showing how it stands up to the challenges of our age.

The three books in this "Developing a Christian Worldview" study series—based on the book *How Now Shall We Live?*—are designed to help you do just that.

Christians must understand the clash of worldviews that is changing the face of society and the world. And we must stand ready to respond as people grow disillusioned with false beliefs and values, and as they begin to seek real answers. We must know not only what our worldview is and why we believe it but also how to defend it. We must also have some understanding of the opposing worldviews and why people believe them. Only then can we present the gospel in language that can be understood.

Only then can we defend truth in a way that is winsome and persuasive.

The twenty-first century promises to be a time of remarkable change and breathtaking developments in science and culture. Before the advent of instant communications profound changes used to take decades; today such changes occur overnight. The question is, What role does the church play—what is the responsibility of the individual Christian—in addressing this? Most Christians are aware of the great commission, but they forget the cultural commission to redeem the culture: saving souls *and* saving culture. The great task in the midst of change is to bring unchanging Truth to bear on a culture going through technological revolution. The only way to do this is to contend for Christianity in every area of life. And that's precisely what this book addresses.

HOW TO USE THIS BOOK

Although this book, the last in the "Developing a Christian Worldview" series, stands alone, it builds on two previous books, *Science and Evolution* and *The Problem of Evil*, which look at foundational worldview questions.

Science and Evolution addresses the most basic question: *Where did we come from, and who are we?* As we discuss and defend our faith, we need to be equipped to counter the prevailing notion that our universe and world are here by chance and that we humans just happened to evolve from amoebas. This book lays out evidence that our world and its inhabitants are the result of the designing hand of a personal Creator. But it doesn't stop there. As it argues for a creationist worldview, it presents reasoned arguments showing the flaws in and implications of the naturalist worldview. As humans, we are created in the image of God, meant to glorify God and enjoy him forever.

That's where the second book, *The Problem of Evil*, begins. God created a world and a host of creatures, including mankind, and deemed that creation "good." But in Eden mankind "fell," and things have never been the same. This raises the second basic worldview question: *What has gone wrong with the world?* And right behind it the third: *What can we do to fix it?* These are the questions addressed in *The Problem of Evil*, which explores the deep questions about sin, evil, and suffering. As in *Science and Evolution*, the second book in the series presents the ineffectual ways various worldviews cast the problem and shows the inadequacy of the promises they make for salvation.

Now in this book, *The Christian in Today's Culture,* we cover
a fourth significant question: *So how, now, shall we live out our
Christian worldview?* What does it mean for us to carry out the
biblical mandates given to us as Christians? Here you'll find
many real-life examples of Christians who are putting feet to
their faith and transforming their families, schools, and neighborhoods as well as the arenas of economics, law and politics,
science, the arts, music, and popular culture. This call to action,
along with the related discussions, will inspire you and equip
you to become part of God's redeeming force in the new millennium.

To help you understand, assimilate, and remember the material
in these chapters, we've incorporated questions and activities for
a six-session group study. Small-group study is one of the most
dynamic ways we as Christians can learn together and support
each other, not only in exploring our worldview, but also in articu-
lating our beliefs in ways that make sense to people who hold
opposing worldviews. At the moment, you may not feel qualified
or confident enough to speak out about your worldview, but we
hope that your group experience will equip you to become an
effective communicator of the truth.

PRACTICAL TIPS

At the beginning of each chapter, you'll find questions to help you
focus on key points as you read. We suggest that you highlight or
underline as you read, marking points you want to remember and
points you want to discuss and clarify with your group. In the text
of some chapters, key phrases are already underlined to facilitate
reading and discussion.

Each study session covers the material in two or three chapters.
At the end of each session you'll find discussion questions. Each
set of questions reviews and reinforces the chapter's content.

It also draws you to a brief passage of Scripture relevant to the chapter content and/or complementary worldview issues.

We've left some blank space after each question, allowing you to jot notes, but with no clear expectation that you will write down exhaustive answers before you get to the group gathering. The emphasis in this guide is on discussion and group dynamics.

Suggested role-play activities at the end of sessions 1 through 5 are not simply entertaining time fillers; they are meant to help solidify the truth in your experience. All of us learn and remember things better when we experience them than when we merely hear or read about them. These role plays may well trigger the piece of information or reasoned argument that you may need to recall in a later conversation with a skeptic.

We suggest you commit ten minutes of a session to the role-play activity; in most of the activities group members practice presenting to a non-Christian what they've learned in this book. Role plays should not be set up in a manner that traumatizes anyone. The goal is encouragement, not intimidation. See further role-play guidelines and instructions in session 1. Role plays can be set up in groups of two or three, or they can be acted out in front of the whole group.

Each session ends with a closing summary question. We suggest that each person in the group verbalize a one-sentence recap: "The one thing that I want to remember from what I read (or heard or did) in this session is . . ."

HAVING AN IMPACT

We trust that this book will provide your group with a forum for lively discussion, a springboard for action, and a tool for accountability. We encourage you to wrestle with ideas presented in the book. Even if you disagree on some points, we're confident that you will come to a deeper understanding of your worldview. Most of all we hope that you are moved to act, to map out goals and strategies for becoming God's redeeming force in this new millennium.

This book is merely a beginning point for you to explore and pursue the truth of what it means to live out a Christian worldview. Take a serious look at the list of resources in the recommended reading section at the end of the book. Choose several titles to deepen your understanding of specific topics that interest you.

ALL THINGS NEW

CHAPTER 1

THE KNOCKOUT PUNCH

As you read chapter 1, keep the following questions in mind:
- What encounters, events, and truths led Danny Croce to Christ?
- What lessons did Danny learn as a young Christian?

Those first nights of his imprisonment in the Plymouth County Correctional Facility, Danny Croce couldn't settle into sleep. Couldn't even come close. He watched and listened as his fellow inmates muttered and the building's old pipes complained. The prison itself seemed restless. Vapory shadows swirled around the bare concrete ceiling, jaundiced by the low light in the hallway.

Wide awake on his bunk, Danny kept descending into deeper shadows, reliving the night that had brought him to this cell. A "village boy" from Brockton, Massachusetts, home of the famous middleweight fighter Marvelous Marvin Hagler, Danny had fought professionally himself. Now the scenes from that night hit him like short punches with plenty of leverage. A pounding he couldn't fend off.

Once again he saw the bus swinging into his lane, its high beams lighting up the curtain of falling rain. He swerved to the right. His car suddenly heaved into the air, the engine racing as the tires spun free. The night's quiet was sheared by the sound of scissoring metal. Danny peered into the sudden blackness, trying to search his way through it. *What's blocking my vision?* The Chevy Nova's wheels touched down at last, thumping into soft earth. The steering wheel played wildly in his hands. Still he could not see. *What* is *that?* He hit the interior dome light, which only intensified the nearness of the thick black covering across his windshield. His blindness lasted a moment's full horrible eternity before the windshield suddenly cleared and he skidded to a stop.

Stumbling out of his car, he saw a splintered police barrier and a man crumpled on the ground. He asked onlookers what had knocked the man down.

"You did," they said.

He looked again and felt a horrible stab of recognition. The man on the ground was police officer John Gilbert. The same John Gilbert who played pool with him in the bar and teased him about keeping in shape for the ring.

Danny's car had carried Gilbert thirty yards, they said. Splayed across the windshield in a black oilskin raincoat, it was Gilbert's body that had blotted out Danny's vision.

Remembering the episode, Danny felt as if that raincoat were covering his own face like a shroud, the rain running down like tears of remorse. Through the nights, the scene played over and over in Danny's head as if God, or maybe the devil, had looped the tape, setting it to replay without end. It was his own hell, which he knew he deserved. And in hell the "if onlys" go on forever.

If only he had left the bar after the first time he nodded off. *If only* his ironworker friend Sully hadn't been juiced up worse than he was and had been able to drive. *If only* it hadn't rained that day and he and Sully had been able to stay and finish out the eighth floor of that building they had been working on. *If only* they had been able to follow the motto of the ironworker: Look where you want to go, and let your feet follow. *If only* he had been able to see the consequences, he would never have followed where that day led. But he hadn't seen a thing.

Danny often wondered whether the freebasing had started the whole chain of events. That was something else he saw in the darkness. The pure white cocaine crystals left after the ethyl ether evaporated. The first of a series of bad choices that had landed Gilbert spread-eagled across Danny's windshield.

When Danny turned in his bunk to stare at the opposite wall, he saw Gilbert's family—his wife, his two kids, the empty chair at their dinner table. He had wanted to apologize to Jeanie Gilbert a thousand times before the sentencing, but his lawyers had said no. So he remained their ghost . . . and they remained his nightmare.

The video began to replay . . . midnight . . . 2:00 A.M. . . . 4:30. Sometimes it felt to Danny as if he were directing the scenes, looking for that undiscovered bridge to a different ending. Sometimes he could only cover up against the assault, both fists clenched over his brow. The memories swung at him—roundhouses, overhands, uppercuts.

Even before Danny got Sully's call about John Gilbert's condition, he had expected the bad news. The same way he had known how the bout would end that time he fought Tommy Rose. Tommy had been the number fourteen–ranked bantamweight at the time, and the matchup was Danny's one moment of boxing glory. Tommy Rose was a fighter going places.

At first Danny thought he had Tommy cornered, and he kept trying to cut him off. He tried to make Tommy think the right was his best shot; that way Tommy would counter weakly, and Danny could step through it and deliver his bomb of a left hook. He did connect with a few shots, but by the end of the third round—or was it the second?—Danny's arms and legs were gone.

He kept standing, like a cow too stupid to fall after the slaughter-house jolt, as Tommy gave him the most vicious beating of his life.

That's what Sully's telephone call was like: knowing his legs were gone, knowing what was coming.

"It's bad," Sully said.

"He's dead, isn't he?"

"Yeah, he's dead."

Except there was a difference. Danny couldn't remember Tommy's punch that put out his lights, but he would never forget the impatient way Sully said "dead"—as if he couldn't wait to clear out of Danny's life.[1]

·   ·   ·

During Danny's first week in prison, he was assigned to a work detail out in the fields, cultivating the hard New England soil, still almost frozen in April. At the end of one shift, as the men drifted toward the water tower to be recounted and escorted back to their cells, Danny heard someone calling him.

"Hey, Croce! Come over here!" A guy by the hay cart. Danny didn't know him, so he kept on walking toward the water tower. But the guy moved out to block his way. He was big in the upper arms and thick through the gut. Danny saw other inmates glancing over their shoulders at the guards in the distance, then converging on the two of them.

"So, Croce, I heard you fought Tommy Rose. Heard you were tough. But the thing is, I don't remember any Croce fighting Rose."

"The promoter called me Rivaro for that one."

"Why? You ashamed of your name? Your wop name—Cro-chay. That's why your family says it's 'Crose,' I bet. Your whole family's ashamed, with a killer like you in it." The guy turned to grin at the onlookers. "A killer everywhere but in the ring."

Danny had known he would have to use his hands in prison. He was surprised only at how soon. "I know the game well enough," he said. "Get out of my way."

"I'm *in* your way, you puke. A real killer, you are. As long as you're driving a car."

The guys around them laughed, and the man rocked his weight back like a Goliath. Then he rushed Danny, throwing a looping right toward his temple.

He threw it as if he had a wrench in his hand, which gave Danny enough time to decide against the typical crossing counter. He didn't want any extra time tacked onto his sentence, so he hoped to take this guy down without marking him too much. He threw a triple combination into the guy's gut—*bm, bm, bm*—and the man's face drained.

He came back at Danny, though. This time he faked with a jab, or threw it so weakly Danny couldn't tell the difference.

Danny popped him in the side of the head with the right, then jabbed him with a left hook, lifting the oaf clean off the back of his heels. He fell dead out like concrete—not even a bounce.

Usually when a fight ended, whether in a bar or in the ring, there was cheering and shouting. But Danny's fellow inmates kept this one quiet. Then something even stranger happened. The onlookers began crowding closer. For a moment Danny thought he was going to have to fight them all. Then he understood. They were walking him away, protecting him.

"The water tower's got a spigot," someone said. They shielded him from view as he washed the blood from his hands. Then they all lined up for the count.

"O'Brien," the guard called out.

"He fell down," someone said. "Back by the hay cart."

"Always sleeping, that mick," the guard said.

Everyone laughed, hearty and false.

At least I won't have to fight again for a while, Danny thought.

.   .   .

Unable to sleep at night, Danny was groggy during the day. He had to find a way to rest, or one of the new arrivals would challenge him, and he would lose his reputation. He dreaded the guards' call of lockdown, the haul and clang of the closing cellblock doors, and time slowing once more as the black moments in that car drained the sweat out of him.

One night, about three months into Danny's sentence, an inmate named John Dunn poked his head into Danny's cell just before lockdown. Danny was not overjoyed to see him. He knew Dunn thought of himself as spiritual.

"We're starting a vehicular-homicide group," Dunn said.

"Like an AA group?" asked Danny.

Dunn nodded. "You get 'good time' for it—time off your sentence," he added. "A day for an hour."

Danny thought about the eighteen-month stretch still ahead of him. "I guess you'll be seeing me, then," he said.

Eventually Danny told his story to the group. When he finished, several of the men said, in one way or another, "It was his time. Everyone's ticket gets punched."

The process was supposed to provide some relief, but Danny felt none. It *wasn't* John Gilbert's time. That was the whole point.

Afterward, a longhaired hippie type came up to him. "Have you ever prayed to God?"

Danny hadn't prayed since he was a kid. He hadn't even thought much about religion. But later that night, back in his cell, he found himself begging, more out of desperation than anything else, "Please, God, let me sleep."

That was the last thing he remembered. Suddenly it was morning, and for the first time in months, he had an appetite for breakfast.

The insomnia returned, though. He waited it out for several

nights, then prayed once more, just as simply. "Please, God, let me sleep."

Again, the next thing he knew, it was morning.

This was so curious that he felt compelled to talk with the long-hair. Danny knew almost nothing about religion. He knew only that whether it was Catholics, Jehovah's Witnesses, or the Four Squares, when they talked at you or handed you a tract, they were carrying "that Book." So he asked the hippie if he had a Bible, and the man loaned Danny his New Testament.

As Danny read the Gospels, he discovered that the Jesus they described appealed to him. Jesus was straight with everyone, and although he was always being set up, he stood his ground. He told people so clearly what was in their hearts that he knocked them out with his words, without throwing a punch—unlike Danny, who had been fighting ever since his family moved into the town of Brockton. "So you think you're too good for us," one of the bigger kids would shout. Or they would yell nasty things about his mother. Anything to start a fight. The first time, he had refused to fight, and they had dropped him into a garbage bin. So he had learned to use his fists. Now, reading the Bible reminded him of how he had become such a tough guy—and what an act it was.

The more Danny felt drawn to Jesus, the more he saw himself in a new light. He was used to comparing himself to the guy on the next bar stool, and that way he usually didn't look so bad. But when he compared himself to Jesus, he started to feel afraid. This man who never raised his fists scared him as nobody else ever had.

He also read the passages about people being "cast into outer darkness," where there was "weeping" and "gnashing of teeth." Danny knew something about darkness. In his mind, he was shut in that car, unable to see, unable to change directions, carrying death along with him—not only John Gilbert's death but also his own.

Lying on his bunk at night, Danny began to review his whole

life, horrified by the person he had become. He saw himself living for his next drink, his next coke party; he saw himself using women. His last girlfriend had been good to him, but he would have thrown her away for the next quarter ounce of coke. In fact, he probably had.

That next Sunday, when the guard called out for people who wanted to be let out of their cells to attend chapel, Danny shouted, "Cell 16." But he sat like a stone through the service, hearing little. He was there to ask a question. Afterward, he approached Chaplain Bob Hansen and asked him if the passages he had read about outer darkness were really about hell.

"Yes," said the chaplain.

"Then I'm in big trouble," Danny said.

"When you get back to your cell, get on your knees by your bunk," said the chaplain. "Confess your sins to God, and pray for Jesus Christ to come into your heart."

Danny did just that. In his cell, he knelt, confessed that he was a sinner, and asked Christ to be his Lord. As he did, he kept remembering horrible things he had done, and the memories brought both pain and an eagerness to be forgiven. Talking to God seemed like carrying on a conversation with someone he had missed all along without knowing it. He could almost hear God replying through a silence that echoed his sorrow and embraced it. Danny not only felt heard, he also felt understood, received.

He slept that night. And every night afterward.

.   .   .

Danny began wearing a cross. He walked the cellblocks with a spiritual strut, a pugnacious witness to the truth he had found. He pumped along with a new confidence, asking everyone he met to come to chapel. Some prisoners even took a step back when he passed, as if he would slam them against a wall if they didn't become Christians.

Inside, Danny resolved that he wouldn't take any abuse for his new convictions. They could call him a Jesus freak, but no one was going to get in his face. He prayed that no one would touch him. He could control himself if they left him alone.

The only fights that broke out were the ones inside him—a war between his new convictions and his old habits.

One day when he was playing Ping-Pong, Danny flipped his usual cigarette into his mouth and flicked his lighter. Suddenly, something said, "Stop." The filter no longer tasted clean. He slipped the cigarette back in the pack and wondered what was going on.

Chaplain Hansen always said to look to the Bible for answers, so Danny actually did a concordance search that night. He found only one passage that said anything at all about smoking; it was in Isaiah and had to do with "smoking flax." Yet he didn't doubt that he had heard a voice say "stop."

Eventually, he discovered 1 Corinthians and gained an understanding that his body was God's house. He shouldn't deliberately damage it. So he prayed for the willpower to stop smoking. The first day he had to pray twenty times . . . as he sat in the mess hall having coffee . . . as he worked in the fields . . . as he played cards at a table in the yard—all the places and times that prompted him to light up again.

The next day he prayed nineteen times. The smoking battle kept him on his knees for weeks.

Danny soon heard that same voice countering most of his lifelong habits. It was a patient voice and said stop to only one thing at a time, but the list was long, beginning with smoking and drinking, then going on to using dope and swearing. He discovered that when he began to clean up his language, he lost half his vocabulary. He also discovered that his first victories produced an overconfidence born of spiritual pride.

One day while playing cards, he said to another Christian

inmate, "What are you putting that cigarette in your mouth for, brother? Don't you know that God will deliver you from that if you ask?"

"Well, I believe it, Danny, but I'm not there yet," his friend said.

Not too long afterward Danny cruised by the showers, where guys smoked dope during the day, back in a hidden area. He could smell the sweet, heavy scent. An inner yearning taunted him, *What would it be like to take just a few more tokes?* He couldn't resist finding out.

When Danny ducked back out, the first person he saw was the brother he had just jumped on for smoking. "Hey, Danny," the guy grinned, gesturing with his cigarette, "guess you're not so perfect either."

Danny went to his bunk and cried out to God for strength. These inner battles with himself were tougher than anything he'd faced in the ring.

Eventually, though, after umpteen prayers a day, the old habits started to fade, and Danny began to feel something like the "new creation" spoken of in the Scriptures.

Then, just before he went into chapel one day, while he was still out in the yard, one of the new inmates started ragging a frail nineteen-year-old called Squeaky. The nickname was apt. The kid, who was in the joint for writing bad checks, really was a mouse. He even looked like one, with his colorless hair and flappy ears.

In contrast, the new inmate looked like a real bad boy, slim but muscled, with things to prove. He pushed Squeaky's shoulder hard with the butt of his hand.

Squeaky did nothing but grab for the place where it hurt.

"You're a tough guy," Danny said, stepping in.

"This punk's been looking at me like he's queer or something."

"He hasn't been looking at you. Squeaky never looks at anything but the ground."

"You calling me a liar?"

"You want to fight someone, fight someone who knows how. Me."

"This shrimp's your whore?"

Danny made no reply.

"Well, I'll fight you, you queer freak. You . . ." He loosed a flood of curses, working up a fighting rage.

His first jab snapped out with greater skill than Danny expected. It went through the block Danny put up and caught him on the side of the head. For a moment Danny anticipated another left, a right, whatever combination the guy's rhythm dictated.

But the newcomer just threw one and stepped away. Threw another and stepped away. Danny blocked and feinted.

When the newcomer yawed the next time, Danny stepped forward quickly and caught him with three close-in shots to the head—*bm, bm, bm.* That left the guy's face a blank, with blood trickling from the brow. The old fury rose up within Danny, and he cleaned the guy with a crossing right. Totally pure. The guy fell on the seat of his pants, bleeding heavily from the mouth. He didn't get up.

"Squeaky's one of Danny's boys now," someone said. "You're gonna have to get born again, Squeaky."

"You don't owe me nothing, Squeaky," Danny said, suddenly feeling as if he had lost the fight.

The buzzer sounded. Time for chapel.

Danny sat through the service, preoccupied with his own thoughts. Afterward, he went up to Chaplain Hansen and asked what he should do.

"You know what you have to do," the chaplain said. "When you offend your brother, you have to make it right. You have to go to the guy."

When Danny appeared at the newcomer's cell, the guy snarled at him, and Danny could hardly bring himself to put his hand forward. "I came by to see how you're doing. I'm sorry for laying you out. I know what I'm doing—too much to hit you like that."

"You proved it," the newcomer said. His mouth was swollen and distorted.

"You don't need to make your rep on guys like Squeaky. Now that you fought me, people will leave you alone. You landed that first shot."

"Didn't slow you down much."

"Like I said, I know what I'm doing. We square?"

"Square," the newcomer said. He stood and shook Danny's hand quickly, then scrambled back to his bunk.

Danny thought of asking the guy to chapel, but he knew that was not the moment for invitations. *He'll be asking about me,* Danny thought. *There'll be other times.*

Back in the dormitory, where he had been permitted to live for the last several months, Danny stood and looked out the window. He could see the water tower and the fields beyond. The rows were filled with lettuce heads, the back fields with waist-high corn. The day was settling down as night came on with a watery blue sky, the clouds blushed with sunset.

All at once, Danny felt free. Standing in the middle of the Plymouth County Correctional Facility, with months still to serve, he felt unfettered as he never had on the outside. There, he had made a prison of his world. Here, in prison, God had set him free. *Look where you want to go, and let your feet follow.* He now saw where the old ways would lead him, and he was free to turn and walk the other way—free to choose the good, even when his old ways still called to him.

Looking at the water tower, he remembered his first fight here, remembered washing the blood off his hands after hammering O'Brien. But it had taken more than the whole water tower to wash John Gilbert's blood off his hands. It had taken Christ's blood—the living water.

.   .   .

Ten years after his release, Danny Croce once again entered the
Plymouth County Correctional Facility. Although the government had closed the old building and built a new one, the Plymouth facility was essentially the same.

He stood in the lock, between the double doors operated by
security. The first door had closed behind him. The second
refused to open. He buzzed again.

"Who are you?" a voice said over the intercom.

For a panicky moment he wondered. He remembered being
in the old prison. Was he the man who had killed John Gilbert?
Yes.

Who else was he? Faces and events rushed through his memory
like a video in fast-forward. The day he was released from prison.
His marriage. His five children. The years working with troubled
kids in Boston. Then the big break: being accepted at Wheaton
College and receiving the Charles W. Colson Scholarship for
ex-offenders. His graduation. His ordination. Yes, he remembered. Both who he had been and who he now was.

"Who are you?" the voice repeated.

"I'm the new prison chaplain," Danny answered.

*Culture in the broadest sense is
the purpose for which God created
man after His image . . . [which]
includes not only the most ancient
callings of . . . hunting and fishing,
agriculture and stock raising, but
also trade and commerce and science
and art.*   HERMAN BAVINCK

CHAPTER 2

SAVED TO WHAT?

**As you read chapter 2, keep the following questions
in mind:**

- What is the cultural commission for humanity? How did
  sin affect it?
- In what ways did Christian missionaries in the Dark Ages
  combine the cultural commission with the "great
  commission" of evangelization?
- Why is today another excellent time for Christians boldly
  to live out and proclaim their faith?

Danny Croce's "wake-up punch" is the perfect punch line for
this book. Not because it's a heartwarming conversion story—
though it is that—but because of what Danny did *after* his
broken life was redeemed. It's the kind of wake-up punch that
contemporary Christians urgently need, as well as an apt metaphor for the theme that will be woven through the rest of this
book.

When Danny Croce became a Christian, he embarked on an
adventure to change the world. First to be transformed was his
own life: He cleaned up his act, got out of prison, got married,
settled down into a respectable life, and earned a college degree.
But changing his own life wasn't the end of things for Danny.
After his graduation, he didn't tuck his Wheaton diploma under

his arm and head off for the comfortable life that his education might have given him. No, he set out to transform the world he had known. He went back to prison.

And transform it he did. The Plymouth County Correctional Facility houses fourteen hundred inmates in twenty-two units, four of which are the "holes," the dreaded segregation and protective-custody units. In each unit, Danny located an on-fire Christian believer, or else he preached and witnessed until God converted someone. Danny then appointed these men to function as elders to help and lead others; to equip them, he continues to disciple and teach them, giving courses on theology and doctrine, often using seminary-level materials. He also holds weekly Bible studies throughout the prison, assisted by Prison Fellowship volunteers. And every day Danny talks with inmates one-on-one, teaching, encouraging, and helping them solve personal problems.

He helps inmates like Peter, who received a letter from his wife telling him she was filing for divorce. Danny prayed with Peter, then drove sixty miles to meet the estranged wife. Many meetings later, Peter and his wife were reconciled, and they are now growing together in Christ.

When God makes us new creations, we are meant to help create a new world around us, and Danny Croce's work at the Plymouth prison offers a striking example. Again and again, I have witnessed this kind of transformation within a rotting prison culture, and the results are measurable in terms of reduced disciplinary problems and reduced recidivism.[1]

MORE THAN A PERSONAL EXPERIENCE

Yes, cultures can be renewed—even those typically considered the most corrupt and intractable. But if we are to restore our world, we first have to shake off the comfortable notion that

Christianity is merely a personal experience, applying only to one's private life. "No man is an island," wrote the Christian poet John Donne. Yet one of the great myths of our day is that we *are* islands—that our decisions are personal and that no one has a right to tell us what to do in our private lives. We easily forget that every private decision contributes to the moral and cultural climate in which we live, rippling out in ever widening circles—first in our personal and family lives, and then in the broader society.

That's because every decision we make reflects our worldview. Every choice, every action, either expresses a false worldview and thus contributes to a disordered and broken world, or expresses God's truth and helps build a world that reflects his created order. Our purpose here is to show you how to make genuinely biblical choices in every area of your life. The three worldview categories—*creation, fall,* and *redemption*—provide a conceptual structure by which we can identify what is wrong with non-Christian ways of thinking and then formulate a Christian perspective on every subject.

The first task, then, is to be discerning, to examine various worldviews by measuring how well they answer the fundamental questions of life: *Creation*—Where did we come from, and who are we? *Fall*—What has gone wrong with the world? *Redemption*—What can we do to fix it? Trace out the way any worldview answers these three questions, and you will be able to see how nonbiblical ideas fail to fit reality. By contrast, the biblical worldview provides answers that are internally consistent and really work.

Finally, when we apply this three-part analysis, we learn how to put biblical principles into practice in every area of life. As we have seen with Danny Croce, *transformed people transform cultures.* And that is what every believer is called to do, as Scripture makes clear.

THE CULTURAL COMMISSION

The scriptural justification for culture building starts with Genesis. At the dawn of creation, the earth is unformed, empty, dark, and undeveloped. Then, in a series of steps, God establishes the basic creational distinctives: light and dark, "above the expanse" and "below the expanse," sea and land, and so on. But then God changes his strategy.

Until the sixth day, God has done the work of creation directly. But now he creates the first human beings and orders them to carry on where he leaves off: They are to reflect his image and to have dominion (Gen. 1:26). From then on, the development of the creation will be primarily social and cultural: It will be the work of humans as they obey God's command to fill and subdue the earth (Gen. 1:28).

Sometimes called the "cultural commission" or "cultural mandate," God's command is the culmination of his work in creation. The curtain has risen on the stage, and the director gives the characters their opening cue in the drama of history.[2] Though the creation itself is "very good," the task of exploring and developing its powers and potentialities, the task of building a civilization, God turns over to his image bearers. "By being fruitful they must fill it even more; by subduing it they must form it even more," explains Al Wolters in *Creation Regained.*[3]

The same command is still binding on us today. Though the Fall introduced sin and evil into human history, it did not erase the cultural mandate. The generations since Adam and Eve still bear children, build families, and spread across the earth. They still tend animals and plant fields. They still construct cities and governments. They still make music and works of art.

Sin introduces a destructive power into God's created order, but it does not obliterate that order. And when we are redeemed, we are not only freed from the sinful motivations that drive us but also restored to fulfill our original purpose, empowered to do what we were created to do: to build societies and create culture—and, in doing so, to restore the created order.

It is our contention in this book that the Lord's cultural commission is inseparable from the great commission. That may be a jarring statement for many conservative Christians, who, through much of the twentieth century, have shunned the notion of reforming culture, associating that concept with the liberal social gospel. The only task of the church, many fundamentalists and evangelicals have believed, is to save as many lost souls as possible from a world literally going to hell. But this implicit denial of a Christian worldview is unbiblical and is the reason we have lost so much of our influence in the world. Salvation does not consist simply of freedom from sin; salvation also means being restored to the task we were given in the beginning—the job of creating culture.

When we turn to the New Testament, admittedly we do not find verses specifically commanding believers to be engaged in politics or the law or education or the arts. But we don't need to, because the cultural mandate given to Adam still applies. Every part of creation came from God's hand, every part was drawn into the mutiny of the human race and its enmity toward God, and every part will someday be redeemed. This is the apostle Paul's message to the Romans, in which he promises that "the creation itself will be liberated from its bondage to decay" (Rom. 8:21). Redemption is not just for individuals; it is for all God's creation.

The Lordship of Christ

Paul makes the point most strongly in Colossians 1:15-20, where he describes the lordship of Christ in three ways: (1) *everything was made by and for Christ:* "By him all things were created: things in heaven and on earth, visible and invisible . . . all things were created by him and for him"; (2) *everything holds together in*

Christ: "He is before all things, and in him all things hold together"; (3) *everything will be reconciled by Christ:* "For God was pleased to have all his fullness dwell in him, and through him to reconcile to himself all things, whether things on earth or things in heaven." Redemption covers all aspects of creation, and the end of time will not signal an end to the creation but the beginning of a new heaven and a new earth: God will make all things new (Rev. 21:5).

The lesson is clear: Christians are saved not only *from* something (sin) but also *to* something (Christ's lordship over all of life). The Christian life begins with spiritual restoration, which God works through the preaching of his Word, prayer, the sacraments, worship, and the exercise of spiritual gifts within a local church. This is the indispensable beginning, for only the redeemed person is filled with God's Spirit and can genuinely know and fulfill God's plan. But then we are meant to proceed to the restoration of all God's creation, which includes private and public virtue; individual and family life; education and community; work, politics, and law; science and medicine; literature, art, and music. This redemptive goal permeates everything we do, for there is no invisible dividing line between sacred and secular. We are to bring "all things" under the lordship of Christ, in the home and the school, in the workshop and the corporate boardroom, on the movie screen and the concert stage, in the city council and the legislative chamber.

This is what we mean when we say a Christian must have a comprehensive worldview: a *view* or perspective that covers all aspects of the *world*. For every aspect of the world was created with a structure, a character, a norm. These underlying principles are God's "laws"—God's design and purpose for creation—and can be known through both *special revelation* (God's words given in Scripture) and *general revelation* (the structure of the world he made). They include both laws of nature and norms for human life.

God's Governing Laws

This point must be pressed, because most people today operate on a fact/value distinction, believing that science uncovers "facts," which they believe to be reliable and true, while morality and religion are based on "values," which they believe to be subjective and relative to the individual. Unfortunately, Christians often mirror this secular attitude. We tend to be confident about God's laws for nature, such as the laws of gravity, motion, and heredity; but we seem far less confident about God's laws for the family, education, or the state. Yet a truly Christian worldview draws no such distinction. It insists that God's laws govern all creation. And just as we have to learn to live in accord with the law of gravity, so, too, we must learn to live in accord with God's norms for society.

The reason these two types of laws seem quite different is that norms for society are obeyed by choice. In the physical world, stones fall, planets move in their orbits, seasons come and go, and the electron circles the nucleus—all without any choice in the matter—because here God rules directly. But in culture and society, God rules indirectly, entrusting human beings with the task of making tools, doing justice, producing art and music, educating children, and building houses. And though a stone cannot defy God's law of gravity, human beings *can* rebel against God's created order—and they often do so. Yet that should not blind us to the fact that there is a single objective, universal order covering both nature and human nature.

All major cultures since the beginning of history have understood this concept of a universal order—all, that is, except postmodern Western culture. Despite the differences among them, all major civilizations have believed in a divine order that lays down the law for both natural and human realms. In the Far East it was called *Tao;* in ancient Egypt it was called *Ma'at;* in Greek philosophy it was called *Logos.*[4]

Likewise, in the Old Testament the psalmist speaks almost in a single breath of God's spreading the snow like wool and revealing his laws and decrees to Jacob, suggesting that there is no essential difference between God's laws for nature and those for people (see Ps. 147:16-19). Both types of law are part of a single universal order. John's Gospel borrows the Greek word for this universal plan of creation *(logos)* and, in a startling move, identifies it with a personal being—Jesus Christ himself. "In the beginning was the Word *[Logos]*," which is the source of creation (John 1:1). "Through him all things were made; without him nothing was made that has been made" (John 1:3). In other words, Jesus himself is the source of the comprehensive plan or design of creation.

As a result, obedience to Christ means living in accord with that plan in all aspects of life. Family and church, business and commerce, art and education, politics and law are institutions grounded in God's created order; they are not arbitrary in their configuration. A school is not a business and shouldn't be run like one; a family is not a state and shouldn't be run like one. Each has its own normative structure, ordained by God, and each has its own sphere of authority under God.[5] For the Christian, there must be no dichotomy between the sacred and the secular because nothing lies outside of God's created order. Our task is to reclaim that entire created order for his dominion.[6]

Spiritual Battleground, but the War Has Been Won

The world is a spiritual battleground, with two powers contending for the same territory. God's adversary, Satan, has invaded creation and now attempts to hold it as occupied territory. With the death and resurrection of Jesus Christ, God launched a counter-offensive to reclaim his rightful domain, and we are God's soldiers in that ongoing battle. "He has rescued us from the dominion of darkness and brought us into the kingdom of the Son he loves"

(Col. 1:13). Redeemed, we are armed for the fight to extend that kingdom and push back the forces of Satan. The fighting may be fierce, but we must not lose hope, for what we are waging is essentially a mop-up operation. Because of the Resurrection, the war has been won; the victory is assured.[7]

The history of Christianity is filled with glorious demonstrations of the truth and power of the gospel. Through the centuries, when Christians have lived out their faith by putting both the cultural commission and the great commission to work, they have renewed, restored, and, on occasions, even built new cultures. They have literally turned the world upside down.

ALL TRUTH IS GOD'S TRUTH

In the first century, a tiny group of Jewish dissidents spread a preposterous message about a condemned felon who rose from the dead. From such ignoble beginnings, Christianity grew into a force that dominated Western culture and eventually the world. How? By believers' dramatic testimony under persecution. Witnessing the peace and joy shining from the faces of ordinary men and women put to death for their convictions, pagans were drawn to Christ and his church.

In the second century, the church father Tertullian even reproached the secular authorities for the failure of their harsh policies: "Your cruelty [against us] does not profit you, however exquisite. Instead, it tempts people to our sect. As often as you mow us down, the more we grow in number. The blood of the Christians is the seed [of the church]." As a result of their striking witness, Christians soon filled every corner of ancient society. "We have filled all you have—cities, islands, forts, towns, assembly halls, even military camps, tribes, town councils, the palace, senate, and forum," Tertullian said, mocking the Romans. "We have left you nothing but the temples."[8]

Even as Christians were growing in number, however, they were also working to transform the culture from within. Another second-century church father, Justin Martyr, showed the way.

As a young man, Justin decided to become a philosopher and studied with teachers of the various philosophical schools of the ancient world, from Stoicism to Aristotelianism to Platonism. Finally he realized that the truth he sought was found in Scripture, and he became a believer, but he did not abandon philosophy. By becoming a Christian, he argued, he had simply become a *better* philosopher: He was now able to gather all the individual truths discovered by various philosophers and make sense of them within the framework of the one perfect truth provided by divine revelation. "Whatever things were rightly said by any man, belong to us Christians," he wrote.[9]

Justin wasn't urging Christians to be complacent relativists, as if all paths lead to God. He was resolutely opposed to the paganism of his day, and he was even put on trial for being a Christian, where he refused to renounce his faith and was executed. No, Justin wasn't one to compromise the truths of Christianity. Yet he did believe that pagans perceive reality in part, and he taught that Christ is the fulfillment of all the partial truths embodied in pagan philosophy and culture.

Following Justin's lead, the early church sought to fulfill both the great commission and the cultural commission, to redeem both souls and society. And when the Roman Empire fell, it was Christians who saved civilization in one of the most inspiring chapters of Western history.

Saving Civilization

The Dark Ages began with a cold snap. In A.D. 406 the Rhine River froze, forming a bridge of ice that allowed a band of barbarians to cross from the Germanic territories into Roman territory. In the following years, successive waves of Vandals and

Visigoths, Sueves and Alans, overran the Roman Empire and Europe, reducing cities to rubble and decimating populations. The entire substructure of Roman civilization was destroyed, to be replaced by small kingdoms ruled by illiterate, barbaric warrior-kings.

As the shadow of the Dark Ages fell over Western Europe, who emerged from the rubble? Who rebuilt Western civilization? The Christian church.[10]

In A.D. 401 a sixteen-year-old British boy named Patricius was seized by a raiding Irish war party, abducted from his Romanized homeland, and sold to a petty Irish chieftain named Miliucc, who sent the boy out to shepherd his flocks. Patricius spent months alone in the hills, hunger gnawing at his innards and the clammy cold biting into his limbs, until finally he sought help from the only source left: he began to pray.

Before this time, Patricius had not really believed in the God his Christian parents had taught him about, and he thought priests were fools. But he found in God a source of strength that helped him endure six long years of bitter isolation and deprivation. "Tending flocks was my daily work, and I would pray constantly during the daylight hours," he wrote later. "The love of God and the fear of him surrounded me more and more—and faith grew and the Spirit was roused."[11]

Then one night, Patricius was awakened by a mysterious voice telling him that he was going home. "Look, your ship is ready," said the voice. Although uncertain of the direction or distance, Patricius set out for the sea. More than two hundred miles later, he found a ship bound for England.

When he reached his homeland, however, Patricius discovered that he no longer fit in with his people. "Hardened physically and psychologically by unsharable experiences, hopelessly behind his peers in education, he cannot settle down," writes historian Thomas Cahill.[12] Then one night, the former slave boy heard

Christ's voice again, this time telling him to return to Ireland. He entered theological training and eventually returned as Patrick, missionary to the Irish.

This was no romantic return, set to the tune of Irish ballads. When St. Patrick began his mission, he faced pagan Irish priests (druids) who still practiced ritual human sacrifice to their monstrous Celtic gods (often portrayed eating people). The fierce Irish warriors, believing that the human head was the seat of the soul, hung their enemies' skulls from their belts as trophies.

Into this bloodthirsty culture St. Patrick brought the Christian message of love and forgiveness and established monasteries throughout the land. The monastic movement in Ireland began to revolutionize the world, replacing the old values of a warrior society with the new values of Christianity. Within St. Patrick's lifetime, warriors cast aside their swords of battle, intertribal warfare decreased markedly, and the slave trade ended. A culture of battle and brute power was transformed by an ethic that sanctified manual labor, poverty, and service. A culture of illiteracy and ignorance became a culture of learning.

Moreover, after Rome fell, the Irish monasteries also became refuges for vast numbers of Christian scholars and monks fleeing the barbarians, streaming in from all across Europe and even from as far away as Egypt, Armenia, and Syria. As a result, says historian Kenneth Clark, surprising as it may seem, "for quite a long time—almost a hundred years—western Christianity survived by clinging to places like Skellig Michael, a pinnacle of rock eighteen miles from the Irish coast."[13] Yet survive it did, and eventually a flood of missionaries from Ireland fanned out across Scotland, England, and the European continent. All along the way the monks established monasteries and carried on their tradition of copying and preserving the Bible, along with every other book they could get their hands on—including the great classics of the Greeks and Romans, some of which had not been seen in Europe for centuries. They also taught their converts Latin, music, and painting.

To give some idea of their success, by the early 600s nearly seven hundred monastic communities had been established along the rocky coasts and mountains of Scotland alone, and between A.D. 650 and A.D. 850 more than half of all known biblical commentaries were written by Irishmen. Everywhere they went, the Irish monks carried their Bibles and books around their waists, just as the Irish pagans had once tied their enemies' skulls to their belts.

This is "how the Irish saved civilization," to use Cahill's words, for it was the disciplined labor of the monks that stanched the tide of barbarism across Europe, preserved the best of Greco-Roman culture, and infused new life into the decadent monasticism of the continent. The monastery became the center of culture, replacing the dying cities and expanding into a vast complex populated by monks, workers, servants, and dependents. Gradually, "the woody swamp became a hermitage, a religious house, a farm, an abbey, a village, a seminary, a school of learning, and a city," writes John Henry Newman.[14]

What's more, this astonishing feat was accomplished again and again throughout the Dark Ages. From the north, Vikings repeatedly swooped down on the coasts or sailed deep inland on the rivers to loot and destroy, murdering people, ruining fields, plundering wealth, and burning cities across Europe. From the east, the Magyars and Avars, the Huns and Mongols, swept successively across the steppes, leaving similar devastation and death in their wake. But each time, Christianity showed its unquenchable, supernatural power of spiritual regeneration. Each time, the monastic communities arose from the rubble to become islands of peace and spiritual order.

The monks' first concern, of course, was to nourish the inner life of faith. But spiritual reform inevitably led to social change as they fulfilled the call to defend the oppressed and to speak boldly against evil in high places. In the monks, says historian Christopher Dawson, "the lawless feudal nobles, who cared nothing for morality or law, recognized the presence of something stronger than brute force—a numinous supernatural power they dared not ignore."[15]

Lasting peace could not come to Europe, however, until the barbarians themselves were evangelized, and one of the most exciting chapters in the history of the Christian church is the transformation of the barbarians from bloodthirsty warriors into peace-loving farmers, determined to live by the work of their own hands instead of by theft and plunder.[16] As the barbarians were converted and the destructive invasions ceased, European society began to flourish. Cities grew, guilds emerged to protect the interests of the crafts and professions, and ideas of representative government took root.

In this setting, Christianity gave birth to a new institution, the university, which developed from schools attached to the great cathedrals in places such as Paris and Bologna, eventually replacing the monasteries as centers of learning and culture. Later, the Reformation would spark a quantum leap in culture formation, inspiring a new work ethic that would fuel the industrial revolution and create a political climate that made free democracies possible.

Inner Life Shapes Actions

This is how Christianity is meant to function in society—not just as a private faith but as a creative force in the culture. The inner life of faith must shape our actions out in the world. In every choice and decision we make, we either help to overcome the forces of barbarism—whether medieval or modern—or acquiesce to those forces; we either help build a life-giving, peace-loving ethos, or fan the flames of egoism and destruction.

THE NEW MILLENNIUM

At the dawn of the third millennium, we face the same challenge
and opportunity that the early church and the medieval monks
faced: to build a culture informed by a biblical worldview. The
most hopeful words from any Christian leader today have come
from John Paul II, who urges believers everywhere to make the
new millennium a "new springtime" for the gospel.[17] Is this false
optimism? On all sides I hear battle-weary evangelicals saying that
we have lost the culture war and that we might as well turn back
to building our churches instead. But in light of our historical heritage, we dare not give in to despair. That would be not only a sin
(lack of faith in God's sovereignty) but also a misreading of our
times. To leave the cultural battlefield now would be to desert the
cause just when we are on the threshold of a great opportunity.

In recent years, all the grand propositions advanced over the
past century have fallen, one by one, like toy soldiers. The twentieth century was the age of ideology, of the great "isms": Communism, socialism, Nazism, liberalism, scientism. Everywhere,
ideologues nursed visions of creating the ideal society by some
utopian scheme. But today all the major ideological constructions
are being tossed on the ash heap of history. All that remains is
the cynicism of postmodernism, with its bankrupt assertions that
there *is* no objective truth or meaning, that we are free to create
our own truth as long as we understand that it is nothing more
than a subjective dream, a comforting illusion.

And as the reigning ideologies crumble, people are caught in
an impasse: Having believed that individual autonomy was the
holy grail that would lead to liberation, they now see that it has
led only to moral chaos and state coercion. The time is ripe for
a message that the social peace and personal fulfillment people
really crave are available only in Christianity. The church has
stood unshaken through the ebb and flow of two millennia. It
has survived the persecutions of the early centuries, the barbarian

invasions of the Middle Ages, and the intellectual assaults of the modern era. Its solid walls rise up above the ruins littered across the intellectual landscape. God forbid that we, heirs of saints and martyrs, should falter at this pivotal moment.

The new millennium is a time for Christians to celebrate, to raise our confidence, to blow trumpets, and to fly the flag high. This is the time to make a compelling case that Christianity offers the most rational and realistic hope for both personal redemption and social renewal.

But if we are to have an impact on our culture, the beginning point must be to take our stand united in Christ, making a conscious effort among all true believers to come together across racial, ethnic, and confessional lines. In his high-priestly prayer, Jesus prayed fervently that we would be one with one another, as he is one with the Father. Why? *So that the world will know* that he is the Christ (see John 17:20-23). The unavoidable implication of Jesus' words is that Christian unity is the key to evangelism and cultural renewal. Much of the church's weakness can be traced to its inability or unwillingness to obey the command to strive for unity in Christ.

This is difficult for many evangelicals (as well as Catholics and Orthodox) to accept, and understandably so. The bloody wounds inflicted in the Reformation and Counter-Reformation remain raw and painful, and deep doctrinal differences continue to divide believers. Conservative believers are distrustful of ecumenism because of the danger of glossing over those differences.

Focusing on worldview, however, can help build bridges. Protestants and Catholics who join together in pro-life demonstrations find that they do indeed share the deepest worldview convictions. They discover what one scholar calls "an ecumenism of the trenches."[18] It was in recognition of this common worldview that in 1992 Father Richard Neuhaus and I organized Evangelicals and Catholics Together (ECT), a nonofficial group seeking

common ground in our witness to the world and our defense of
Christian truth. ECT's joint statements have emphasized the
great truths of the faith we hold in common without compromising the very real doctrinal differences that continue to exist.

Our efforts have been controversial, but they should not be.
Abraham Kuyper, a committed Calvinist, saw more clearly than
any other modern figure that the battle of our times is worldview
against worldview, principle against principle, and that in this
battle against the forces of modernity, Catholics and Protestants
must stand side by side. More than a hundred years ago in his
famous Stone Lectures at Princeton, Kuyper argued that when
we understand Christianity as a worldview, we "might be enabled
once more to take our stand by the side of Romanism in opposition to modern pantheism." For "what we have in common with
Rome . . . are precisely those fundamentals of our Christian creed
now most fiercely assaulted by the modern spirit." If Roman
Catholics "take up the sword to do valiant and skillful battle"
against the same enemy, Kuyper concluded, "is it not the part of
wisdom to accept their valuable help?"[19]

Yet Kuyper was only echoing themes expressed back in 1541.
In the very midst of the Reformation battles, a group of Catholic
and Protestant leaders, including a cardinal from the Vatican, met
at Regensburg, Germany, in the Colloquy of Ratisbon. The group
reached agreement on the doctrine of justification, which had
been the great opening wedge of the Reformation (though discussions foundered on other issues, such as the Mass). One of the
Protestant participants wrote a letter to a friend, in which he said,
"You will be astonished that our opponents yielded so much . . .
[they] have thus retained the substance of the true doctrine."[20]
The writer of that letter was a young aide to the Protestant nego-
tiators. His name was John Calvin.

Today we need the kind of stand Calvin sought and Kuyper so
powerfully urged on us. We need what C. S. Lewis called mere

Christianity: believers standing together, rallying around the great truths of Scripture and the ancient creeds. Only when such unity is visible in the world will we truly experience the power of the gospel.

Then, standing together as the people of God, we must obey the two great commissions: first to win the lost and then to build a culture. Christians must seize this moment to show the world, just as the Irish did centuries ago, that Christianity is not only true . . . it is humanity's one great hope.

The Christian and the Materialist
hold different beliefs about the
universe. They can't both be right.
The one who is wrong will act in
a way which simply doesn't fit the
real universe.   C. S. LEWIS

CHAPTER 3

DON'T WORRY,
BE RELIGIOUS

As you read chapter 3, keep the following questions
in mind:
- What are the results of rejecting the biblical views of
  creation, the Fall, and redemption?
- What is the "modernist impasse," and why does it make
  the Christian message attractive to people?
- What medical and social research results indicate that
  faithful Christian living is worthwhile—in concrete terms?

How do we redeem a culture? How do we rise to the opportunity before us at the start of a new millennium?

The answer is simple: from the inside out. From the individual
to the family to the community, and then outward in ever widening ripples. We must begin by understanding what it means to
live by Christian worldview principles in our own behavior and
choices. Unless we do, we will interpret the biblical commands
according to the spirit of the age and will therefore be conformed
to the world rather than to God's Word.

Some years ago, in the middle of a doctrinal discussion, a young
man differed with Nancy over a point the apostle Paul makes in
1 Corinthians.

"I disagree with you," he said.

"No, you disagree with Paul," Nancy corrected him gently.

"Okay, then, I disagree with Paul," he said and shrugged.

He went on to explain that as he saw it, the Bible was written long ago for a different age and that today the Holy Spirit can reveal new truth—truth that might even contradict what the Bible teaches. Now, this young man was a sincere Christian—president of a Christian campus group and a leader among his peers—but he had absorbed the mental framework of a secular culture and was reinterpreting Scripture in the context of that framework. He had lost his understanding of truth and revelation, of a worldview that roots Scripture in the God who is ultimate reality. This carried over into his personal choices, evidenced by the fact that he was sleeping with his girlfriend. He was not untaught in biblical ethics; and he was not deliberately backsliding. His honest convictions told him that the Bible consisted of nothing more than human documents and, therefore, was not normative for his life. Whenever he read Scripture, it was filtered through a mental grid set by a non-Christian worldview, resulting in a distorted understanding of doctrine and personal ethics.

If we want to transform our pagan culture as the monks did in the Middle Ages, we must start with ourselves, understanding what a Christian worldview means for our own moral and lifestyle choices. This is more important today than ever because individual moral choices determine the health of the entire society. Polls consistently show that Americans worry most about social and moral decay—crime, family breakdown, drug abuse, sex and violence in the entertainment media—all results of moral choices made ultimately by individuals.[1]

VALUES-FREE LIFE?

Given these facts, one might expect the nation's bully pulpits would be devoted to encouraging people to take responsibility for their lives, to exert the self-discipline needed to change their behavior. Instead, for the past few decades, the dominant cultural voices have argued that individuals have a right to live in any way they choose and that *society* has a responsibility to pick up the tab for any negative consequences that result.

This attitude was cleverly illustrated in the comic strip "Outland" during the controversial health-care debate in 1993. In the opening frame, the penguin Opus and his friends are perched precariously on a tricycle at the edge of a precipice. Posted all around are warning signs: Danger! Stop! A surgeon general's warning says "Plummeting down cliffs is hazardous to one's health." But the characters ignore the signs and go careening down. The tricycle topples over, of course, and they all fly off. From the mud, Opus reaches out his hand and demands, "Quick! Free unlimited health care!"[2]

Sadly, this is the attitude many Americans have taken toward the pathologies plaguing both our personal lives and society at large: that our behavior is our own business and that society has a duty to compensate for any negative consequences of our autonomous choices.

Sexual behavior is a prime example. Sexual relationships outside marriage are responsible for the spread of sexually transmitted diseases (STDs), for most abortions, for fatherless homes, and for chronic welfare dependency. But did this social wreckage cause sex educators to teach young people to refrain from sex outside marriage? Hardly. From the 1960s through the 1980s, public school sex-education programs and their advocates were adamant that sexual activity was entirely a matter of the student's personal choice. And when the inevitable consequences followed, these same educators pressed for government solutions to bandage over the negative effects. To avoid STDs, the government supplied condoms in the schools. When homosexual promiscuity led to fatal diseases, the government was blamed and shamed into picking up the tab for more research. When sex led to pregnancy, the government was expected to pay for abortions or supply welfare support to fatherless families.

This attitude began in the 1960s, when a new concept of public morality took hold, stated baldly in the words of sociologist Christopher Jencks. Speaking of fatherless families, Jencks argued that if people "truly prefer a family consisting of a mother, children, and a series of transient males, then it is hardly the federal government's proper business to try to alter this choice." What *is* the government's business then? It "ought to invent ways of providing such [single-parent] families with the same physical and psychic necessities of life available to other kinds of families."[3]

Note carefully what Jencks is saying: The government *must not* seek to help shape the nation's moral climate or discourage irresponsible behavior. Instead, its job is to "invent ways" to compensate for any disadvantages created by the bad choices people make. As psychiatrist David Larson puts it, the government is supposed to make sure people have their cake and eat it, too![4]

This attitude is not confined to the government. It's amazing how many ordinary Americans have fallen into the trap of expecting someone else to pick up the costs of their own irresponsibility. The American Medical Association says the growth in health-care expenses today can be traced largely to "lifestyle factors and social problems." Some studies indicate that up to 70 percent of all diseases result from lifestyle choices.[5] People know they should stop smoking, cut out junk food, and get regular exercise. But how many take these basic steps in preventive care? And when their unhealthy habits give them heart disease or lung cancer, they expect the health-care system to protect them from the consequences of their own bad habits.[6] The Opus cartoon is uncomfortably close to the truth.

Where did this idea of value-free lifestyles come from? What are its worldview roots? How do the categories of *creation, fall,* and *redemption* help us to diagnose what's wrong with the predominant secular view—and to see how a Christian worldview leads to a better, healthier, and more rational way of living?

In a nutshell, if we reject the biblical teaching about creation, we end up with nature as our creator. Morality then becomes something humans invent when they have evolved to a certain level. There is no transcendent source of moral standards that dictates how we should live. Each individual has the right to chart his or her own course. And if we reject the idea of sin and the Fall, nothing is objectively wrong, and there is no real guilt; there are only false guilt feelings that result from social disapproval. The logical conclusion of this thinking is that redemption means freeing ourselves from false guilt and restoring our natural autonomy by eliminating the stigma from all lifestyles. And the role of public authorities is to mobilize resources to make sure that no negative consequences follow from the choices any individual may make. For if all choices are morally equal, then no one should suffer for the choices he or she makes.

By contrast, Christianity claims that God created the universe with a definite structure—a material order and a moral order. If we live contrary to that order, we sin against God, and the consequences are invariably harmful and painful, on both a personal and a social level. On the other hand, if we submit to that order and live in harmony with it, then our lives will be happier and healthier. The role of public authorities is to encourage people to live according to the principles that make for social health and harmony.

Over the past four decades, our public discourse was dominated by the value-free model. Yet today, its disastrous consequences are becoming abundantly clear. Even determined secularists have begun to see that society simply can't keep up with the costs of personal and moral irresponsibility: Over those same four decades, abortion and teen pregnancy soared; the welfare system grew overloaded; crime rates shot up, especially among juveniles; health-care costs climbed so fast that the government keeps threatening to take over (even as Medicare projects bankruptcy in a few years). It is becoming increasingly obvious that the welfare state has *not* been able to "invent ways" to give fatherless families "the same physical and psychic necessities of life available to other kinds of families," as Jencks put it.[7] Instead, welfare has helped create a permanent underclass that is disordered and demoralized. By compensating for irresponsible behavior, government has, in essence, subsidized it, thus encouraging more of it.

Americans have reached "the modernist impasse": <u>They were told they had a right to be free from the restrictions of morality and religion, yet as unrestricted choices have led to social break-down, they have begun to long for the protection that morality once provided.</u> After all, we didn't *have* epidemics of crime, broken families, abortion, or sexually transmitted diseases when Americans largely accepted biblical morality. Many are beginning to understand that morality is not merely an arbitrary constraint on individual choice but a protection against social disintegration.

That's why, after decades of public rhetoric about individual rights, we now hear cultural leaders struggling to find some common secular language to revive a sense of civic duty and virtue. Organizations like David Blankenhorn's National Fatherhood Initiative are emerging to halt family breakdown. Sex educators are beginning to talk about teaching kids to delay sexual involvement (if not until marriage, at least until adulthood). Character education is making inroads into classrooms.

BENEFITS OF CHRISTIAN LIVING

This new openness to moral arguments gives Christians an extraordinary opportunity to make our case that living according to the biblical moral order is healthier for both individuals and society. And there's a growing body of scientific evidence we can use to back up our argument. Medical studies are confirming that those who attend church regularly and act consistently with their faith are better off, both physically and mentally. Consider a few recent findings.[8]

Alcohol Abuse

Alcohol abuse is highest among those with little or no religious commitment.[9] One study found that nearly 89 percent of alcoholics said they lost interest in religion during their youth.[10]

Drug Abuse

Numerous studies have found an inverse correlation between religious commitment and drug abuse. Among young people, the importance of religion is the single best predictor of substance-abuse patterns. Joseph Califano, former secretary of the department of Health and Human Services and an architect of Lyndon Johnson's Great Society, did an amazing about-face when he became head of Columbia University's Center on Addiction and Substance Abuse. In 1998, Califano invited me, along with General McAffrey, Clinton's antidrug czar, to join him at a press conference where he released the results of a three-year study showing the relationship between substance abuse and crime. The statistics were startling: In 80 percent of criminal offenses, alcohol or drugs were implicated.[11] Then Califano pointed at me and told the assembled press gathering, "He has the answer. Every individual I have met who successfully came off drugs or alcohol has given religion as the key to rehabilitation." Califano now vigorously supports public funding for drug-treatment programs that "provide for spiritual needs."[12]

Crime

There is also a strong correlation between participation in religious activities and the avoidance of crime. In one study, Harvard

professor Richard Freeman discovered that regular church attendance is the primary factor in preventing African-American urban
young people from turning to drugs or crime.[13] Another study
revealed that regular attendance at a Prison Fellowship Bible study
cut recidivism by two-thirds.[14]

Depression and Stress

Several studies have found that high levels of religious commitment correlate with lower levels of depression and stress.[15] In
one Gallup survey, respondents with a strong religious commitment were twice as likely to describe themselves as "very happy."[16]
Armand Nicholi, professor of psychiatry at Harvard Medical
School and a deeply committed believer, argues from his lifelong
experience that Christians are far less likely to experience mental
disorders than their secular counterparts. Why? Because "the one
essential feature that characterizes all types of depression" is "the
feeling of hopelessness and helplessness," and Christians are never
without hope.[17]

Suicide

Persons who do not attend church are four times more likely to
commit suicide than are frequent church attenders. In fact, lack
of church attendance correlates more strongly with suicide rates
than with any other risk factor, including unemployment.[18]

Family Stability

A number of studies have found a strong inverse correlation
between church attendance and divorce, and one study found
that church attendance is the most important predictor of marital
stability.[19] Religion has also shown itself to be an important factor
in preventing teen sexual relations, babies born out of wedlock,
discord between parent and child, and other forms of family
breakdown.

The classic sociological research project "Middletown" studied the inhabitants of a typical American town three times, first in the 1920s and for the third time in the 1980s. The data over this extended period indicated a clear "relationship between family solidarity—family health, if you will—and church affiliation and activity."[20] In a study of the factors that contribute to healthy families, 84 percent of strong families identified religion as an important contributor to their strength. In yet another study, African-American parents cited church influence as significant in rearing their children and providing moral guidelines.[21]

Marital and Sexual Satisfaction

Lest one think these numbers mean that religious people are staying in unhappy marriages from a sense of duty, consider these statistics. Churchgoers are more likely to say they would marry the same spouse again—an important measure of marital satisfaction. A 1978 study found that church attendance predicted marital satisfaction better than any other single variable.[22] And the 1994 Sex in America study showed that very religious women enjoy a higher level of sexual satisfaction in their marriage than do nonreligious women.[23]

Physical Health: Studies have shown that maternity patients and their newborns have fewer medical complications if the mothers have a religious affiliation. Belonging to a religious group can lower blood pressure, relieve stress, and enhance survival after a heart attack. Heart surgery patients with strong religious beliefs are much more likely to survive surgery. Elderly men and women who attend worship services are less depressed and physically healthier than their peers with no religious faith. They are also healthier than those who do not attend worship services but watch religious television at home. People who go to church have lower blood pressure, even when risky behaviors such as smoking are factored in.[24]

Church attendance even affects mortality rates. For men who attend church frequently, the risk of dying from arteriosclerotic heart disease is only 60 percent of that for men who attend infrequently. The death rates of churchgoing men from pulmonary emphysema are less than half and from cirrhosis of the liver only 25 percent as high as for nonchurchgoing men.[25] Science seems to be confirming the teaching of Proverbs: "The fear of the Lord adds length to life" (Prov. 10:27).

.   .   .

This does not mean that every person of faith is healthy and happy, but the statistics do "make a powerful statement about the typical human condition," writes Patrick Glynn in *God: The Evidence*. Both clinical experience and research data suggest that "among the most important determinants of human happiness and well-being are our spiritual beliefs and moral choices."[26]

The statistics are so compelling that even a confirmed secularist ought to be convinced that religion is good for society. In fact, that's exactly what Guenter Lewy concludes in his recent book *Why America Needs Religion*. Lewy started out to write a book defending secularism, but after surveying the data, he ended up arguing, to his own surprise, that belief in God makes people happier and more fulfilled. "Whether it be juvenile delinquency, adult crime, prejudice, out-of-wedlock births, or marital conflict and divorce, there is a significantly lower rate of such indicators of moral failure and social ills among believing Christians."[27] In short, a person *can* live a moral and healthy life without God, but statistically speaking, the odds are against it.

Furthermore, the benefits of Christianity are not solely a matter of attitude and lifestyle. It is impossible to dismiss the frankly supernatural. Dr. Dale Matthews has documented experiments in which volunteers prayed for selected patients with rheumatoid arthritis. To avoid a possible placebo effect from knowing they were being prayed for, the patients were not told which ones were subjects of the test. The recovery rate among those prayed for was measurably higher than among a control group, for which prayers were not offered.[28]

It is time for the medical profession to recognize the healing potential of the spiritual dimension, says Harvard professor Herbert Benson. Though not a professing Christian himself, Benson admits that humans are "engineered for religious faith." We are "wired for God. . . . Our genetic blueprint has made believing in an Infinite Absolute part of our nature."[29] That is about as close as a nonbeliever can get to confirming the biblical claim that the human spirit was created in order to live in communion with God.

These findings do not mean, however, that just any kind of religion is beneficial. Gordon Allport, the great psychologist of religion, drew a distinction between *intrinsic* and *extrinsic* religion. Extrinsically religious people use religion for external purposes, like the politician who attends church to gain respectability or the person who prays for purely material benefits. But intrinsically religious people serve God without ulterior motive: They pray in order to commune with him and understand his truth; they give without any utilitarian calculation. In Allport's professional experience, improved mental health correlates only with intrinsic religion. The benefits go to those who genuinely believe, not to those who use religion for ulterior purposes.[30] These findings seem to shatter the Freudian stereotype of religion as mere wish fulfillment, something we make up to obtain certain benefits. For if we were to make up a religion for external purposes, we would be more miserable than ever.

Similarly, benefits accrue only to those who practice their faith, not to those who merely profess it. In fact, the Larsons' studies have found that it is extremely *un*healthy to hold strong religious beliefs without practicing them. People exhibit high levels of stress if they believe in God but neglect church attendance, fail to read and meditate on Scripture, omit prayer before meals, or fall into sin. One study of chronic alcoholics found that a surprisingly high number hold conservative religious beliefs but are not acting on them. The Larsons suggest that the stress caused by this contradiction between belief and practice may contribute to their alcoholism.[31]

In short, the inconsistent Christian suffers even more than the consistent atheist. The most miserable person of all is the one who knows the truth yet doesn't obey it.

THE BEGINNING OF WISDOM

The growth in scientific evidence validating the Christian worldview has been greatly inspired by the work of one man, David Larson, president of the National Institute for Healthcare Research. Larson's story illustrates not only how Christians should persevere in their convictions but also what we can achieve when we do.

When Larson began his training in psychiatry, one of his professors tried to discourage him. "Tell me, Dave," the professor said. "Your faith is important to you, isn't it?"

"Yes," said Larson.

"Then I think you should put aside the idea of becoming a psychiatrist. For psychiatric patients, religion can only be harmful."

Larson's professor was stating the conventional wisdom among psychiatrists and psychologists, handed down from Sigmund Freud, the founder of psychoanalysis, who defined religion as "a universal obsessional neurosis," an "infantile helplessness," and "regression to primary narcissism." The terminology has changed since Freud, but most psychologists and psychiatrists retain the assumption that religion is a negative factor in mental health and that it is associated with mental pathologies.[32]

Yet Larson refused to be deterred. And as he continued his studies, he noticed a very interesting pattern: Religion was not associated with mental illness after all. In fact, quite the opposite: Religion actually helped protect *against* mental disorders.

This insight spurred Larson to conduct his own research, and today his work has begun to turn around an entire profession. "Growing numbers of psychologists are finding religion, if not in their personal lives, at least in their data," reports the *New York Times*. "What was once, at best, an unfashionable topic in psychology has been born again as a respectable focus for scientific research."[33] The data is showing that religion, far from being a mental illness, is actually beneficial to mental health, physical health, family strength, and social order.

This new scientific data provides a wonderful tool for apologetics, for it shows clearly that if we ignore biblical principles, we end up living in ways that run against the grain of our being, and we pay a steep price in terms of stress, depression, family conflict, and even physical illness. Rather than being an arbitrary set of rules and restrictions that repress and distort our true nature, Christianity actually describes our true nature and shows us how to live in accord with it. And when we do so, we enjoy the fruits of operating the way we were made to. "The fear of the Lord is the beginning of wisdom. . . . For through me your days will be many, and years will be added to your life" (Prov. 9:10-11). The evidence is a powerful validation of Proverbs; a biblical view of human nature does indeed conform to reality.

Recognizing these concrete benefits of faith, many Christians are joining together for their own financial, spiritual, and emotional advantage—as well as to provide an effective witness to the broader culture. For example, the Florida-based Christian Care Medi-Share Program offers members 100 percent coverage for far less than most conventional group insurance programs—a little under $200 per family, per month. In return, members commit to living a healthy lifestyle: no smoking, no illegal drugs, no sex outside marriage, moderation in alcohol use. They also pray for one another. When a group member suffers illness or injury, others pray and write letters of encouragement. John Reinhold, founder and president of Christian Care Medi-Share Program, says, "Our members believe in sharing and caring, but they do not wish to subsidize those . . . who choose to live in a way which inevitably leads to a premature breakdown in mind and body."[34]

We cannot escape the consequences of our own choices. In our bodies, we flesh out either the biblical worldview or a worldview that is in opposition to the Bible. And when we incarnate the truth of God in our lives and families, we help bring new life to our neighborhoods and churches, our cities and nation, in an ever widening circle.

DISCUSSION QUESTIONS

CHAPTER 1

1 Trace Danny Croce's spiritual journey to Christ. Who said what to him? What did he read and see? How direct or indirect was the witness he received? How does this compare to your own conversion? Though the Spirit works differently with each person, are there patterns evident in your group?

2 As a new Christian, what did Danny expect from himself? What did other people expect from him? How did other people react to him—positively or negatively? What was he free to do, and why? Compare his journey to your own. What parallels do you see?

CHAPTER 2

3 What if John Donne had written a meditation with the line "Everyone is an island" (rather than "No man is an island, entire of itself; every man is a piece of the continent, a part of the main" *Devotions upon Emergent Occasions,* 1624, "Devotion 17")? Come up with more lines—metaphorical or descriptive— to describe the isolated people and the landscape (seascape). What evidence do you see that "everyone is an island" is a prevailing byword of our contemporary culture? What unhealthy symptoms does this philosophy cause?

4   "We first have to shake off the comfortable notion that Christianity is merely a personal experience, applying only to one's private life." Discuss whether or not you think this is true. If you agree with the statement, does the truth of it feel threatening? Why or why not?

5   What is the cultural commission of humankind? How did sin affect it?

6   Read aloud Colossians 1:13-14. What does this passage say we are saved from? What has this meant in your own life?

7   Read and discuss the paragraph on pages 21–22 about Colossians 1:15-20, the lordship of Christ. Then read aloud 2 Corinthians 5:14-21. If you have been given a "ministry of reconciliation" and you are "Christ's ambassadors," what is your relationship with, attitude toward, and message to

other Christians?

nonbelievers?

the culture at large?

the created world?

yourself?

Christ?

8 What does salvation mean or involve? What does it mean that Christians are saved not only *from* something but also *to* something?

9 What is the fault inherent in the modern distinction between facts and values? What is the relationship between God's governing laws and a Christian worldview?

10 What makes this time in history an excellent time for Christians boldly to live out and proclaim their faith? (Discuss this in light of material in chapter 3 also.)

CHAPTER 3

11 What are the results of rejecting the biblical views of creation, the Fall, and redemption? (If you have studied the first two books in this series, this question serves as a review.)

12 The redeeming "ripples" of the Christian worldview start with, but go beyond, the individual. Go through the long list of issues for which studies show that Christians come off looking pretty healthy and well adjusted compared to the population at large. How does this compare with your own observations?

13 Have there been seasons in your life when you sensed the truth of this comment: "The most miserable person of all is the one who knows the truth yet doesn't obey it"? Share your experience if you think others could learn from it.

14 Starting today, what can you do to realize more of the positive benefits of the Christian worldview in your own life? How can you help one another overcome any obstacles in your path?

ROLE PLAY

Role plays can be "no pressure" ways for participants to practice explaining the Christian worldview to skeptics. Remember a few ground rules. Any comments from listeners should be made (and received) as encouragement, not as personal criticism. "You might add this point . . . "; "You might smile more and maintain a friendly tone"; "You might start with a more basic premise. . . ."

Choose one option, depending on the size of your group and group dynamics.

1. In front of the whole group, ask two people to volunteer to act out a conversation between a skeptic and a Christian. The large group can give constructive feedback. If time allows, another pair can follow.

2. Have all participants pair off. The two people can take turns assuming the roles, each taking the role of a Christian and of a skeptic.

3. Have people form groups of three. One person takes the role of the Christian. The second person takes the role of a skeptic. The third is an observer who gives feedback. Alternate roles.

CONVERSATION STARTER

Assume your neighbor says, "You won't smoke; you won't drink. You Christians never have any fun." Review some of the benefits of the Christian worldview that you've realized in your life. (If it's true that you never do have much fun, maybe this session will serve as a wake-up call, and this role play can become a vehicle for your helping one another learn how to tap into the "joy of your salvation.")

CLOSING SUMMARY

What is the one thing you want to remember from what you read (or heard or did) in this session?

Consider sharing this with the group.

AT HOME,
AT SCHOOL

If the family trends of recent decades are extended into the future, the result will be not only growing uncertainty within marriage, but the gradual elimination of marriage in favor of casual liaisons oriented to adult expressiveness and self-fulfillment. The problem with this scenario is that children will be harmed, adults will probably be no happier, and the social order could collapse.

DAVID POPENOE

CHAPTER 4

GOD'S TRAINING GROUND

As you read chapter 4, keep the following questions in mind:

- In what ways is the clash of worldviews evident in the contemporary definitions of "family" and in family issues?
- What subtle distinction is at the heart of contemporary moral conflicts?
- How does the philosophy of the "unencumbered self" affect the family and other social institutions?
- What does the Christian worldview say about the family?

Imagine your children bringing home a library book that assures them divorce is nothing serious, just a transition some families go through. Or *don't* imagine it. Go to the library yourself, and you'll find a rainbow of children's books that downplay the importance of an intact marriage.

"There are different kinds of daddies," one book for preschoolers reassures them. "Sometimes a daddy goes away like yours did. He may not see his children at all." In other words, divorce is just a normal variation on fatherhood. "Some kids know both their mom and their dad, and some kids don't," says another book. Still another treats divorce as an awkward moment that can be mastered by applying a few practical tips. "Living with one parent almost always means there will be less money. Be prepared to give up some things."[1]

The message? That daddies who stay and daddies who leave are just "different kinds of daddies" and that divorce has no moral significance.

The message does not end with picture books for young children. When the Institute for American Values surveyed twenty of the most widely used college textbooks in undergraduate courses on marriage and family, it uncovered a shockingly negative outlook on the subject.[2] The textbooks emphasize problems such as domestic violence while downplaying the benefits of marriage. They warn women that marriage is likely to be psychologically stifling and even physically threatening. "We do know," states one textbook, ". . . that marriage has an adverse effect on women's mental health," an assertion that has no support in empirical data. In fact, most studies find that both men and women report higher levels of happiness when they are married.[3] Meanwhile, these volumes all but ignore the well-documented negative effects of divorce on children, only half even mentioning the fact that family breakdown correlates strongly with increased juvenile crime.

It would not have been surprising if the Institute for American Values study had found a few ideologically biased textbooks. What is disturbing is the finding that virtually *all* the textbooks used by students across the nation are preaching the views of radical feminism and the sexual revolution to our nation's future teachers, guidance counselors, and caseworkers.

Out of sheer self-interest, if for no other reason, nearly every civilization has protected the family both legally and socially, for it is the institution that propagates the human race and civilizes children. Yet in postmodern America, the family is being assaulted on many fronts, from books to popular magazines, on television and in movies, through state and federal policies. This systematic deconstruction of the oldest, most basic social institution is a prime cause of the social chaos in America in recent decades.

As we move out from the range of individuals and their choices, the first circle of influence is in the intimate relationships of the family. Nowhere is the clash of worldviews more pronounced than here. Nowhere are its effects more disastrous. Nowhere does it touch more deeply on the natural order that underlies all civilizations. And nowhere is it more evident that we Christians must take a worldview approach if we are going to make a difference. Many believers have become politically active over issues related to the family, yet typically our efforts are reactive rather than proactive, largely because we have failed to confront the underlying worldview assumptions.

THE FAMILY IN AN AGE OF MURPHY BROWN

Conflicting worldviews over the family were displayed sharply in 1992 when then Vice President Dan Quayle delivered his infamous "Murphy Brown" speech, which evoked howls of ridicule from one end of the country to the other. Many Americans tuned in to the next season's opening show just to hear Candice Bergen's response. And the star did not disappoint. As Murphy Brown, she looked straight into the camera and lectured viewers that there is no normative definition of the family. All that matters, she intoned, is "commitment, love, and caring."

Shortly afterward, however, Bergen was interviewed in *TV Guide* and took quite a different line. "As far as my family values go," she said, "my child and my family have always been my top priority." Bergen even claimed that she had been one step ahead of Dan Quayle, having warned the show's producers not to "send out the message . . . to young women especially, that we're encouraging them to be single mothers." She ended by declaring that "I myself

. . . believe the ideal is that you have a two-parent family. I'm the last person to think fathers are obsolete."[4] When speaking as cultural icon Murphy Brown, she insists there is no normative family structure. But as Candice Bergen, wife and mother, she enthusiastically supports the committed, two-parent family.

If we are to understand contemporary moral liberalism, we must dissect this puzzling inconsistency. We live in an age in which liberty has been defined as absolutely free choice. It doesn't matter *what* we choose; the dignity of the individual resides in the mere capacity to choose. So we are perfectly free to favor marriage and traditional values, just as long as we don't deny others the right to choose other values. That is, as long as we don't claim that our choice is based on an objective, normative standard of truth that applies to everyone.

So Bergen feels perfectly free to reveal her own adherence to traditional ideals for the family because all she's doing is expressing her own private, personal, subjective opinion. But when Dan Quayle expresses identical ideals, he is savaged in the media and ridiculed by late-night comedians. Even Bergen condemned him as "arrogant," "aggressive," and "offensive"—even though she apparently holds precisely the same views.[5] Why? Because Quayle is presenting these views not as personal preferences but as objective moral truths.

This subtle distinction is at the heart of the moral conflicts dividing our culture today. As a result, we cannot determine people's worldview simply by asking about their position on particular moral questions: Are you for or against abortion? Are you for or against homosexual marriage? Instead, we must ask how they *justify* their views. Many Americans retain traditional ideals but regard them as matters of personal choice, refusing to insist on them as objective, universal norms. The most familiar example is those who are "personally opposed" to abortion yet defend the right of others to make their own choice. In their own lives, many

Americans practice exemplary ethical behavior, yet when asked to articulate objective principles to justify that behavior, they can offer nothing beyond, "It feels right for me."[6]

This is certainly true when it comes to family and sexuality. People use the traditional terms *marriage* and *family*, but the words no longer muster a sense of objective obligation. Many Americans no longer treat marriage as a moral commitment with its own definition and nature, a commitment that makes objective demands of us, regardless of what we might prefer. Instead, marriage is regarded as a social construction, as something one can define according to one's own preferences. Even some who wear the mantle of moral conservatism fall into this trap. At the 1992 Republican National Convention, former First Lady Barbara Bush came out with this fuzzy statement: "However *you* define family, that's what we mean by family values."[7]

It's important that we cut through the rhetoric and get to the root of this conflict, which again hinges on our basic assumptions about *creation, fall,* and *redemption.* The Christian worldview teaches that from the beginning, God created individuals in relationship. By creating human beings as male and female, God established the interrelatedness of human sexuality, the marital relationship, and the institution of the family, each with its own divinely given moral norms. While there can be great variety in the cultural expression of these institutions, when we enter into the covenant of marriage and family, we submit to an objective and God-given structure.

But during the Enlightenment, philosophers began rejecting the doctrine of creation and substituting a hypothetical presocial, prepolitical "state of nature." In this primeval state, individuals are the only ultimate reality; social bonds are created by the choices individuals make. That's why French philosopher Pierre Manent says the basic tenet of modern liberalism is that "no individual can have an obligation to which he has not consented."[8]

This radically changes one's view of marriage, for if it is not rooted in the way we were originally created, but only in individual choice, then it is also something we can *alter* by choice. What's more, all choices become morally equivalent, and there is no justification for favoring some choices over others. If someone wants a traditional marriage, that's fine. If someone else wants a same-sex marriage or some other variant, well, that's fine, too.

This moral equivalence has led to an aggressive defense of deviant practices. In Hollywood, for example, it's become normal to have children out of wedlock and to grow patchwork families from various couplings. For these people, foregoing marriage is not merely a matter of unrestrained sexual urges but an expression of genuine conviction, an assertion that cohabitation is as morally acceptable as marriage.

Film critic Michael Medved found that out when he commended the film production work of a particular Hollywood couple, referring to them as "married." This was a natural assumption, since they had been together more than fifteen years and had given birth to two children. Ah, but one can no longer assume such things, and Medved received an angry letter from a friend of the couple, saying that the two were certainly *not* married and that they would be "offended" to hear themselves described that way.[9]

Offended? Assuming that someone is married is now an insult? What we're seeing is that challenges to traditional morality are themselves treated as moral crusades. For if no choices are wrong, then no lifestyle may be criticized, and one must never be made to feel guilty. Indeed, doing so is positively wrong. Put in worldview terms, in modern liberalism, the only "sin" is hemming others in with oppressive rules and artificial moral codes; "redemption" means restoring the freedom once enjoyed in the original state of nature. As political philosopher John Stuart Mill once wrote, "the mere example of nonconformity, the mere refusal to bend the knee to custom, is itself a service."[10] Now, *there's* a positive spin on immorality: If you deliberately reject moral and social rules, you're actually performing a service, helping to free people from the grip of oppressive moral traditions.

The Unencumbered Self

This is the philosophy of the "unencumbered self," says Harvard political philosopher Michael Sandel, a worldview that depicts the isolated self as prior to all commitments or moral obligations. In traditional societies, a person's identity was found in and expressed through the social roles he or she played in the family, church, village, trade, tribe, and ethnic group. Today, however, roles and responsibilities are regarded as separate from, even contradictory to, one's essential identity, one's core self. The self can either accept or reject them in the process of defining itself.[11]

This may sound abstract, but it has intensely practical consequences. One of the themes of the radical feminist movement has been that women are stifled by the roles of wife and mother and must discover their true self *apart* from these relationships. As a result, the past few decades have seen a vast migration of women into the paid workforce, as personal fulfillment became more important than marriage and family to many women. The sharp rise in abortion can be seen as a strong indicator of a decreased interest in bearing children. Similarly, the increased use of day care reflects in part a lower commitment to being the primary caregiver for one's own children. Dr. Stanley Greenspan, pediatrics professor at the George Washington University School of Medicine, observes that this is the first time in history that there's been a growing trend for middle-class families "to farm out the care of their babies."[12]

The source of these trends, however, is not solely feminism. One reason women found the theme of autonomy so persuasive is that it had already been adopted by *men* for nearly half a century. In colonial times, manhood was defined in terms of responsibility for the family and the common good; today, "true" masculinity tends to be defined as individualistic, aggressive, and self-assertive. This new image emerged at the end of the nineteenth century in cowboy and adventure fiction that "celebrated the man who had escaped the confines of domesticity."[13] By the 1950s, *Playboy* came on the scene, warning that marriage is a trap that will "crush man's adventurous, freedom-loving spirit."[14] The roles of husband and father, instead of being God-ordained responsibilities that express a man's essential nature, came to be seen as restricting conventions that contradict a man's true self. This bore deadly fruit as men deserted their family responsibilities, a trend so widespread today that the dominant social problem in America is male flight from the family.[15]

The notion of the "unencumbered self" has caused both men and women to view family relationships as arbitrary and confining roles. That's why people like sexuality researcher Shere Hite can insist that "the breakdown of the family is a good thing," because it liberates us from restrictive roles and rules.[16]

This negative view of marriage has yielded consequences across the entire culture. If people dare to say that marriage is superior to other arrangements, they are accused of "discrimination." Elayne Bennett, founder of Best Friends, a program that teaches girls to delay sexual involvement until after high school, was once asked why she did not urge girls to delay sex until marriage. "If we talk about marriage," she said, "the schools won't let us in."[17] Let that sink in for a moment: Many public schools today *won't even consider* a program that holds up marriage as an ideal. In addition, many public policies no longer protect marriage as a unique social good. In tax law, there's the marriage penalty; in business, there are spousal benefits for people who are not married; in the courts, there are rulings that put homosexual unions on the same level as marriage.[18] The family is treated as a loose collection of rights-bearing individuals who hook up with others in whatever ways they choose to for their own benefit.

Popular culture echoes this message. The same people who bring us those heartwarming Hallmark family films also produced a wedding card that reads, "I can't promise you forever. But I can promise you today." Equally telling, a cartoon in a major magazine depicts a young man saying to his girlfriend, "It's only marriage I'm proposing, after all, not a lifetime commitment." Acclaimed novelist Toni Morrison has said the nuclear family "is a paradigm that just doesn't work. . . . Why we are hanging on to it, I don't know."[19] And popular entertainment consistently portrays divorce and adultery as forms of liberation. In the closing scene of the hit movie *Mrs. Doubtfire,* the central character reassures a young girl after her parents' breakup that after divorce some parents "get along much better . . . and they can become better people and much better mommies and daddies."[20]

Reality Check?

How about a reality check here? Social science statistics show that divorced parents *don't* generally become "better mommies and daddies." Few fathers even see their children regularly, and mothers spend less time with their children, too, because of the emotional devastation they suffer and the increased responsibilities they bear. In fact, the negative consequences of divorce are being measured over and over again, and the findings are grim.[21]

Consider these statistics. Children in single-parent families are six times more likely to be poor, and half the single mothers in the United States live below the poverty line. Children of divorce suffer intense grief, which often lasts for many years. Even as young adults, they are nearly twice as likely to require psychological help. Children from disrupted families have more academic and behavioral problems at school and are nearly twice as likely to drop out of high school.[22] Girls in single-parent homes are at much greater risk for precocious sexuality and are three times more likely to have a child out of wedlock.[23]

Crime and substance abuse are strongly linked to fatherless households. Studies show that 60 percent of rapists grew up in fatherless homes, as did 72 percent of adolescent murderers and 70 percent of all long-term prison inmates. In fact, most of the social pathologies disrupting American life today can be traced to fatherlessness.[24]

Surprisingly, when divorced parents marry again, their children are not any better off, and some studies actually show that the children develop increased pathologies. Preschool children in stepfamilies, for example, are forty times more likely to suffer physical or sexual abuse.[25]

Adults are also profoundly harmed by divorce. A study that examined the impact of divorce ten years after the divorce found that among two-thirds of divorced couples, one partner is still depressed and financially precarious. And among a quarter of all divorced couples, *both* former partners are worse off, suffering loneliness and depression.[26]

Divorce affects even physical health. Children of divorce are more prone to illness, accidents, and suicide. Divorced men are twice as likely as married men to die from heart disease, stroke, hypertension, and cancer. They are four times more likely to die in auto accidents and suicide, and their odds are seven times higher for pneumonia and cirrhosis of the liver. Divorced women lose 50 percent more time to illness and injury each year than do married women, and they are two to three times as likely to die of all forms of cancer. Both divorced men and women are almost five times more likely to succumb to substance abuse.[27]

The impact of divorce on health, says David Larson, president of the National Institute for Healthcare Research, "is like starting to smoke a pack of cigarettes a day."[28]

And the effects don't stop with the families directly involved. When family breakdown becomes widespread, entire neighborhoods decay. Neighborhoods without fathers are often infected with crime and delinquency. They are often places where teachers cannot teach because misbehaving children disrupt classrooms. Moreover, children of divorce are much more likely to get divorced themselves as adults, so that the negative consequences pass on to the next generation. In this way, family breakdown affects the entire society.[29]

Generation Xers often sense these truths better than their baby-boomer parents do. Many have suffered through their parents' divorce(s) and typically say they desperately hope for a marriage that will endure, while at the same time they are profoundly pessimistic about marriage. When grunge-rock star Kurt Cobain committed suicide, reporters digging into his private life discovered that when he was eight years old, his parents divorced, sending him into a sharp downward spiral. "It destroyed him," admits his mother, Wendy Cobain. "He changed completely." The experience was so painful that when Cobain made an earlier suicide attempt in 1994, he had a note in his pocket that said, "I'd rather die than go through a divorce."[30]

The time is ripe for Christians to make a persuasive case for a biblical view of marriage and family, using statistics like these to frame a convincing argument that people are happier and healthier in stable families. And then we must learn how to model the biblical view before a watching world.

MARRIAGE AS A MYSTIC MIRROR

What does the Christian worldview say about the family? The doctrine of creation tells us God made us with a definite nature (in his image) and gave us a definite task: to nurture and develop the powers of nature (fill the earth and subdue it) and to form families and create societies (be fruitful and increase in number). The image of God is reflected, in part, in the differentiation of humanity into two sexes: "God created man in his own image, . . . male and female he created them" (Gen. 1:27). The implication is that to be a husband or wife, a father or mother, is not an artificial or arbitrary role separate from our "true" self, a threat to authentic personhood. Instead, these relationships form an intrinsic part of our fundamental identity, of what makes us fully human. Liberation is not found by escaping these roles but by embracing them and carrying out our responsibilities in a manner faithful to God's ideals.

In other parts of Scripture, we learn that marriage is also rich in spiritual symbolism and meaning—a mystical mirror of the relationship between God and his people. Ancient fertility religions often imagined God to be both male and female, and pagan theology was expressed in fertility celebrations involving ritual fornication in temple prostitution. That's why, in the Old Testament, idolatry is often called fornication. But biblical theology was expressed in marriage, with the faithful love between husband and wife as an image of God's faithful love for his people. In the New Testament, Paul likens the relationship between a husband and a wife to the "profound mystery" of Christ's union with his bride, the church (see Eph. 5).

As husband and wife come together, they form a family, the core institution of human society—the training ground, in fact, for all other social institutions. Human sexuality is not designed only as a source of pleasure or a means of expressing affection. It was designed as a powerful bond between husband and wife in order to form a secure, stable environment for raising vulnerable children to adulthood. Family life is the "first school" that prepares us to participate in the religious, civic, and political life of society, training us in the virtues that enable us to place the common good before our own private goals. Saying no to sex outside marriage means saying yes to this broader vision of marriage as the foundation of an enduring institution that not only meets personal needs but also ties us into a wider community through mutual obligations and benefits.

It's not enough to insist that sex outside marriage is sinful or that practicing homosexuality is wrong. We must learn to articulate in a positive way the overall biblical worldview that makes sense of these moral principles. We must explain what it means to live within an objective, created moral order instead of perpetuating the chaotic reign of the autonomous self.

HOW TO BE A MARRIAGE SAVER

How well has the church taught this biblical model and helped believers to live it? Some of the best work has been done by parachurch organizations such as James Dobson's Focus on the Family. Dobson's books, articles, and radio programs have been singularly effective, and we cannot know this side of heaven how much they have done to help strengthen families and increase their dedication to living by biblical principles.

Sadly, local churches have not always been as effective. Their response to the decline of marriage has often been helpless handwringing and haranguing against a decadent culture. Few clergy have been equipped to put the brakes on the destructive trends that have torn marriages apart at ever increasing rates, even within their own congregations.

Solid Principles

What are some of the most important principles that churches can teach families? For starters, believers should be encouraged to treat their own families as a ministry—a mission to the surrounding culture. Many friends of mine have this kind of vision for their families, and one family in particular has achieved bountiful success. As a young couple, Jack and Rhodora Donahue decided that their job as Christians was to produce a strong family. Today, they have 13 children and 75 grandchildren, and all are committed Christians. Some are clergy, some are involved in starting Christian schools, and most are active in lay ministries such as Young Life and Prison Fellowship. And the Donahues continue to educate their children and grandchildren, often holding dinner parties where they invite speakers to address topical issues, then spend the entire evening discussing related theological, philosophical, and moral questions.

As a stirring historical model, consider Jonathan Edwards, the Congregational pastor, scholar, and leader of the First Great Awakening. He and his wife, Sarah, reared 11 children; and by the year 1900, the family had 1,400 descendants, among them 13 college presidents, 65 professors, 100 lawyers, 30 judges, 66 physicians, and 80 prominent public officials, including 3 governors, 3 senators, and a vice president of the United States.[31] With families of such learning and distinction, it's no wonder the Puritans did so much to shape the American mind and character. If modern evangelicals hope to leave the same powerful legacy, we need to realize that the task of culture building requires a long-term commitment, and we must focus on nurturing godly families to influence future generations.

Whether your family is small or large, whether your resources are sparse or extensive, every Christian parent is called to make the home a ministry. That means educating our children in a biblical worldview and equipping them to have an impact on the world. In the long run, this is the best way that Christians can restore and redeem the surrounding culture.

Church Strategies

How can the church nurture such families? A few years ago, Washington journalist Michael McManus searched out the best programs for engaged couples, for marriage enrichment, and for rescuing seriously troubled marriages. What started out as research for writing columns has ended up as a ministry. Mike has organized an overall strategy he calls Marriage Savers, and the programs in this positive, biblically based approach are mak-

ing a difference across the country. When several churches in
a community agree to adopt the Marriage Savers strategy, it
does lower the local divorce rate and make marriages stronger.[32]

Consider some of the effective programs that Marriage Savers
brings together:

Smart Dating: A couple's habits of relating to one another are
formed long before they walk down the aisle. That means the
church must begin by helping dating couples, and the first message they need to hear is that if you want a good marriage, avoid
premarital sexual relations. The National Survey of Family
Growth found that women who were not virgins when they got
married have a 71 percent higher divorce rate. Saying no to premarital sex means saying yes to a stronger marriage.[33]

Trial Is Error: Many couples regard living together as a sort
of trial marriage, a way to test their compatibility, making for a
better marriage later. But the reality is just the opposite: Cohabitation is almost certain to *destroy* their chances of a good marriage.
About 90 percent of the couples who live together say they want
to get married, but the National Survey of Families and Households found that almost half break up before signing a marriage
license. Those who do marry are 50 percent more likely to divorce.
Living together is not preparation for marriage; it literally sets up
couples for failure.[34]

Engaging Couples: Many churches have become "blessing
machines," willing to marry any couple that comes knocking, without giving them any training in how to have a strong marriage.
In fact, three-quarters of all weddings are blessed in a church or
synagogue, which means churches are implicated in the nation's
staggering divorce rate. Yet churches have access to excellent and
effective programs such as PREPARE (Premarital Personal and
Relationship Evaluation), which helps couples identify their
strengths and weaknesses so they can iron out major conflicts *before*
saying "I do." Another effective program is Engaged Encounter, an

intensive weekend program that teaches couples how to relate more
effectively. Both can prepare couples to face the difficulties that
beset even the best marriage.[35]

Wedding Shock: After the romantic enchantment wears off,
many couples face the most critical time of marriage, for most
divorces trace back to habits established in those early years.
ENRICH is a program to support fledgling marriages by enabling
couples to inventory their strengths and weaknesses, identifying
key problem areas.[36] In Old Testament law, a recently married
man was exempt from military and other duties for one year so
he could "be free to stay at home and bring happiness to the wife
he has married" (Deut. 24:5). Clearly, the biblical principle is to
protect and nurture young couples.

Divorce Insurance: No church needs to stand by while couples in
the congregation break up. One of the best programs available to
help couples is Marriage Encounter, an intensive weekend retreat
with a 90 percent success rate in strengthening marriages. And for
seriously troubled marriages, there is Retrouvaille (a French word
meaning "recovery"), which works on the Alcoholics Anonymous
model, with personal counseling by couples who themselves have
worked through serious marriage problems. Of the couples who
have attended Retrouvaille, nearly half were already separated or
divorced, yet 80 percent have reunited and stayed together.[37]

In fact, all Marriage Savers programs rely on older couples as
mentors. Whether working with engaged couples, newlyweds, or
seriously troubled marriages, the most effective counselors are couples who have successfully worked through their own difficulties.

Community Policies

Sometimes pastors are hesitant to require couples to undergo
counseling, for fear they will simply go to another church down
the street. To forestall that, McManus has established Community Marriage Policies, in which several churches in a city agree

together to impose uniform minimal requirements on couples
who want to marry. The results have been dramatic. The first city
to adopt this policy was Modesto, California, where clergy from
ninety-five churches agreed to require couples to undergo four
months of marriage preparation, take a premarital inventory, and
meet with a mentor couple. A decade later, the city's divorce rate
had dropped 40 percent, despite a large increase in the population.
In the two years that a Community Marriage Policy has been
in effect in the Kansas suburbs of Kansas City, divorces have
dropped by more than a third (while in the Missouri suburbs of
the same city where there was no program, divorces increased).
By the end of 1998, a hundred cities had adopted Community
Marriage Policies, and nine have been in place long enough to
produce a measurable drop in the local divorce rate.[38]

Community Marriage Policies have been so successful that
in some places they have attracted attention outside the church.
In Grand Rapids, Michigan, the mayor of Kentwood, a major
suburb, persuaded more than two thousand leaders from local
businesses, universities, and government to come together and
examine how "current policies . . . may undermine marriage formation," and to outline changes that might "promote marriage
and stable families." Mayor Bill Hardiman made his appeal not
on the basis of religion but on the need to "improve the well-being
of children."[39]

In another part of Michigan, District Court Chief Judge James
Sheridan persuaded the clergy of sixty churches to sign a Community Marriage Policy. Then, in an unusual step, Sheridan also
elicited a voluntary agreement among all the judges, magistrates,
and mayors who perform civil weddings to require couples to go
through premarital counseling. "Divorce is a community issue, not
just a religious matter," Sheridan explains, and he is quite right.
"Divorce affects my caseload as a judge, and that of every judge in
the U.S." He cites the statistics: "The number of alcohol-related

problems doubles as you go from married to divorced. The mortality rate of both men and women is much higher if you're divorced. People tend to have accidents or illnesses that cause community expense." Then, too, many divorced mothers need government assistance. "Where does the money come from to take care of kids on welfare? From taxes." The entire community pays the price of marriage breakdown, and as a result, the entire community has an interest in programs that make marriages stronger.[40]

Renewed Effort, Redemptive Force

Much of this renewed effort is the result of the pressure exerted by Michael McManus, and he is an inspiring example of the difference just one Christian can make. A friendly giant of a man, McManus and his wife, Harriet, a tiny woman who mirrors his enthusiasm, are changing the way churches minister to married couples. And the surrounding culture finally seems ready to hear what the churches are saying as well.

Back in the 1970s, books touted divorce as liberation, with titles like *Creative Divorce* and *Divorce: The New Freedom*.[41] The common presumption was that divorce creates only temporary distress and that individuals soon bounce back and go on to form new and more meaningful relationships. Divorce was even presented as a chance for inner growth and self-actualization. But the moral tides are turning, and people are showing a growing concern for the social cost of family breakdown, reflected in titles such as *The Case against Divorce* by Diane Medved, *Divorce Busting* by Michele Weiner-Davis, and *Rethinking Divorce* by William Galston.[42] There are even efforts under way to eliminate no-fault divorce, which gives all the legal power to those who walk away from their family commitments. Christians ought to line up behind efforts like these to build moral accountability back into family law.

The family is one arena where we as Christians can and must

be a redemptive force. Yet as we work to incorporate biblical principles within our own families, we inevitably come up against the counterforce of public education. Nowhere has the secular worldview gained a firmer foothold than in our nation's schools, and since the education of our children shapes the future, we must begin to take our redemptive message right into the classroom.

CHAPTER 5

STILL AT RISK

As you read chapter 5, keep the following questions
in mind:
- Historically in America, what were the two tasks of public
  education, and how are schools addressing these tasks today?
- How has a faulty view of creation, fall, and redemption
  influenced American public education?
- What are strengths and weaknesses of various educational
  options available for Christian children today?

In 1983, the National Commission on Excellence in Education
published "A Nation at Risk," a shocking assessment of American education. Today the risk is even graver. American high
school seniors are among the worst educated in the world. In
one study covering twenty-one nations, American students placed
nineteenth in math and science, and dead last in physics.[1] Even
students in well-endowed Ivy League colleges show gaping defi-
ciencies in their knowledge of American history and civics. For
example, three out of four cannot identify the author of the Get-
tysburg Address. Facts every immigrant has to master in order
to gain U.S. citizenship seem to elude the young people destined
to become our nation's next generation of leaders.[2]

Even more disturbing is the decline in moral education. In a
study by the Josephson Institute of Ethics, two-thirds of the high

school students surveyed admitted to cheating on an exam within
the past year, one-third said they had stolen something, and more
than a third said they would lie on a job application.³ Clearly,
American public education is no longer successful at its two historic tasks: academic training and moral education.

What has caused this disastrous decline? It's a well-known
fact, of course, that schools have replaced time-tested methods
of teaching with trendy techniques, from values clarification to
multiculturalism. But the basic question is *why*. Why did educators
buy into these methodologies in the first place, and why do they
cling to them when it is obvious they are not working?

We can start by looking at the schools that train the nation's
teachers and administrators. The typical curriculum in colleges of
education, says Rita Kramer, author of *Ed School Follies*, is "all too
often a grab bag of pieties about the influence of race, ethnicity,
and gender on learning." Future teachers do not take courses on
the subject matter they will be teaching; instead, their schedules are
crammed with courses that focus on self-esteem and social equity.
One professor told future teachers of language arts: "More important than content or thinking [are] the students' feelings. You are
not there to feed them information but to be sensitive to their need
for positive reinforcement, for self-esteem." A UCLA professor
cautioned a class of young teachers against correcting children's
spelling and punctuation: "It's more important for them to create
than follow rules."⁴

No wonder American kids score at the bottom in terms of skills
but at the top in terms of self-esteem. We've made them feel good
about doing badly.

WORLDVIEW RAMIFICATIONS

Where have these ideas about education come from? Once again,
the answer lies in a shift in worldview. Every educational method

grows out of a broader philosophy that addresses certain fundamental questions: Who are we as humans? What is our task in life? How can we prepare ourselves to perform that task? The best way to critique contemporary education is to examine the answers that have been offered to these basic questions, using the framework of *creation, fall,* and *redemption.*

Process over Content

John Dewey, America's most influential educational theorist, applied Charles Darwin's ideas to education. Dewey rejected the biblical view of the child as a creature of God and maintained instead that the child is nothing but a biological organism. Thus the mind is merely a complex organ, evolving through adaptation to the environment, trying out different responses until it finds something that works. These assumptions led to pragmatism, a philosophy that says there are no transcendent, unchanging truths but only pragmatic strategies for getting what we want. Applying this philosophy, Dewey came up with an educational theory that stressed process over content. Children should not be taught facts and truths; they should be taught how to conduct a process of inquiry.[5]

A current version of this philosophy is "constructivist" education, today's most popular pedagogical technique, which is based on the idea that knowledge is not objective but a social construction; therefore, children should not be given the "right" answers but should be taught to construct their own solutions through interaction within a group. In the words of education theorist Catherine Fosnot, "Constructivism does not assume the presence of an outside objective reality that is revealed to the learner, but rather that learners actively construct their own reality, transforming it and themselves in the process."[6] Children are taught to construct their own math rules, their own spelling systems ("invented spelling"), their own punctuation, and so on, and teachers are urged not to tell students whether their answers are right or wrong.

Dewey applied the same process view of knowledge to ethics. If we experiment by selecting different responses to particular conditions, he taught, then over time we will develop a "science" of ethics, identifying those actions that predictably lead to enjoyable and satisfying consequences. The hitch, of course, is that what satisfies me may not satisfy you. Thus, Dewey's philosophy inspired the relativistic methods of moral education in vogue in the classroom today, including Sidney Simon's method of "values clarification" and its seven-step process for choosing values—followed by Lawrence Kohlberg's method of "moral reasoning," Clive Beck's "reflective approach," and many others. What all such methods have in common is that teachers are rigorously instructed not to be directive in any way but to coach students in a process of weighing alternatives and making up their own minds. Students' choices are considered acceptable not because the choices agree with a transcendent standard but because the students have gone through the required process—regardless of the outcome.[7]

Myth of Innocence

A faulty view of creation has led directly to the conceptual and moral relativism that plagues modern public education. Equally disastrous has been the loss of the biblical teaching on sin and the Fall. Jean-Jacques Rousseau shocked the world by pronouncing that human nature in its natural state is innocent—that people are made evil only by the constraints of civilization. And where do we see human nature in its spontaneous, natural state, he asked, before it is ruined by rules and inhibitions? Why, in the child. The child reveals the full range of human potential, the glory of the indeterminate self, open to all possibilities.

And so was birthed a utopian view of the child. "Trailing clouds of glory do we come, from God, who is our home: Heaven lies about us in our infancy," in the words of the romantic poet William Wordsworth.[8] Gone was the biblical notion that children are affected by the Fall, their nature distorted by original sin. Gone was the idea that children are capable of genuine wrongdoing and thus need moral boundaries and training. As a result, the romantics set about crafting radical new ideas about the way children should be raised and educated.

In the nineteenth century, for example, the German educational theorist Friedrich Froebel founded the first kindergarten, which literally means "children's garden," where he fleshed out a radically new utopian approach to education. Whereas the goal of classical education is to transmit a cultural heritage, in Froebel's utopian vision, education is seen as the means of humanity's passage to the next stage of evolution. Whereas in classical education children are taught to imitate the best of the past, in utopian education they are taught to reject the past and create something new. Whereas classical education teaches children to adapt their lives to eternal principles, utopian education seeks to free them to unfold and develop new ideas and ways of living out of their own experience. Froebel's kindergarten pictured the child as a plant whose growth must be allowed to proceed according to its own inner law of organic development, lest we stunt its evolution. Old standards of truth and virtue must be cast off to give freedom to the New Man, who is even now in process of evolving through our children.[9]

Another nineteenth-century educator, Francis Wayland Parker, went so far as to call the child divine: "The spontaneous tendencies of the child are the records of inborn divinity."[10] In Parker's child-centered theory of education, the most important thing is for the adult to get out of the way of the child's natural tendencies, to refrain from stifling the child with either academic requirements or moral demands.

Educators like Froebel and Parker assumed that children, left to themselves, would spontaneously tend toward love, selflessness, hard work, creativity, and all the other Christian virtues. In other words, they assumed that human nature is naturally good, and they saw no danger in getting rid of externally imposed training and objective standards.[11] Today the same utopianism is at work in nondirective values-education programs, which, as we saw earlier, are based on the assumption that if children are merely taught a process of inquiry to evaluate their options, they will choose wisely and rationally.

The rejection of the biblical view of the Fall has led to unrealistic and unworkable educational methods that are blind to our children's need for moral direction. Is it any wonder that many kids are cheating, stealing, and even assaulting one another in the classroom?

Political and Therapeutic Redemption

If a faulty understanding of the doctrine of the Fall has undermined moral education, what about the effects of a faulty doctrine of redemption? Redemption is certainly alive and well in the classroom today, but it's political redemption—a reflection of the kind found in wider society. Many children know more about acid rain and gay rights than they do about Shakespeare and George Washington. Education is being turned into the means for lifting society to the next stage in social evolution.

In the 1930s, the influential educator George S. Counts explicitly called on teachers to begin "controlling the evolution of society." He urged them to "redeem" society, to stop being merely transmitters of the culture and become "creator[s] of social values." Educators should reach deliberately for power to "build a new social order," raising students' consciousness about social problems and encouraging them to come up with alternative ways of ordering society.[12] Today schools are doing just that . . . with gusto.

Increasingly, classroom time is taken away from studying the classics of Western culture and is devoted to politically correct causes, based on a philosophy of postmodernism that reduces truth to power politics and treats all ideas as expressions of race, class, or gender. Most educators no longer define education as fostering the search for truth and transmitting a valued heritage, says Frederic Sommers of Brandeis University; instead, they define education as a means to "empower students by alerting them to the need for struggle against patriarchy, racism, and classism."[13] Nancy's son discovered this recently when he entered a state university. His honors English course was taught by a radical feminist who devoted the entire curriculum to contemporary works by feminists and homosexual-rights activists. Instead of being an arena where students can learn to weigh conflicting ideas dispassionately, the classroom is becoming a place where students are indoctrinated in political radicalism and enlisted in the culture wars.

At the same time, education has been greatly influenced by a therapeutic model of redemption, in which teachers treat children's psyches while teaching them the ABCs. The source of this widespread trend is the philosophy of existentialism, which casts each individual as an *autonomous self.* According to this worldview, people must create their own purpose by making choices, even though there is no standard to tell them whether or not the choices they are making are right.[14] The resulting theory of education is sometimes called humanistic education, after the great humanistic psychologists of the 1970s—Carl Rogers, Rollo May, and Abraham Maslow—who pioneered the use of therapeutic techniques in the classroom as a way of freeing students from psychological barriers so they could become autonomous decision makers. Teachers became amateur psychologists, exploring the student's personality with techniques borrowed from encounter groups and sensitivity training.

But education is not the same as therapy, and the impact of existentialism in the classroom has been disastrous. Educator William Coulson, once a colleague of Carl Rogers, tells a fascinating personal story that illustrates why humanistic education fails. In 1967, Coulson and Rogers received a grant to conduct the first large-scale systematic study of the effect of encounter groups in the classroom. Their laboratory consisted of some sixty schools within the Catholic school system in Los Angeles, and they began by holding workshops for the nuns who taught in the schools (the Sisters of the Immaculate Heart of Mary). To Coulson's surprise and consternation, many nuns responded to the training by removing their habits and leaving the Catholic church. The message they got from the workshops was that to be "authentic" individuals, they must free themselves from all external authority and make their own choices. Of course, as Coulson points out, in leaving the church, the nuns were not really liberating themselves from external authority at all. They were simply trading in one authority (the Catholic church) for another (the workshop leaders).[15]

Coulson's experience was not unique. When Abraham Maslow translated his humanistic theory of psychology into educational practice, he discovered that his students developed an "almost paranoid certainty of their own absolute virtues and correctness."[16] Having been taught that they were autonomous selves who must make up their own minds about right and wrong, his students became unteachable. No wonder research shows that students who take "lifestyle" courses employing nondirective decision-making methods end up being *more* likely to engage in destructive behavior.[17]

Students who are taught to look only to their own feelings soon lose all sense of accountability to any external moral standard. One teacher found this out when she used a values-education program with her low-achieving eighth graders. The program required students to list the things they loved doing, which turned out to be "sex, drugs, drinking, and skipping school." The teacher was horrified but powerless. Her students had clarified their values, and the nondirective program gave her no way to challenge them to aim for something higher.[18]

The decline in American public education is not due to poor teaching or lack of funding; it is due to educational theories that deny the existence of transcendent truth and morality, that renounce standards of excellence, and that ultimately render children unteachable. If we hope to reform the educational system, we must learn to analyze and critique the worldviews that have spawned these disastrous teaching methods and then offer an alternative worldview that is decisively Christian—one that will yield a theory of education capable of improving the schools for all students.

TRUTH IN TEACHING

What is the Christian view? It was captured in a dramatic moment in the movie *Witness*.[19] In a powerful scene involving a big-city detective and an eight-year-old Amish boy named Samuel, the boy spots the detective's pistol in a drawer and reaches to pick it up.

"Samuel!" the detective says sternly. "Never play with a loaded gun!"

The detective doesn't ask Samuel how he feels about what he's doing. He doesn't allow the boy to make up his own mind about whether playing with a loaded gun is right for him. Instead, a knowledgeable adult in a directive manner informs the boy of the dangers of playing with guns.

This example illustrates an approach to teaching that is directive and objective, and we suggest that it also reflects the biblical model. Christian education is not utopian; it does not assume that children (or the rest of us) are capable of determining ultimate truth on their own in the vacuum of subjectivism. Instead, God has communicated with us through the Bible, revealing an objective standard of truth and morality for all people. Our lives are guided by revealed truths that are much greater than anything we could possibly conceive on our own.

What are those truths? First, children are not merely biological organisms adapting to the environment; they are created in the image of God and bear all the dignity of beings capable of recognizing truth, goodness, and beauty. The goal of education should be to feed children's souls through a directive presentation of these objective ideals.

But that's only part of the story. We must also take into account children's capacity for selfishness and willfulness. Moral education should likewise be directive, teaching the biblical virtues and enforcing them with consistent classroom discipline.

Finally, education is one of the ways we seek to reverse the effects of the Fall and restore humanity to its original dignity and purpose. The goal of learning, wrote the great Christian poet John Milton, "is to repair the ruins of our first parents."[20] Teachers should recognize the moral and spiritual drama taking place in their students' souls, helping them see how that same drama is the stuff of history and literature and philosophy. Education is a major arena in the spiritual battle raging in the world, a battlefield where we should be bringing a Christian worldview to bear: pushing back the power of the adversary and claiming for Christ the entire territory of the mind and spirit.

Christian Schools

Scripture constantly enjoins Christians to teach their children and to pass on the great truths of the faith from generation to generation. So it's not surprising that Christians have historically accorded great importance to education, founding schools and teaching literacy wherever they went around the globe. Almost every major college in the first two centuries of American history was founded by Christians. (In fact, Harvard, Princeton, and the other Ivy League universities were founded to train pastors.) Today Christians continue to establish schools, often with the goal of reaching out to a decaying culture. In city after city, Christian and parochial schools educate a substantial number of inner-city students, producing higher test scores at a fraction of the cost of public education.[21]

Christian education is not simply a matter of starting class with Bible reading and prayer, then teaching subjects out of secular textbooks. It consists of teaching everything, from science and mathematics to literature and the arts, within the framework of an integrated biblical worldview. It means teaching students to relate every academic discipline to God's truth and his self-revelation in Scripture, while detecting and critiquing nonbiblical worldview assumptions.

For those seeking guidance on how to do it right, good models abound. In Detroit, my close friend Mike Timmis heads a coalition of leaders from local churches, businesses, and community organizations that has founded four Christ-centered, ecumenical schools in urban neighborhoods. With an enrollment of nearly seven hundred students, Cornerstone schools run eleven months of the year, and parents must sign a "covenant" to actively support the school. Chapel attendance is mandatory, and every student participates in a Bible study group. Privately funded by corporations and foundations, the schools also draw in ordinary people as "partners," who not only contribute $2000 a year to support one student but also commit to forming a friendship with that student. The students, 98 percent of whom are minorities, finish far above the national average in standardized tests, and the number of disciplinary violations is far lower than in public schools.[22]

One of the more interesting experiments in recent years has been the growth of the Christian classical school movement. Classical education is based on the idea that in any subject there is a three-stage development of learning. Students must (1) know the basics of the subject (what the ancient Greeks called "grammar"); (2) be able to reason clearly about it ("logic"); and (3) apply it in a creative, persuasive manner ("rhetoric"). Classical education teaches students how to use these basic tools of learning to appreciate the best of Western culture's classical heritage. Students listen to symphonies, study paintings, and read great works of literature by Homer, Plato, Dante, Shakespeare, Dickens, and Dostoyevsky. This approach is having a dramatic effect in creating academically stellar Christian schools across the country.[23]

Homeschooling

The most radical alternative for Christian parents is to take on the task of educating their children themselves, becoming part of the fast-growing homeschooling movement. In earlier centuries, many of our outstanding national leaders were educated, at least partly, at home: Patrick Henry, William Penn, Daniel Webster, Wilbur and Orville Wright, Abraham Lincoln, and Thomas Edison. Today some 1.7 million American children are being homeschooled, and on the 1997 ACT test, the average score of home-schooled students was above the national average.[24]

Meg and Steve Garber of Burke, Virginia, are teaching their nine-year-old twins at home, and the Garbers demonstrate how a curriculum can be unified across several subjects for greater learning effect. Last fall, while studying a unit on Colonial America, the twins read books on the subject and practiced writing by composing a journal of the everyday life of a colonial child; they cooked colonial food and read about nutrition and farming; they sewed colonial-style clothing and took a field trip to colonial Williamsburg. At the same time they kept up with drills in math, phonics, and composition, not to mention soccer, basketball, ballet lessons, and raising chickens in the backyard.

Of course, many Christian families choose to send their children to public schools either because they cannot afford private school or because they are committed to working within the public school system. But these families also have an educational task to do at home, teaching their children an overarching Christian worldview by which to interpret and critique what they learn at school. In this sense, all Christian parents must be home schoolers. And all need support from the church, which means local churches need to encourage youth group leaders to go beyond volleyball and pizza parties and begin to teach apologetics and worldview issues.

Summit Ministries in Colorado is pointing the way. Perched high in the Rocky Mountains, every summer Summit packs in high school students who want to learn how to defend their faith against the ideological trends of the day. Founder David Noebel has developed a curriculum that gives Christian kids a crash course in apologetics, teaching them how to deal with the intellectual challenges they face in high school and college. They learn how to analyze and critique the New Age movement, humanism, Marxism, feminism, evolutionism, and whatever other "ism" happens to be gaining a foothold in contemporary American culture. Churches and Christian schools ought to take a page from Summit's book (or use Summit's own book *Understanding the Times*) and begin preparing young people to face an increasingly hostile culture.[25]

Reforming Public Schools

But even as we shore up Christian education, we cannot retreat from the challenge to reform public education. The future of any society depends on the way it teaches its children. That's why one of the first measures taken by revolutionary governments is to place all educational agencies under the direct control of the state, giving schools a central hand in building the new society. That's also why one of the fiercest battles in today's "culture war" is over education. If Christians are going to be "salt," if we are going to restore order and justice throughout the culture, we must restore high-quality education.

We can begin by supporting curricular reforms that restore an objective focus to the public school classroom. In state schools we cannot push for an explicitly Christian approach to education, of course, but we *can* play an active role in promoting the teaching of general principles of truth and morality that, though ultimately derived from Scripture, can also be supported on rational grounds. Because of common grace, these principles are often recognized by people of other faiths (such as Jews, Muslims, Mormons, and the like) as well as by nonbelievers, allowing us to work together as allies in the fight. For example, we ought to support groups such as the Character Education Partnership, which seeks to teach the virtues on which a majority of citizens can agree.[26]

Reform efforts can be effective, as evidenced by Piscataquis Community High School, an impoverished rural school in Maine. A decade ago, the school's scores on a state achievement test were among the lowest in the state. Today they are among the highest. The secret? Discipline and a demanding curriculum. Or, as Norman Higgins, who was principal for ten years, puts it, "High standards for students, high standards for teachers, high standards for schools." Higgins brought in a classical curriculum in which all students, not just those bound for college, are required to learn algebra, biology, chemistry, physics, and foreign languages. "We are a New England private school in a poor public school setting," Higgins says.[27]

Individual Christians working within the public school system can also have an enormous impact. For thirty years, an African-American woman named Barbara Moses was a public school teacher in Philadelphia, where she led thousands of kids to straighten up their lives by sharing God's love with them. She prayed with kids, invited them to accept Christ, visited their homes, got to know their families. Few individuals have had greater impact on their local schools, demonstrating what one Spirit-led believer can do.[28]

Charter Schools

One of the most creative means of reforming public education is the charter-school movement. Charter schools are public schools, but the difference is that teachers survive on merit, not tenure, and they don't have to teach the state curriculum. In exchange for this freedom, charter schools must meet strict performance standards. The idea is to allow a wide range of experimentation while subjecting the students to rigorous academic standards so the state will be able to determine which methods work best.

An example of what charter schools can accomplish can be seen at Wesley Elementary in the violent, drug-infested Acres Homes section of Houston, Texas. The school is surrounded by barbed-wire fencing and boarded-up houses, and several years ago, only 18 percent of Wesley's third graders were scoring at grade level in reading comprehension. But after Thaddeus Lott became the principal in 1975, that number shot up to 85 percent. To achieve this astounding turnaround, Lott got back to the basics: strict discipline, high expectations, and a curriculum that stresses drills and sequential learning (Direct Instruction). His approach was so successful that he was asked to take over several additional troubled schools. These became the first charter schools in Texas, and their success is being replicated in charter schools around the country.[29]

Supplemental Programs

Christians can also create ways to supplement the public school system. This was the tactic adopted by Jerry McNeely, an ordained minister in the African Methodist Episcopal church, who set his sights on William D. Hinton School, a public elementary school in south-side Chicago, where gunfire and sirens are common background noises and the sidewalks are littered with empty liquor bottles and crack vials. These days something astonishing happens at Hinton School. Twice a week, as soon as the last bell rings, several students rush to take over an empty classroom, pull out their homework, and start comparing notes. Then Jerry McNeely arrives, opens a large box of chemicals, and the students are soon engrossed in a science project.

These kids are participants in one of the hottest after-school programs in Chicago: the Urban Pioneers, a component of the Chicago Urban League's Black Churches Project. McNeely is the director of Urban Pioneers, with a vision to help inner-city kids go on to earn graduate degrees in science and math. As a result, hundreds of students in grades five through eight spend four hours a week exploring the world of science and mathematics in hands-on experiments.[30]

One of the best programs for helping students succeed in school is Kids Hope USA, a program founded by Virgil Gulker, who was horrified by rising rates of violence, gang activity, and suicide, even in the youngest grades. When he interviewed experts across the country, he repeatedly heard the same refrain: We don't need any more programs. What we need are more caring adults to put their arms around troubled children and say, "I love you."

So Gulker founded a program in which a church "adopts" a local elementary school, and members of the congregation conduct one-on-one tutoring. Each volunteer meets with his or her student on school grounds, then sends the teacher a progress report after each session. The academic goal is for the students to acquire basic skills in reading and computation, but the personal goal is to sustain a long-term, consistent, trusting relationship between a Christian volunteer and a needy kid—the only kind of relationship with a proven record of giving these kids the hope they need.[31] Kids Hope USA currently has sixty participating churches in six states.

School Choice

The best hope for reforming our public schools may be the voucher system, which provides low-income families with some choice over their children's schooling.

In Cleveland, Ohio, Delvoland Shakespeare was horrified when he visited the school his five-year-old son would attend in the fall. At the intersection outside the school, drug dealers occupied one corner, winos a second corner, prostitutes a third, and men shooting dice on the fourth. Inside the school, he saw students bouncing around without any discipline, and battered textbooks with no covers. In the boys' bathroom, a man tried to sell him drugs. "[My son] had to walk through this war zone, and once we get in the school grounds, he is still in a war zone," Shakespeare said. "No way was I going to send him into that school."[32] The young African-American father moved his family into an attic so he could afford to pay for a private Catholic school. Finally, two years later, when Ohio began a voucher program that permitted parents to use the vouchers at religious schools, the Shakespeares won vouchers for both of their sons. Freed from tuition expenses, the family was able to move out of the attic and into their own home.

Vouchers are perhaps the best route to educational equity, giving low-income parents equal opportunity to take their kids out of failing public schools and enroll them in good private schools. According to a Harvard study of the school-choice program in Milwaukee, Wisconsin, minority children improved their reading scores by 3 to 5 percentage points and their math skills by 5 to 12 percentage points. Opponents continue to challenge voucher programs in court, but in 1998, by a vote of 8 to 1, the Supreme Court refused to block Wisconsin's program.[33]

Vouchers are beneficial for public schools as well, for they create the competition needed to break the monopoly of the public school system and force the schools to improve. Yet school-choice measures are often blocked politically by powerful teachers' unions and educational lobbies. As a result, some innovative business people are organizing private voucher systems. In Indiana, Golden Rule Insurance Company established America's first private voucher program, the Educational CHOICE Charitable Trust.

Funded through private donations from individuals, corporations, and foundations, the program contributes half the tuition for a child from a low-income family to attend a private or church-run school.

CHOICE has been so successful that it has attracted many imitators. For example, financier Ted Forstmann and Wal-Mart heir John Walton started the Washington Scholarship Fund, a privately financed scholarship program that enables about thirteen hundred children every year to escape one of the country's worst school systems (Washington, D.C.) and attend private schools. They also started the Children's Scholarship Fund, putting up $100 million to give scholarships to children in cities around the country.[34]

■   ■   ■

What the schools do today determines what society will be tomorrow. That's why reforming education, from preschools to universities, is one of the most crucial cultural tasks that Christians face. We have an opportunity not only to have an influence on our public institutions but also to create Christian centers of education that will become sources of cultural renewal much as the monasteries did in the Middle Ages. Though secularists once condemned biblical faith as irrational and contrary to reason, ironically Christianity now stands poised to become the great defender of reason.[35]

But just a step beyond the schoolyard is the neighborhood, another arena ripe for renewal, as one man discovered in his efforts to bring restoration in the midst of crime and decay.

DISCUSSION QUESTIONS

CHAPTER 4

1 What subtle distinction is at the heart of contemporary moral conflicts? Why is it difficult to ask people to justify their views? Why is it difficult to justify your own views?

2 Do you see marriage and family as a "social construction" or as an "objective obligation"? Compare and contrast the underlying meaning and ramifications of these two views.

3 In a culture where "no choices are wrong," what is viewed as the only "sin"?

"redemption"?

a "service" to humanity?

4 Without "haranguing against a decadent culture," discuss the challenges you face in presenting to your children or friends a Christian view of marriage and family.

5 Read aloud Matthew 19:4-12, a teaching of Jesus in which he quotes from the Genesis creation account. List and discuss elements of God's design for sexuality and marriage.

6 If you have ever tried to "find" your "unencumbered self," where did such a search lead you? How has reading this chapter changed (or solidified) the way you define yourself?

7 Read aloud Ephesians 5:15-25. What foundational principles for family living do you see in this passage? The Three Musketeers lived by a slogan: "All for one and one for all." Brainstorm applicable slogans that can help you remember to "make the home a ministry."

8 What can you as a group or church do to promote healthier families among your members and in the larger community?

CHAPTER 5

9 What evidence do you see of Dewey's educational philosophy: process is more important than content? Compare and contrast benefits and liabilities of the effects of this philosophy.

10 Discuss, from personal observation, the results of children's actions and choices when they are chronically left "undirected"? Does your experience align more closely with the Christian or the secular view of the Fall?

11 Compare and contrast the goals and methods of *(a)* classical education and *(b)* education based on the utopian view of the child. What value, if any, do you see in children being taught to imitate "the best of the past"?

12 Read aloud Ephesians 6:1-4. In practical terms discuss ways— specific phrases—you can use to teach your children responsibility and require accountability but without crushing their spirits.

13 Discuss the statement: "Education is not the same as therapy." What problems arise when we—children or adults—look only to our own feelings for direction?

14 Drawing on your collective memory, create a list of the "best old books" suitable for children and adolescents. Brainstorm ways to motivate your church children (individually or as groups) to read and get the most value from these books.

15 In what ways must all parents be "homeschoolers"?

16 To what extent and in what ways is it possible for parents in your community to take an active role in the education of the community's children?

17 In what ways can you—and your church—begin to take a more active role in seeing to it that your own children receive an education that is consistent with the biblical worldview?

ROLE PLAY

Refer to the directions for role play, at the end of session 1 (pp. 52–53).

CONVERSATION STARTERS

a. Assume a "marriage skeptic"—twenty years old and unmarried— says to you, "Marriage just doesn't work." As part of your conversation, cite some of the evidence to the contrary (see chapter 4, subhead "Reality Check," p. 65).

b. Act out a second conversation, in which the marriage skeptic is unhappily married. How would your conversation and response be different?

CLOSING SUMMARY

What is the one thing you want to remember from what you read (or heard or did) in this session?

Consider sharing this with the group.

TRANSFORMING COMMUNITIES

CHAPTER 6

ANYTHING CAN
HAPPEN HERE

As you read chapter 6, keep the following questions in mind:
- Note each aspect of Sal's job. At each site, what is Sal doing and why?
- What effect does Sal have on the neighborhood?

The first day at Special Post 1 on DeKalb Avenue, Bed-Stuy in Brooklyn, Officer Salvatore Bartolomeo keeps his eyes open, watches, gives himself time to learn the beat. In the early morning he marches past corner bodegas, brick tenements, storefronts with their iron gates still locked. One of the bodegas already has a line out the back. He's sure they're running numbers, not selling milk.[1]

It's a cold, overcast November day, and people on the street are digging their hands into coat pockets. He passes an abandoned car, its stripped carcass halfway out into the street. The whole neighborhood looks similarly scavenged. Twenty dilapidated, garbage-strewn, pot-bunkered blocks. Every street has its burned-out husk of a building, its sooty abscess. Officer Sal understands why nobody else wanted this job, why it remained unfilled for months. Anything can happen here. Anything does. Daily.

The Lafayette Towers, the high-rise projects, loom ahead. First-day jitters tell him that galleries of thousands are watching his every move as three teenagers in army fatigue jackets and baggy pants approach.

"Hello," says Officer Sal. "How you doing today?"

The kids look down and keep walking.

"You in a hurry to get to school?" he asks. "Can't wait to start algebra?"

They stop. One of them, more powerfully built than the other two, quirks his thick eyebrows and says to his friends, "We're only walking the street, and this cop has to be talking to us."

"I'm saying hello," Sal says. "Like in . . . hello, how are you?"

"Do you know me?" the youth asks, finally looking directly at the outsider.

"I'm the new beat cop. I'm trying to get to know the neighborhood. You live in the Towers?"

The leader says to the others, "I didn't think he knew us."

"There's no reason for him to know us," the tallest kid says.

"Look, don't be saying hello to us if you don't know us," the leader says. "We don't like cops. Especially beat cops that get busted out of their cars. What'd you do? Kill somebody on Long Island, so they sent you here?"

"Hey, Mr. Mayor, I volunteered for this job," Sal says.

The three grin widely. They call him "stupid," followed by an obscenity, then walk off in a hail of cursing and jackal laughter.

I'm Brooklyn just like you, Sal wants to say. *I grew up here. My father was raised right on these streets—at DeKalb and Marsey.*

For the rest of the morning he walks DeKalb, says hello, and learns his beat. He walks by a burned-out area behind the welfare building on Skillman Street, with two abandoned, half-charred houses that have fallen against one another, their roofs tangled in the telephone wires. His eyes survey the surrounding lots filled with weeds, garbage, and abandoned cars. These abandoned buildings get as much traffic as the bodegas. Mostly individuals, but occasionally a couple, with the woman dressed to party at ten in the morning.

Sal always sees a black-jacketed kid stationed beside the handball courts in Lafayette Towers—somebody who can see for several hundred yards in every direction. This sentry says a word or two to everyone who passes. When somebody stops to talk, the sentry shakes hands at their parting. *He's either running for office or dealing drugs,* thinks Sal. There are others like him at various locations around the precinct. They've all got a good long view, and they'd be long gone before he could get to them.

He could have that abandoned car towed, though. It would be a start at cleaning up the neighborhood. His assignment here is part of New York City's experiment with a new theory of crime reduction, and his job is to start with the simple things, the first steps in restoring public order. He'll figure out how to bring down the dealers later.

■   ■   ■

As Sal becomes familiar with his beat, he begins to time his movements according to the neighborhood's schedules and rhythms. In the morning, the kids are on their way to school, so he walks the streets close to one of the neighborhood schools, in random order. The grade-schoolers begin to come up and hold his hand and are soon calling him "Officer Sal." They're glad to see him; he scares off the big kids and bullies. The middle schoolers, hanging back on street corners, start threading their way toward their homerooms when he shows up. The high schoolers are sometimes more stubborn about standing their ground, but then he has a chance to go up and ask them, "How's it going?" He quickly becomes a celebrated pain in the neck, a favorite target for the put-down artists.

"Yo, Rocky, Mr. Italian Stallion. There ain't no Mona Lisas here. You go back to AA-drii-ann before she gets the idea you got jungle fever."

"Yo, MC Mickey Mouth," Sal says, "you the one got the fever. But there ain't no Minnie for rats like you!" Sal always gives as good as he gets. In a few weeks he can call dozens of the kids by name, and sometimes his greetings are actually returned.

By the time the merchants open up in the morning, he's back on DeKalb Avenue and stops in at all the shops. Most of the shopkeepers have a story to tell of break-ins and robberies, and they seem surprised when he listens. He asks about delivery times, whether they have a bank-run routine, what their security measures are like. In their embittered manner he can sense the question, "What makes you think *you're* going to make a difference?"

The bank gets busy at eleven-thirty in the morning and stays that way until one-thirty. The check-cashing store gets most of its traffic at the end of the business day.

The first time Sal posts himself by the check store, sipping coffee out of a paper cup, he sees a panhandler within a hundred feet, a tall, thin man whose bony knees have nearly worn through his jeans. The guy doesn't have any signs that promise work for food, or gimmicks like a cute pet dog. He squats on the stoop and whispers, reaching out his hand. He keeps at it until Sal is right over him.

"How you doing this afternoon?" Sal asks.

The whites of the man's eyes are clear. Either he hasn't been on the streets long, or begging isn't his only profession.

"I'm fine," he says. "Taking the sun." He tilts an eye up at the heavy cloud bank and grins.

"You could do with some exercise," Sal says. "I'd like you to step off now." He holds out an arm as if to usher the man through a door.

"No harm in sittin'," the man says.

"Step off," Sal repeats, "or I'll run you in for panhandling."

"This is the United States." The man's flat face goes hard. "Why you troubling me if I ain't doin' nothin'?"

"Loitering here is illegal. Panhandling here is illegal. What else you are doing in your spare time, I don't know, but I can make it my business to find out."

The man rises slowly to his feet, stretches his neck until it pops. "You miss your chance to join the gestapo or what? This is America."

"Yes, it is. A country where people can go into a store without fear of being knocked over the head when they come out."

"Have I knocked anybody over the head?"

"If I have to ask you for your identification, I'll find out. Then I won't have any choice about what to do."

The man's expression grows serious for a moment. He twists his mouth as if working a toothpick around in it. Then he sets his head back and regally strolls away.

Sal shoos off another panhandler as well, then walks back to the check-cashing store. He sees an elderly woman still fidgeting with her purse as she's walking out the door. She's about to turn in the direction the panhandlers went.

"Ma'am," says Sal.

She takes a quick, cringing look to see who's talking to her.

"Would you like me to walk along with you down that way?"

Her shoulders settle. She steps closer to him. "Is there trouble?"

"No, there's not going to be any trouble. Not today."

∎   ∎   ∎

Sal not only patrols the streets but also conducts "vertical searches," climbing the stairs of the walk-up tenements. On one such venture he finds the body of a young woman, sexually abused, then shot in the back of the head, execution-style. She is only one of the many young people who will die by violence on his beat. In Sal's years on DeKalb Avenue, the funeral home becomes almost another stop on his rounds. He always goes in, says a prayer. It doesn't matter what kind of gangster the young man or woman might have been. He kneels down and prays.

Sal also frequents the places where people congregate so he can meet neighborhood residents. He likes stories, and he tries to have a "joke of the day" ready. The young mothers congregate by the swing sets in Lafayette Gardens playground. When he spots a new mom, he always goes over and puts a ten-dollar bill in the baby's hand. With his jokes and his baby kissing, he's kidded about running for mayor.

Mothers with older children begin to notice the protection he gives their kids in the mornings on the way to school and afterward in the park. One day, outside one of the small grocery stores, Destin's mother asks, "Officer Sal? You any good at math? Can you look at Destin's math homework here?"

The boy has a workbook page crumpled in his hand.

Sal thinks of where he and the boy might go—a place they can sit down together, with at least a little privacy. "Come into the store," he says, leading them into Marvelous Mart. "Bernie, let me sit over here in the corner for a while. I'm checking Destin's homework."

Sal gets a look he takes for permission. The little desk in the corner becomes his tutoring station as Destin is joined by many others. Sal teaches Sam how to make his *B*s. He practices fractions with Monique and helps Saleesha with phonics. Checking the kids' homework becomes one more important part of his job.

He starts building a photo collection of "his kids." When school pictures are taken, the mothers come up to him and give him their children's pictures, signed by the child on the back. "You helped Destin with his homework." "You made sure Roderick made it all the way to school." "Clay thinks you hung the moon." "Natasha wants to be a cop now, too."

.   .   .

Pickup basketball games run year-round, and Sal uses the game to stay fit. He has to, the way the beat calls for him to hang out his gut every day, chasing down perps, subduing them one-on-one. When he has weekend duty, he spends time at the parks and the courts.

Eight-year-old Donzell always comes over and wants to watch his cap and nightstick for him. He lets the kid put the cap on and strut around with the stick while he plays basketball. Sal and his mostly teenage opponents play serious half-court games. Sal plays all comers and beats most of them, which irritates the losers so much he knows they would try to punch him out if he weren't a cop. He earns the nickname "Officer Bird"—after the famous basketball player Larry Bird—because of his athletic skills, light brown hair, and green eyes.

After one matchup, a teen named Shawn loses his temper, mostly because his friend Dennis becomes more and more derisive as "Whitey" keeps scoring. He shoves his friend hard, and they start beating on each other.

Salvatore retrieves the nightstick from Donzell, all the time thinking they'll get in a few punches and calm down on their own. But they don't, and they soon start drawing blood. When Sal rushes in, most of the punches in the melee miss him, but not the body shots.

"What are you doing? What are you doing?" he screams. "Shawn! Dennis! Stop fighting! Stop fighting! I mean it!"

They finally break apart, breathing hard, although they're still guarded, as if recovering for the next go.

"Look, you two, cut it out." Sal reaches into his pocket and fishes out a five from his money clip. "Here. Go have a drink together and cool down, or I'll arrest you both. Is that what you want? Huh?"

Sal watches them play his offer against what's happened. He can see that their last thought comes down to remembering he's a cop.

"Take it," he urges. "Or don't pass go and proceed directly to jail."

Their breathing slows. They slump into sullen and self-protective postures, arms folded, feet twisting.

"Uh, you want something to drink, Shawn?" Dennis asks.

"Yeah, I guess."

They walk off together, still keeping a cautious distance between them.

.   .   .

The abandoned buildings on Skillman behind the welfare building—the ones that get all the traffic—become the site of Sal's first stealth operation. The buildings are close to another beat cop's area, and he persuades the officer, Joey Francioso, to help him find out what's happening in there.

They position themselves in what was the back room of a double parlor in the ground-floor unit. The rooms are filled with trash, fallen plaster, and nail-studded fretwork. It's so dark they hardly have to hide themselves. They crouch down on the floor and look through a hole in the back-parlor wall toward the front. The first time they stake the place out, time passes so slowly that Sal finds himself counting each *woosh* of a passing bus or truck. He hears litter rustling as the rats scamper along the floors.

Soon enough, though, there's a flare of light in the front parlor. A user's crack pipe is being lit. The ammonialike scent hits them. They turn on their big heavy flashlights and come down on the crackhead almost before he looks up.

They take him out the back way, see that he's processed, then return.

A string of users and prostitutes is caught this way.

.   .   .

At DeKalb and Tenth there's a stoplight where the street angles, allowing drivers to see in both directions. Another light sits only thirty feet beyond, and then there's not another light for three blocks. People habitually run the light at DeKalb and Tenth, even when Sal is right there, blowing his whistle.

One day when it happens, some of the neighborhood bad boys are hanging around, and they're on Sal immediately. "Hey, Robo Cop, you fast enough to catch that car? No one going to pay attention to you if you can't catch somebody running a red light! Nobody care about you and that little whistle!"

Then they laugh and carry on, and the people standing around shake their heads and look sour.

The next time Sal sees someone run a light there, he hops into the back of a Yellow Cab. "You know what they say in the movies!" he yells at the driver. "Follow that car. He'll have to stop at the next light."

"Officer, I—"

"Just pull two or three car lengths ahead of him, and then you can scram as soon as I get out."

With that, the chase is on. The cab swings wide into the left lane at the next light and stops three car lengths in front of the offender.

Sal gets out and strolls over to the rusted-out Chevy that's shaking on its frame as if it has a case of the D.T.'s. The driver can't go anywhere, so now he's "awfully sorry" that he "didn't hear the officer's whistle." Then he's even sorrier because his registration has expired. Much sorrier because he has no insurance. Sorrier still because his multiple outstanding tickets have long ago resulted in a warrant for his arrest. And truly distraught when he steps out of the car and Sal sees the bag of marijuana on the floor.

Before long, Sal finds cabs nearly as useful as his old cruiser. Almost everyone he catches running that light has multiple unpaid tickets—at the very least. Nabbing people who run red lights is netting him drug dealers and muggers.

.   .   .

Sal's successful use of cabs gives him an idea of how he might take a run at the drug dealers by the handball courts. He asks the driver of a *New York Daily News* truck if he can hitch a ride. As the truck lurches down the street, Sal stands on the rear steel bumper and clings to the latches that lift the gate.

He catches a break when the truck has to stop for traffic and his perch winds up almost directly in front of the courts. A deal is going down, and for the moment the dealer's eyes are on his customer's hands and pockets.

Sal starts his rush. The dealer looks up. His face registers total shock. His mouth drops; his eyes grow big. The customer jets toward another building in the projects.

Sal goes after the dealer, registering where the vials drop, hoping a few are still on the ground after he grabs the kid.

The dealer runs for building 5. If the kid gets inside an apartment, Sal knows he'll never find him. The back entrances lead to multiple stairwells and elevators.

As they reach the building's terracelike entrance, the dealer jumps the low steps and stumbles. Sal dives and delivers a rolling tackle to the back of the dealer's thighs just as he leaps for the door. They fall together, and Sal catches an elbow to the side of his head. The dealer rises to his knees. Sal holds the kid's plaid Pendleton-like jacket in his left hand and pops the kid with a straight right. That finally stops him, but it makes the arrest ugly as the kid's nose pours blood over his mouth and down his chin.

People begin to gather as Sal stands the dealer up and puts cuffs on him. The crowd keeps growing, and their attitude is increasingly unfriendly. "What's he done? That's Jimmy. Jimmy ain't done nothin'. Why'd you beat him like that?"

Sal realizes he's one Italian cop in the midst of the Towers' thousands of African-Americans and Hispanics. He has to be cool. This is how riots start. An arrest becomes a brawl . . . a brawl becomes South Central L.A.

The building's security guard shows up, but he's a retirement-age rent-a-cop whose obvious fear only spurs on the dealer's defenders.

"Why you tossing Jimmy?" someone asks again. "Look here, he's bleeding all over. You the one who needs to be arrested. Jimmy be needin' an ambulance."

Sal turns on the crowd. "Jimmy's been dealing, and if the ones that are in it with him stick around, I'll take you in, too."

"He thinks Jimmy's some kind of drug dealer? Where are the drugs then? Where are the drugs?" Enough people echo the speaker that the crowd is on the verge of chanting.

By now, Sal's on the radio, calling for help. He'll stay in front of the building, waiting for the backup to arrive. He's safer here than he would be running the gauntlet back out to the street. He takes the dealer over to the steel bike rack, detaches one cuff, locks it down on the rack. Sal can face the crowd now, although he's conscious that parking the dealer almost invites someone else to get in his face.

"Now I told you, if you don't let me do my job here, I'll take somebody else in. My backup will be here in another minute."

A tall, graying man, in an old-fashioned overcoat and oversized wing tips that turn up at the toes, steps toward him and then turns around to the crowd. "What are you people giving the officer here a hard time for? You know this punk is dealing. I see him about every time I go to work. I know what he's doing. Everybody does. 'Cept my six-year-old son, Mattie. And I don't want Mattie *ever* to know. Of course he will soon enough. But if I can have one more day without his knowing, I'll take it. The ones of you that care about your children, your brothers and sisters, leave with me. Let the officer haul off the rest of the scum that don't."

Without ever turning around to face Sal, the man walks off. The citizens join him. The gangsters reluctantly follow.

Sal's backup finally walks through the dispersing crowd, glancing from side to side to see why everyone's leaving.

■   ■   ■

With time, Sal's tactics become more sophisticated, and he knows how to take advantage of the neighborhood's layout as well as or better than the crooks. The bad guys are always checking out his movements, his schedule. One day he gets an inquiry that's more particular than most.

A dealer he knows as Sonny asks, "What time you getting off today, Officer?"

"You got a big deal going down, Sonny? You want to know when the coast's clear?"

"Officer, it's cold out here. I'm just worried 'bout you coming in from the cold."

"I'm off at four o'clock, Sonny. That doesn't mean the neighborhood's without a presence, you know."

"I hope not. Enough people getting killed already."

"You got that right."

"You have a nice day, Officer. You get out of the cold soon as you can."

Close to four o'clock, the time he told Sonny his shift would end, Sal makes sure he passes the same corner at DeKalb and Spencer where he and Sonny had their talk earlier. Then Sal walks around the block and enters the welfare building the back way. He takes the elevator, then an interior stairwell, and posts himself in an office where the view takes in Sonny's field of operation. The welfare building, where the blinds are always drawn, provides perfect cover.

Sal watches Sonny's crew set up. The dealer posts lookouts on each side of the street, both ways, and four more on the cross street. He must be getting ready to move more than just daily hits. Three more people appear with him, and then he moves away toward the curb as they recede into doorways. The three shadows must be carrying the product while Sonny handles diplomacy.

Sal hits his radio and says, "This is Beat 12, central. We've got drug dealing on the corner of DeKalb and Spencer. I want the SNEU [Streets Narcotics Enforcement Unit] team to set up here. The buys are going to be coming in soon, and they look to be heavy."

In short order, SNEU sets up its units two blocks away.

Sonny must have told his customers he was having a sale because within the next two hours, nearly a dozen buys go down. Sal sits in the welfare building, directing traffic, while SNEU picks up the buyers a block or more from the dealer's spot. They hold them, collecting evidence.

Suddenly Sal sees the lookouts start to drift away. "Now! Now! Now!" he shouts into his radio. SNEU swarms in on Sonny & Company from every direction, cars screaming, weapons drawn.

.   .   .

The man who had supported Sal earlier begins to have quieter partners among the kids.

"You see that phone booth," says a gangly kid with his hair shaved close. "I left something in there. Read it carefully."

The note, tucked in the coin return, lists a place and a time. Sal knows there's nearly always a dealer stationed where he's being directed and figures a fresh supply of crack is being delivered. He takes the risk that the kid knows what he's talking about and has SNEU set up on it.

The delivery comes in right on schedule, only this time it's the cops, not the gangsters, who score big.

.   .   .

Sal receives a call from detectives at the 67th Precinct. "You see the papers about the drug hit in Flatbush? That family?"

"I think so. Yeah."

"What happened was, the father of this family ripped off his drug partners. So they came to the house to get him. When he wasn't there, the partners decided to send a message. They blindfolded the women and children, gagged them with duct tape, and then shot them. *Bing, bing, bing.* A .44 special. All dead except an older daughter, who played dead. She got up after they left and called 911. The father came home eventually, and we got him. He says his former associate, named Scanlon, must have been the hitter. Scanlon's from your territory, the 79th."

"Scanlon? There's a Scanlon I met at a block association meeting. He's in insurance. Maybe a relative?"

"Find out for us, would you?"

Sal makes preliminary inquires that establish the insurance agent as the accused hitter's father. Sal likes Mr. Scanlon and goes to the apartment with mixed emotions, keeping a hand on his gun as he knocks on the door, in case the son is there.

"Come in, come in, Officer Sal," Mr. Scanlon welcomes him. He urges Sal to sit and insists on bringing him a Coke.

"Here's the situation," Sal says. "We think your son Harvey might be involved in something. Something pretty bad. Has he been around here?"

"Just went out. He came back home last night and has been running around ever since. That's his bag right there, by that chair. He packed like there was no tomorrow. I expect him to breeze in here and breeze out again anytime."

"You mind if I take a look in his bag, Mr. Scanlon?"

"You have to ask?"

"Well, actually, I do."

"Go ahead, go ahead!"

Sal goes through the bag. He finds the .44 special stuffed in a sock. There's also lots of ammo, along with canned beans, corn, peas, and carrots. "Does your son have a room, Mr. Scanlon?"

"Through there."

Sal finds clothes piled on the bed. Obviously this guy is planning to head underground. Sal calls for his precinct's detectives to come over and keep watch with him. While they do, Mr. and Mrs. Scanlon keep wanting to serve them food.

Harvey never shows. Someone must have tipped him off. So Sal puts the word on the street. Anyone know where Harvey Scanlon might be?

Soon little eyes and ears want to know if he's heard about Harvey's girlfriend over in Flatbush. He gets an address. An accurate one. The detectives at the 67th find Harvey, only blocks from where the hit occurred.

Sal gets a letter of commendation, but what he's concerned about is the Scanlons. He goes back to visit.

Mr. Scanlon greets him just as warmly as before, if not more so. He even calls in his wife and daughters. "My son was out of control with those drugs," Mr. Scanlon says. "We were afraid he'd hurt *us*. Thank you for finding him. He's going to be away for a long time, but at least he'll be alive. Maybe he'll think about things."

"Sure. Sure he will," Sal says.

After that, when Sal sees the family on the street, the mother and daughters always have a kiss for him.

■   ■   ■

As many times as Sal rousts people out of the abandoned buildings on Skillman, the users and the couples always come back. People even shoot up and defecate in the abandoned cars that the empty lots breed.

One of Sal's jobs is to reduce crime by destroying its protective surroundings, so he goes to work with the sanitation department's Bob Tolito—a nice guy who also cares about the neighborhood. It takes a while, because Bob can pull only so many strings.

One day, however, the neighborhood sees a transformation. The sanitation department arrives with a regular mechanized army. With the assistance of a crane and wrecking ball, the giant earthmovers raze the abandoned buildings. The wrecked cars are towed at the same time. John Deere tractors as big as the ones that ply Midwest wheat fields level the whole area and drag it smooth. Then the earthmovers come back, this time with gigantic boulders that they station at the area's perimeter. The sanitation department then installs a hurricane fence topped with barbed wire around the whole area. The users and abusers have no place to hide anymore.

Anything can *happen here!* Sal thinks.

■   ■   ■

Sal gives seminars to churches, schools, block associations, and senior citizens' groups.

"If you want to show us you care, just dial the phone," he tells them. "We won't ask what your name is. We don't have to know it. The phone number you're calling from is going to come up on our screens, you know that. But we're not going to give you up to the people we arrest. If you'd like a code number as a block watcher, we have those, too. You can just say, 'I'm 0573.' You don't have to give your name."

A woman stands up in the back. Sal remembers her and wonders what she will say.

"This doesn't have anything to do with what we're talking about," she says. "But I just want the rest of you to know that this man saved my life."

He remembers the day. He had been hiding out in the welfare building again, directing traffic for another SNEU drug bust, when he saw her faint right there on the street below him. He dashed down the stairs and out the building. When he checked for a pulse, he found she had none. Zero. He thought she was gone. He radioed for help and started giving her CPR. He kept at it until the paramedics came.

Here she is, big as life, telling them all about it.

At the end of the session, he gives out a lot of code numbers.

■   ■   ■

Late on a Thursday night, Sal stops by the liquor store on DeKalb Avenue across from the welfare building. It's Mr. King's shop, and Sal keeps a close watch on his store at closing time. "How are you doing, Mr. King? Everything all right? Closing up?"

"We'll be out of here soon, Sal."

"Okay. I'll just be up the street."

Sal steps back through the door and . . . *boom, boom, boom.* By the time he uncovers from hiding, he sees a young man sitting on the ground, shot. Shot bad. The perp is walking away, not even running. He turns the corner.

Officer Sal starts to run. His leather soles slapping the pavement, along with his jingling keys and cuffs, finally signal the shooter that he'd better run, too. "Stop! Police! Don't move!"

The shooter turns and unloads his 9 mm in Sal's direction. Bullets whang against poles, thunk into cars, ricochet off the street.

Sal zigzags between the cars, ducking. He's got his own weapon out, and he gets the shooter in his sights. Sal looks beyond his target and sees people sitting out in their folding chairs, baby strollers parked beside front steps. It's dark. Sal knows that if he misses, he might hit a bystander. He slows, holsters his weapon, but stays in pursuit, walking now. He sees the shooter jump into an abandoned lot filled with bushes and shrubs, and by the time Sal reaches the lot, the guy is gone.

He calls in the situation, and he and his backup spend the rest of the night searching the area. They don't quit until one-thirty in the morning, by which time the temperature has fallen to twenty degrees. Tired and cold, Sal just wants to go home. But when everyone from the community has dispersed, bored now that the manhunt is over, four guys come up to him.

"We were watching you," the leader says. "We waited until the crowd cleared out. Meet us at the elementary school. On the playground. We got what you need."

"Okay, guys. Sure, all right. I'll take a stroll over there." Sal speaks coolly, casually. To any possible onlookers, he wants it to look like they're shooting the breeze—as unlikely as that might be, here at a crime scene at one-thirty in the morning.

When the four guys leave, Sal gathers the undercover officers and tells them about the invitation. "Look, guys, throw your radios on channel 10 and come up in your cars as quietly as you can. No lights. If I need you, you've got to be there before I ask! I don't know if I'm being set up or what, and I've been shot at enough for one day."

Sal walks the familiar route to the school. He can sense the undercover officers rolling through the streets behind him. He keeps his own radio open to channel 10. "This is Sal. C-Pop 12."

"We're here, Sal. We can see you."

The four young men are waiting in the schoolyard, as promised. He walks up to them as casually as he can.

"Listen, we know the guy," says the talker in the group. "He lives at his father's place over on Spencer."

"You got a number?" Sal asks, taking out his memo pad.

"It's the tan building right across from the dry cleaner's." After they give him the apartment number and the guy's name, they say, "We don't want anybody messing with you. You're okay, Robo Cop. Nobody needs to be shooting at *you*."

Sal thanks the guys and strolls away, confident that they have more than a good chance of nabbing the shooter. Beyond that, he basks in something more personal. The community has been noticing the time and attention he's put in. It's making a difference.

The next day, when the stakeout team finally sees the shooter show up at his father's apartment, the detectives grab him.

∎   ∎   ∎

Walking DeKalb late one afternoon, Sal runs into Shawn and Dennis, the two guys he broke up in the basketball fight. They talk about the Knicks, whether Patrick Ewing is mobile enough to win a championship.

Suddenly, from across the street, they hear shouts. "Stop him! Stop him! He's got my purse. Somebody help me! He's got my purse!"

They see the snatcher headed toward Spencer Street. Sal dashes at an angle across four lanes of traffic, bringing the southbound lanes to a screeching halt.

"Stop! Police!" he shouts at the thief.

Behind him, he hears someone else running. By the time he reaches the far curb, Shawn and Dennis have pulled ahead of him and are flying after the snatcher like gazelles. They dodge past the folks who can't think fast enough to get out of the way. Dennis actually jumps all the way over a short man.

Sal's sore hips begin to slow him. He's been on this beat for many years now, and both of his hip joints are worn down painfully. The jolt of each stride jacks up the pain voltage. He's hobbling as he rounds a corner, and then he sees both Shawn and Dennis flatten out in the air, double-teaming the snatcher to the ground. Whoa! That's a citizen's arrest for you!

∎   ∎   ∎

In the spring of 1993, Sal receives an invitation to a block party. The Marsey Street Mavens, as they style themselves (a neighborhood watch association), are cooking for the community on May 26. This is the first time anyone has dared to hold such an event, and Sal is glad to see it happen on the street where his dad used to live.

The first party is quickly followed by others. People are no longer frightened to be out on the streets, at least in the daytime. The neighborhood has gone from a living hell to at least a borderline place. Now anything truly *can* happen here, including community events.

.   .   .

By 1994, Sal's hips and legs are telling him that his days as a street cop have come to an end. He applies to go back into a cruiser, and the transfer comes through. His beat will be close to DeKalb, though, so he'll be able to roll back through and see his friends.

On his last day, while he's making his tour through Lafayette Towers, a group of people come up to him. The elderly woman to whom he gave CPR. Two block-association presidents. The tough kid who mouthed off at him the first day on the job. About forty people in all. They are, almost to a person, his favorites, and he wonders how they know about each other.

The security guard in the Towers steps forward. He's carrying a trophy, a loving cup. "Officer Sal," he says, "we know you're being reassigned. But before you go, we want to say thanks. We got you this trophy. You won a lot of battles here, and you helped us win back our neighborhood."

Everyone cheers, applauds.

Sal looks at the inscription on the cup: "To Officer Salvatore Bartolomeo. 'Robo Cop.' Six Years' Dedicated Service."

Official commendations are one thing. This is different, and much better. Sal never heard of a beat cop being given a trophy before. "I don't deserve this," he says. "You made it so easy."

Everybody laughs. "Right, easy," they mutter.

"No, I mean it! I mean it!"

Yes, something good *is* happening here.

The crumbling of order and resulting
self-destruction of the community start
with broken windows not being fixed;
next prostitutes and vagrants are
allowed to loiter; soon delinquents and
youth gangs realize they can act with
impunity; and by then the neighborhood
is well on its way toward disintegration.
ANDREW PEYTON THOMAS

CHAPTER 7

THERE GOES THE NEIGHBORHOOD

As you read chapter 7, keep the following questions in mind:
- What new concept of civil liberties swept through the courts in the 1970s and 1980s and why?
- What is the broken-window theory, and what makes it "old news"?
- What does *shalom* mean, and in what ways are Christians working toward *shalom* in their communities?

Salvatore Bartolomeo's policing of the streets of Brooklyn illustrates an exciting new approach to crime prevention. As Officer Sal pounded his beat, he dealt, of course, with serious crimes like murder, drug dealing, and robbery. But he also helped clear out the things that attract crime to a neighborhood: the signs of social disorder and decay, such as loitering, panhandling, graffiti, abandoned cars, vacant buildings, and littered lots. The success of this form of policing in New York City suggests that it may well be the key to restoring America's crime-ravaged inner cities. And significantly, it builds on the classic Christian understanding that civil peace comes only from a just and responsible social order— an insight sorely needed in our culture.

Over the past few decades, both crime and public disorder have risen sharply. High on the list of causes is the demographic shift that occurred when the baby boomers hit the crime-prone teen years. Another cause is the misguided policies of the 1960s and 1970s, shaped by the assumption that the cause of crime is poverty, an approach that seemed to excuse crime by blaming it on the environment.[1] At the same time, drug use was soaring, causing a domino effect of crime; and Great-Society welfare programs were weakening family structure, which led to gangs of poorly parented juveniles roaming the streets. The resulting social chaos turned America's inner cities into combat zones, and nothing seemed able to stop the downward spiral. Violent crime (per 100,000 persons) grew from 161 in 1960 to 758 in 1992, a 470 percent increase. Property crimes (per 100,000 persons) grew from 1,726 in 1960 to 4,903 in 1992, a 284 percent increase.[2]

Our inability to respond to crime effectively was often blamed on the sheer fact that in many cities the police were outnumbered and outgunned. But it wasn't just insufficient manpower and firepower that allowed crime to flourish. It was also a flawed worldview.

NEW CONCEPT OF CIVIL LIBERTIES

In the 1970s and 1980s, the courts introduced a novel concept of civil liberties that transformed disorderly and disruptive public behavior into a civil right. Most significant were two Supreme Court cases, one in 1972 and the other in 1983, striking down statutes against vagrancy and loitering. In the 1972 case, Justice William O. Douglas waxed colorful about the rights of "rogues and vagabonds" to roam the countryside as "loafers or litterers," as if drunks and panhandlers were merely romantic wanderers. The real culprits, the Court suggested, were the uptight middle-class moralists who were trying to force all dissenters to conform.[3]

In throwing out laws against vagrancy and loitering, however, the high court departed from a legal tradition that extended as far back as the Middle Ages, and even to ancient Athens. Historically, these laws were designed to discourage "the extreme individualistic license" that marks people who flout social convention and disrupt social order, explains attorney Andrew Peyton Thomas. The laws especially targeted those once referred to as "hobos," "tramps," or "bums"—drifters and transients who "rebel against family and career commitments" and prefer a rootless, roaming existence, sleeping in public places and begging from responsible citizens. "Vagrancy laws sought to uphold public order and personal responsibility by encouraging gainful employment and stable ties to family and neighbors."[4]

It was this attempt to "uphold public order" that was abruptly abandoned by the Court in its two landmark cases. Vagrants and drifters were no longer regarded as a danger to social stability but as a persecuted class deserving protection. It was civilized society that the Court condemned for shirking its obligations to misfits and miscreants.

A domino effect followed from these cases, as lower courts overturned state and municipal laws that had given police authority to restrain behavior in public places. Before long, the streets, parks, and subways of our major cities were filled with panhandlers, prostitutes, drunks urinating on the sidewalks, and people sleeping on heating grates.

The same concept of civil liberties captured the mental-health profession, as psychiatrists like R. D. Laing began to argue that there is no generally applicable standard of normalcy and that the mentally ill simply hold a different, but equally valid, perspective on life. Civil libertarians began to portray the mentally ill as just another oppressed group, while championing the absolute right of all people, sane or insane, to live by their own perceptions of reality. The American Civil Liberties Union pressed the point home

with several lawsuits. The result was a massive movement to
de-institutionalize the mentally ill, unleashing a flood of mentally
unstable, disoriented people onto the streets of the nation's cities.
Many promptly became homeless, often acting in ways that were
menacing or intimidating to ordinary citizens.[5]

So at the same time that crime was soaring and the mentally
ill were taking over parks and other public spaces, the courts
were handcuffing the police in their ability to curb antisocial and
disorderly behavior. The symbol of the times was "The Wildman
of 96th Street," a crack-addicted veteran who for years stalked
women, pushed people in front of cars, and generally terrorized
people on Manhattan's Upper West Side because authorities were
unable either to jail or institutionalize him. Repeated across the
country, such incidents sent a clear signal that authorities were
unable or unwilling to prevent minor forms of disorder—and
therefore were unlikely to prevent major crimes as well. As a
result, law-abiding citizens began to move out of the cities, while
lawbreakers moved in.

Underlying Worldview Issues

If we hope to restore our cities, we must understand and critique
the worldview that unleashed this disorder. This novel view of
civil liberties was the direct result of rejecting the biblical doctrine
of creation, which teaches that humans were created to live in
community, and replacing the Garden of Eden with a hypothetical "state of nature" (see earlier discussion in chapter 4). In this
secularized myth of human origins, individuals are the only ultimate reality, and individual rights trump all others; the requirements of public order are outweighed by the imperious demands
of individual autonomy. Thus civil liberties came to be defined in
excessively individualistic terms, denying the right of communities
to promote their values or to insist on standards of public behavior. This definition was adopted by sociologists, aggressively

promoted by civil-liberty organizations, enshrined in court decisions, and finally even accepted by the police themselves.

The solution, therefore, is not simply a matter of building more prisons and incarcerating more criminals. Indeed, America has tried that route. The 1970s saw the biggest prison-building boom in our nation's history. Speeches sprinkled with slogans about "law and order" and "getting tough on crime" were sure winners on the campaign trail. Arrests rose, prisons became overcrowded . . . and yet crime continued to rise.

Winds of Change

Then, in the early 1980s, a breakthrough came when social scientists George Kelling and James Q. Wilson advanced what became known as the broken-window theory. They discovered that if a broken window in a building is left unrepaired, soon all the windows are knocked out. Why? Because damage left untended sends a message that no one cares, that no one is in charge, and that further vandalism will incur no penalty. A single broken window soon attracts the kind of people who will smash more windows. Likewise, a city that allows pockets of public disorder, starting with graffiti and litter, sends a message that authorities are either unwilling or unable to enforce standards of behavior—to control their space and their citizens. And once a city sends that message, law-abiding citizens leave, and the criminal element is attracted—exactly the cycle that has ravaged America's major cities.[6]

In the early 1990s, New York Police Chief William Bratton took the broken-window theory to heart and persuaded New York's newly elected mayor and tough ex-prosecutor Rudolph Guiliani to give the theory a try. The order went out to police in Precincts 69 and 75 and to Brooklyn, where Officer Sal was stationed, to "fix broken windows"—that is, to arrest petty offenders and clean up the neighborhoods. The police adopted a policy of zero tolerance for any violation of public order, and in the process they soon discovered that there is indeed a "seamless web" between controlling petty crime and restraining major crime. Whereas before they had ignored turnstile jumping at subways, officers now nabbed the offenders, who, as often as not, turned out to be muggers. Whereas before they had turned a blind eye to minor traffic violations, they now stopped all traffic violators, which often led to the discovery of drugs and guns in the cars. They chased away loiterers and panhandlers, many of whom were drug dealers looking for a sale. In three years in Precinct 75, once one of the most dangerous places in America, the number of homicides dropped from 129 to 47.[7]

Civil libertarians attacked Bratton's crime-prevention program repeatedly and even sued the New York Police Department, citing the earlier Supreme Court decisions and arguing that the program targeted people simply because they were poor or homeless. But Bratton had framed his policies carefully to penalize behavior, not status (e.g., homelessness), and the courts denied the challenges of civil libertarians. (One suspects that judges were also responding to public clamor to end the chaos.)[8]

Cities around the country began imitating New York, with equally dramatic results. Politicians were quick to trumpet their successes anywhere they could find a camera or microphone. It was as if they had discovered the Holy Grail, the long-sought answer to crime. Yet all that Guiliani and the others have "discovered" is a well-established, fundamental biblical truth.

REAL SHALOM

Thousands of years before the broken-window theory, the Jewish people had already captured the idea in *shalom*. Although popularly translated "peace," the connotations of the term are actually much broader than the absence of hostilities. *Shalom* refers to peace in a positive sense, the result of a rightly ordered community. When people live together according to God's moral order—in *shalom*—there is civility and harmony. <u>The best way to reduce crime is not to react after the fact with punishments and rehabilitation but to discourage it before it happens by creating an ordered and civil community life.</u>

The biblical basis for this approach is the doctrine of creation, which tells us we were created for community. Contrary to the notion of a "state of nature," with its war of all against all, the Bible teaches that we are not autonomous individuals. Instead, we are created in the image of the One who in his very essence is a community of being—that is, the Trinity. God's very nature is reciprocal love and communication among the persons of the Trinity. We were created as inherently communal beings, and the God-ordained institutions of society make rightful, normative demands that we are morally obligated to fulfill.

These institutions are not impositions on our freedom but expressions of our inherently social nature. "God might have created men as disconnected individuals," writes Kuyper. Instead, he created an original couple, with the result that, by birth, each of us "is organically united with the whole race."[9] This social nature is expressed through our social institutions, and these institutions need some kind of authority structure to direct their activities to the common good. Thus to create and maintain order in our political communities, God has ordained the state. All of us have a moral imperative to obey proper authority and to work for justice and *shalom*.

In the fourth century, in his classic work *The City of God,* St. Augustine taught that peace *(shalom)* is "the tranquillity produced by order" *(tranquillitas ordinis).* A political community can enjoy peace and harmony only by following the moral order, he wrote; for only an ordered civil life allows fallen human beings to "live and work together." Therefore, the primary role of the state is not to chase down criminals after the fact but to nurture the *tranquillitas ordinis,* using its unique powers of coercion to that end. Pursuing *tranquillitas ordinis* is also the duty of every Christian, for though our sights are set ultimately on the "City of God," as long as we live in the "City of Man," it is morally imperative for us to work for the peace of that city. This is not optional; it is the only way to keep evil in check.[10]

For centuries this biblical view of communal order dominated Western thought. In the last century, William Wilberforce, the great evangelical British statesman, noted that "the most effectual way to prevent the greater crimes is by punishing the smaller, and by endeavoring to repress the general spirit of licentiousness, which is the parent of every kind of vice."[11] The same philosophy influenced the original principles of policing laid out by Sir Robert Peel in 1829. The first job of the police, said Peel, is not fighting crime but keeping the peace.[12] Seventy years later, in the first New York City charter, the same principles were repeated: "It is hereby made the duty of the police department to especially preserve the public peace, . . . remove all nuisances in the public streets, . . . restrain all unlawful and disorderly conduct."[13] As a result, at the turn of the century it was the police who developed the first food and soup lines; they built police stations with extra space where migrants could stay until they found work; they referred beggars to charitable agencies; and yes, they even helped lost children find their way home. Officer Sal would have been right at home.

The success this approach has demonstrated in restoring America's major cities underlines the wisdom of the classic biblical view and provides powerful evidence that it is, in fact, true—true to our nature, true to who we are. By contrast, the chaos of the last few decades attests to the disastrous consequences of living by a false philosophy of human nature, one that denies the biblical teaching of creation and substitutes a secular myth of our origins and our nature. The secular view has been tried and found wanting, and its failure opens a wonderful opportunity for Christians to make a case for a biblical view of human nature and community.

FIXING BROKEN WINDOWS

What does the biblical approach look like in practice? In Newport News, Virginia, police grew weary of constantly answering calls about burglars and drug dealers in a run-down housing project, and the entire project was finally scheduled for demolition. In preparation for new construction, the officers decided to clean up the area: They carted away trash, removed abandoned cars, filled in potholes. To everyone's surprise, burglary rates suddenly dropped by 35 percent. The police had inadvertently stumbled on the broken-window theory. Similarly, Baltimore police worked with local agencies to clean up a housing project—to upgrade street lighting, trim shrubbery, clean alleys, and build a play-ground—with the result that burglaries were reduced by 80 percent and auto larceny by 100 percent. Restoring order really does create "the tranquillity of order."[14]

One of the most successful examples is in Charleston, South Carolina, where Police Chief Reuben Greenberg decided to fight crime by cleaning up inner-city neighborhoods, getting rid of lit-ter, used needles, and graffiti. To keep costs down, he employed prisoners from the local jail. Soon formerly crime-ridden areas were clean and neat, signaling that disruptive and disorderly behavior would not be tolerated.

Greenberg then went after open-air drug dealing, which had taken over entire sections of the city. He simply placed uniformed police officers on every corner where drugs were being sold. The officers didn't question anyone; they just stood there. Yet the impact on business was immediate. No one came near the drug dealers, not even to say hello. They were forced to leave the area or go out of business altogether.

Next Greenberg revived the original 1930s vision of public housing as a refuge for the poor, not a haven for crime. The housing authority began to screen tenants, refusing to accept violent criminals, and today public housing is one of the safest places to live in the entire city.

Finally, to fight soaring juvenile crime, Greenberg reintroduced truant officers. If school-age children were spotted anywhere in the city during school hours, a truant officer was dispatched to pick them up and return them to school. Results were immediate: a 24 percent permanent decrease in such daytime crimes as purse snatching, car theft, and shoplifting.[15]

In some places, citizens themselves are taking the initiative to restore neighborhoods. A good example is Bryant Park in New York City, once a haven for drug dealers and other lawbreakers, the site of one hundred fifty reported robberies and ten rapes a year. Finally, neighbors and property owners formed an association and leased the seven-acre park from the city. They tore down iron fencing and high hedges that made easy hiding places for criminals; they remodeled the rest rooms and kept them clean and safe; they hired unarmed security guards to patrol the park to deter small misdemeanors such as wading in the fountains or walking in the flower beds. Today, while remaining virtually free from crime, Bryant Park draws thousands of New Yorkers every week to sunbathe, picnic, and attend artistic events.[16]

Even kids can get in on the act. A few years ago, in Montgomery, Alabama, fifty Christian teenagers armed with hedge clippers and Weedwacker trimmers descended on a neighborhood of mostly elderly people. Determined to tackle the overgrown bushes that provided hiding places for vandals, burglars, and muggers, the kids trimmed towering hedges, thinned low-hanging tree branches, even replaced burned-out lights and installed peepholes in doors. The project was called Youth Cutting Down on Crime, and it was organized by Neighbors Who

Care, a Prison Fellowship ministry that mobilizes churches to help crime victims.

Why does establishing order work so well as a crime preventive? Because it expresses an underlying moral order and shows that the community is willing to enforce it. Such is the finding of one of the largest studies ever undertaken into the causes of crime and delinquency. Researchers at Harvard University, the Kaiser Institute, and the University of Chicago joined together to survey 382 Chicago neighborhoods, all with different ethnic, racial, and economic characteristics. They could find no common thread in traditional demographics. In some minority communities crime was high, while in others it was low. The same was true of poverty. The only common pattern researchers found was that rates of violence were lower in areas that had a strong sense of community values and a willingness to impose those values on the public space—for example, where neighbors felt free to step in and discipline kids who skip school or scribble graffiti on the walls or hang out on the streets. In other words, even disadvantaged communities can overcome adverse conditions if they have common values and are willing to enforce them, especially among the young.[17] As a *Boston Globe* reporter put it, somewhat tongue in cheek, the level of violence is mostly influenced by "such things as being willing to look after other people's children and mind others' business."[18]

This is what Roberto Rivera, one of our Prison Fellowship colleagues, calls the "Mrs. Greene syndrome." Rivera grew up in a racially mixed, big-city neighborhood presided over by an imposing woman named Mrs. Greene. She had three children of her own, but she considered it her business to watch out for everyone else's kids, too. "If she saw you doing something stupid or dangerous, she would not hesitate to call you on it," Rivera recalls. "Even worse, you could count on her telling your parents. It was almost impossible to get away with anything when Mrs. Greene was around."

Social science is proving that it's the Mrs. Greenes of this world who enforce community values and keep neighborhoods safe. And values, in turn, derive ultimately from biblical religion. Several recent studies show a direct connection between the influence of Christian faith and crime reduction. Independent studies have shown that crime is highest in neighborhoods with the most bars and liquor stores, and lowest in areas with the most churches.[19] A landmark study by Richard Freeman of Harvard found that young people who are active in church are more likely to finish school, avoid out-of-wedlock pregnancies, keep a job, and stay out of trouble with the law. In preventing crime, church attendance rates even higher than family structure, a highly significant finding, given that growing up in a fatherless home has also been proven to have a severely negative impact. The power of religion comes from the fact that it instills a sense of purpose and value to life; it also teaches a standard of morality that acts as a restraint on antisocial and criminal behavior.[20]

The same effect has been proven historically as well. James Q. Wilson found that crime fell dramatically in the latter half of the last century despite rapid industrialization. He traced the cause to a widespread revival (the Second Great Awakening), when Christians created an extraordinary number of associations to help the poor, the needy, unemployed men, and abandoned women.[21] Their success in transforming society gives persuasive evidence that Christians can do the same today.

In fact, it is only Christians who have a worldview capable of providing workable solutions to the problems of community life. Thus, we ought to be in the forefront, helping communities take charge of their own neighborhoods. Whether it's mobilizing efforts to paint over graffiti and clean up vacant lots, or political activism to pass laws enforcing standards of public behavior, we should be helping to restore order in these smaller areas as the first step toward tackling major social ills.

We can take our lead from the stunning successes of inner-city churches that have assumed an active role in recapturing their neighborhoods. Take, for example, the Reverend Eugene Rivers, who leads Azusa Christian Community, a Pentecostal congregation in Boston's impoverished Dorchester area. Rivers, a former gang member who went on to graduate from Harvard, was inspired to restore his community after witnessing a shocking tragedy. In the spring of 1992, gang members entered a church in the middle of a funeral and stabbed a teenager from a rival gang, then shot up the church. Rivers, joined by more than forty other pastors, set out to rescue inner-city kids from gangs and drugs. The churches started offering after-school tutoring ("latchkey learning") and Bible studies; they formed neighborhood patrols to offer kids safe conduct to and from school; they counseled juveniles on probation; and they made contacts with Christian businessmen to help teens get jobs.[22] After Boston went two years without a single gun-related homicide among teens, even national magazines such as *The New Yorker* took notice: "You couldn't function effectively without the ministers in Boston," former Boston police commissioner William Bratton told the magazine. "Those churches and leaders like Gene Rivers were a very significant reason for our success."[23]

Princeton professor John DiIulio was so impressed with ministries like the one in Boston that he reduced his teaching load at Princeton and created an organization called PRRAY (Partnership for Research on Religion and At-Risk Youth) to research and help fund faith-based programs. DiIulio describes such ministries in dramatic terms: Church volunteers "go right on the street, right to the gangs, right to the heart of the action. Kids are stunned. Police don't even go in there." But committed Christians go where police fear to tread, bringing the bold message that "God loves you and has something better for you."[24]

In 1996, I visited the Allison Hill section of Pennsylvania's capital city, Harrisburg, a desperate ghetto, its alleys reeking of old garbage and its abandoned lots littered with bullet casings and used needles. I saw sidewalks stained with blood from drug deals gone bad.

But shortly afterward, the Reverend Ana Martinez, copastor of First Spanish Christian Church, opened a small storefront office of Neighbors Who Care, a Prison Fellowship ministry to victims of crime. One night Ana and her coworkers Rosalie Danchanko and Paulita Vido led a prayer march through Allison Hill. Volunteers wearing bright yellow T-shirts printed with "When Neigbors Care, Crime Goes Down" handed out hot dogs and balloons. Face-painters and clowns entertained the children. And the crowds grew. Spontaneously, five hundred people began walking together down the littered streets, holding hands, singing hymns, and praying out loud. "Shine the Light," the people sang. "Shine the Light on Harrisburg!"

As they marched, people poured out of the local bar to see what was happening. A young woman, high on drugs, stumbled after them. "I need help," she sobbed. (Rosie and the volunteers later connected her with a treatment program and led her to Christ.) Kids sailing by on skateboards joined the procession.

The crowd approached a corner where a cluster of black-clad gang members were milling around, edgy with tension, and Reverend Ana called out in a booming voice, "The Lord loves you. We love you. But we don't love what you're doing. Come join us!" One teenage boy, his young face already hard from years on the streets, slowly backed away from the gang on the corner and joined the Christians.

Meanwhile, carloads of teenagers tried to disrupt what was going on, gunning their motors, honking their horns, blaring their radios. The marchers prayed even more loudly. Men were crying, women shaking. The prayer rose like a great roar, filling the streets and alleys.

When you walk the streets of Allison Hill today, you will find the syringes gone, the ranks of the drug dealers thinned out. As the prayer warriors keep marching, there is hope in Harrisburg, signs of shalom.

"It was the soccer ball and the Bible that worked," says Kathy Dudley who, with her husband, founded Voice of Hope to restore neighborhoods in West Dallas. "We would go to a street, gather up all the kids, take them to a playground, and play ball," she says. "Then we would tell them Bible stories." From that first soccer ball, Voice of Hope has grown into a successful community-development program with after-school tutoring, job training, housing rehabilitation, a dental clinic, a thrift store, and a gift shop.[25]

Under way at Chicago's Lawndale Community Church are similar efforts begun by Wayne Gordon, who founded the church with a group of teenagers in 1978, having sensed the call to revive one of the city's toughest inner-city neighborhoods. Lawndale Community Church has become a safe refuge for kids, with a gymnasium and after-school tutoring. In the College Opportunity Program, eighth-graders commit themselves to a five-year program of twice-weekly study sessions at the church's learning center. If they maintain a 2.5 grade-point average, they receive a $3,000-per-year, four-year college scholarship. If the kids or their family members get sick, they can go to the church's full-service medical center for a minimal fee, and Lawndale's job-training program helps the unemployed find work. The church also has a housing ministry to rehabilitate abandoned buildings and give the poor an opportunity to become homeowners.[26]

In Baltimore, Sandtown was once a neighborhood of boarded-up row houses and littered alleys, with drug dealers on every corner—that is, until New Song Community Church was founded. Now the church reaches people like Torey Reynolds, mother of four, who was addicted to crack and on welfare. With the church's help, she went through job training and is now employed as a community health-care worker. Her children attend New Song's Learning Center, and when they're sick, she takes them to New Song Family Health Center. Torey and her husband are also proud first-time homeowners of one of the row houses rehabilitated through the local Habitat for Humanity.

In Memphis, Tennessee, the same vision for restoring social and moral order inspires the members of Mississippi Boulevard Christian Church. The church runs a housing-rehabilitation ministry, a Christian school, the Manna Food Center for distributing food to the poor and elderly, and the Family Life Center with everything from youth basketball and volleyball teams to roller skating, a handball court, and a bowling alley. The church also has a clothing pantry, a job-placement program, a bookstore, and counseling services.

All of these examples were originally inspired by a vision for Christian community development that was first born in the hearts of my friends John and Vera Mae Perkins. John grew up picking cotton in Mississippi, suffered beatings during the civil rights movement, and then founded Voice of Calvary ministry in Mendenhall and Jackson, Mississippi. Today these ministries have grown to include housing rehabilitation, a thrift store, job training, a school, day care, a food co-op, and a medical center. The Perkins's model of Christian community development is now being imitated across the country.

In recent years, John and Vera Mae have taken their vision to the drug-infested northwest corner of Pasadena, California. The first time I visited the Perkins's new home, I saw drug dealers on the street outside, pulling up in their limousines to do street-corner deals amid the garbage and litter. I prayed with John and Vera Mae in their living room, sitting by a window that still had a bullet hole from a drive-by shooting.

But within months, the Perkinses had turned their backyard

into a play area where neighborhood kids could play safely and listen to Bible stories. Soon they bought up adjoining properties and renovated them; they opened a youth center and additional family services. They encouraged other Christians to buy properties close by and open related ministries. Over time, the drug dealers disappeared, crime abated, and children were playing in their front yards once more. When I returned for another visit, I could not believe the transformation.

What is happening in Boston, Harrisburg, Dallas, Chicago, Baltimore, Memphis, Mendenhall, Jackson, and Pasadena is what Christians should be doing everywhere: converting chaos into the *tranquillitas ordinis,* one house at a time, one block at a time, one neighborhood at a time, one community at a time. Although our citizenship is in the "City of God," we know that God has placed us in our cities and neighborhoods to reflect his character and to restore his righteous dominion in the midst of a fallen world. We begin with our personal lives and habits, move out from there to our families and schools and then into our communities—and from there into our society as a whole.

*"Why, sir, if he really believes there
is no distinction between virtue and
vice, let us count our spoons before
he leaves."* SAMUEL JOHNSON
(when told that a dinner guest
believed morality was a sham)

CHAPTER 8

CREATING THE GOOD SOCIETY

As you read chapter 8, keep the following questions in mind:

- Why doesn't relativism or pragmatism provide a foundation for a safe and orderly society?
- What is integrity, and why is it important?
- What does it take to create the "good life"?

What does it take to achieve the good life? Not the Budweiser "good life," but a life of virtue? Our Founding Fathers understood that this is a crucial question for any society, for virtue is essential to freedom. People who cannot restrain their own baser instincts, who cannot treat one another with civility, are not capable of self-government. "Our Constitution was made for a moral and religious people," said John Adams. "It is wholly inadequate to the government of any other."[1] Without virtue, a society can be ruled only by fear, a truth that tyrants understand all too well.

The same critical question, then, confronts us as we move beyond our families and neighborhoods to consider our common life together: How can we achieve the virtue necessary to maintain a good society and to preserve liberty? And how do the worldview categories of *creation, fall,* and *redemption* help us analyze the false views we confront in our culture today?

Sadly, in our relativistic age many people, even Christians, have lost the ethical categories of right and wrong. A few years ago, a young acquaintance of mine, who is a member of a good church, attended a four-week ethics course at Harvard Business School— a course that was started in response to the Savings and Loan scandals in the 1980s. On his return, he raved about the course.

"What kind of ethics are they teaching?" I asked.

"Well, the professor really summed it up the last day when he said, 'Don't do anything that will get you in the newspapers. It's bad for business.'"

"But that's pure pragmatism," I replied in astonishment. " 'Don't get caught.' 'Don't get the company in trouble.' What's that got to do with ethics?"

"But that's the point, isn't it?" said the young man. "To stay out of trouble."

Unfortunately, this perspective is quite common. Yet I have no grounds for self-righteousness, for when I was in politics, I practiced similar principles. I would not do anything I knew to be illegal, but I felt entitled to do to our opposition whatever they had done to us when they were in power (a sort of reverse Golden Rule). That's why the Watergate scandal was so frequently defended with the excuse "Everyone does it." Why was a little bugging of the Democratic headquarters so bad when we knew that President Johnson had bugged the Nixon campaign plane in 1968? And President Clinton resorted to exactly the same defense when challenged on campaign abuses in 1995.

Is it any wonder our country has been in an ethical free fall for the past three decades? A generation ago, the Watergate scandal rocked the nation; today, countless "gates" later, the public treats such scandals as routine.

The problem is that relativism provides no sure foundation for a safe and orderly society. If all people are free to choose for themselves what is right, how can a society agree on, and enforce, even minimal standards? And if there is no ultimate moral law, what motivation is there to be virtuous? The result is the loss of community. If you thought your neighbors had no clear definition of right and wrong, would you sleep well at night or let your children play in their yard?

Throughout most of Western history, the moral consensus was largely informed by the Judeo-Christian tradition. But with the Enlightenment, intellectuals began to argue that since God was no longer needed to explain creation, he was no longer needed to establish moral laws. Reason alone would form the basis for morality. Since then, the great question that has faced Western society is the one posed by the great Russian novelist Fyodor Dostoyevsky: "Can man be good without God?"

IS REASON ENOUGH?

Can reason alone come up with a viable moral system? The answer is no, and the failure of reason alone to generate moral norms was illustrated forcefully some years ago by the fate of the Conference on Science, Philosophy, and Religion. In the summer of 1939, with Nazi armies occupying Czechoslovakia and poised to strike at Poland, the last hopes for appeasing Hitler were finally shattered, and the world girded itself for the horrors of another world war. Realizing that the moral resolve of the Western world must somehow be reinforced, Louis Finkelstein, chancellor of the Jewish Theological Seminary in New York, began planning for a grand conference where the greatest scholars from every discipline would draw on their collective wisdom to devise a universal code of ethics to provide the moral foundation for democracy. The conference was announced in June 1940 in a statement signed by seventy-nine leading intellectuals, including Albert Einstein. The *New York Times* printed the announcement in full on page one, breathlessly hailing it as an "intellectual declaration of independence."[2] A week later the *Times* published an editorial, "To Defend Democracy," which concluded that "we need a new Social Contract, a new Declaration of the Rights of Man."[3]

When the group convened later that year, the goal was what Finkelstein called "corporate thinking"—that is, an effort to synthesize Judeo-Christian ethics with Enlightenment humanism and modern science, in order to create a new foundation for democratic societies. Yet even before the opening gun—during the organizing session—the battle lines were drawn between traditionalists and modernists. On the side of the traditionalists, Mortimer Adler, editor of the Great Books series, declared, "We have more to fear from our professors than from Hitler," referring to those intellectuals who had abandoned historically accepted moral truths. His adversary, Sidney Hook, responded that Adler was promoting a "new medievalism." "The only absolute is science," Hook contended, and called for a pragmatic approach to morality. The modernists contended that all values are relative—except, of course, the value of tolerance.[4]

Notwithstanding the difficulties of the first conference, hopes continued to run high for the second one. Surely the best minds of our nation could agree on universal norms of conduct so that out of the ashes of war would emerge a new world of hope. The press continued its effusive coverage.

It was not until the third conference that the optimistic fervor began to subside as the debate came to a stalemate over which morality should be adopted. Around the country, editorialists began to reduce expectations slightly with headlines such as "Scholars Confess They Are Confused."[5]

The Conference on Science, Philosophy, and Religion continued to meet through the war years and after, debating issues such as the atom bomb, one-world government, and the end of Western colonialism. By the 1948 meeting, reports Fred Beuttler of the University of Illinois, "the biggest fear of most academic intellectuals was dogmatism and indoctrination." In other words, the relativists had carried the day. "All absolutist thinking," they said, "has totalitarian potential." By the early 1960s the conference was disbanded. The original goal of defining "cultural universals" had proved impossible.[6]

Think of it: For two decades some of the world's greatest minds engaged in stimulating debate and produced . . . nothing. Why? Because they disagreed about the proper starting point of ethical knowledge. The traditionalists, like Adler, understood that in order to have objective, universal ethical principles, there must be an absolute source, a transcendent authority. The modernists started with the assumption that science is the only source of sure knowledge, that nature is all there is, and thus that morality is merely a human invention that can be changed to meet changing circumstances in an evolving world. The two sides started out with conflicting worldviews, and in their fruitless exchanges were merely playing out the logical consequences of their starting points.

The grandiose endeavor of Louis Finkelstein brings into focus the failure of efforts to derive ethical rules from reason alone. Today ethics has degenerated into relativism, with each individual carving out his or her own private truths to live by. In the words of Father Richard John Neuhaus, we are "herds of independent minds marching towards moral oblivion with Frank Sinatra's witless boast on our lips, 'I Did It My Way.'"[7]

In this climate, it is considered offensive to assert in polite company that Western civilization, under the influence of the Judeo-Christian tradition, might enjoy any moral advantage or that its historic beliefs might be drawn on to arrest our moral free fall. When one of the Bass brothers of Texas gave $20 million to his alma mater, Yale University, stipulating that the grant be used for the study of Western civilization, the university hemmed and hawed. The faculty wanted a multicultural curriculum, not one that favored the Western tradition, so they dragged their feet until Lee Bass finally asked that his gift be returned.[8]

In our public schools it has become nearly impossible to teach traditional precepts of right and wrong—which has led to disastrous consequences. "For generations," writes theologian Michael Novak, "the primary task explicitly assigned public schools of the nation was character formation."[9] No longer. A few years ago, a *New York Times* reporter visited a New Jersey high school classroom in which students were discussing the case of a woman who had found $1000 and turned it in. All fifteen students said she was a fool. But the real shocker came after class, when the reporter asked the teacher why she had not told the students they were wrong. The teacher replied, "If I came from the position of what is right and wrong, then I'm not their counselor."[10]

Don't educators understand where this kind of value-free teaching must lead? A nation without virtue cannot govern itself. "Our people are losing virtue," Novak says bluntly. "That is why we have been losing self-government."[11] And if we cannot govern ourselves, then we invite others to govern us. The death of virtue threatens our very liberty as a people.

At root, this great struggle is between worldviews, and it poses the question: How now shall we live—by the Judeo-Christian tradition or by the moral nihilism of today's relativistic, individualistic culture?

A SOCIETY GUARDED BY 250 MILLION POLICEMEN

By examining these conflicting worldviews through the analytical grid of *creation, fall,* and *redemption,* we see clearly the cause of our ethical malaise. Creation tells us that we owe our existence to a holy God, whose character is the standard of all righteousness, the measure of all morality. "Be holy because I, the Lord your God, am holy" (Lev. 19:2). The clear failing of the secular worldview is that it tells us we owe our existence to natural forces acting at random; therefore, there can be no ultimate source of moral norms.

The second category is just as crucial. The Fall tells us we are prone to evil and thus need moral restraints for society to function. "What comes out of a man is what makes him 'unclean.'" (Mark 7:20). But secularism fails to understand the nature of our moral dilemma, leading to the false assumption that since people are basically good, a virtuous society can be formed by creating the right social, political, and economic structures.

But the truth is that <u>a virtuous society can be created only by virtuous people, whose individual consciences guard their behavior and hold them accountable.</u> Without conscience, a society can be held in check only through coercion. Yet even coercion ultimately fails, for there is no police force large enough to keep an eye on every individual. "This country ought to have, when it is healthy and when it is working as it is intended to work, 250 million policemen—called *conscience*," says Michael Novak. "When there are 250 million consciences on guard, it is surprising how few police are needed on the streets."[12]

The emphasis on social justice at the expense of private virtue is not only mistaken but downright dangerous. People without personal morality inevitably fail in their efforts to create public morality. "There is no social sin without personal sin," writes Georgetown University professor James Schall. "Our youth today are almost invariably taught they must change the world, not their souls. So they change the world, and it becomes worse."[13] Moral crusaders with zeal but no ethical understanding are likely to give us solutions that are worse than the problems.

What's more, when we focus young people's moral attention solely on public issues and causes, they fail to treat the personal realm as morally serious. Some years ago, Christina Hoff Sommers, philosophy professor at Clark University, wrote an article entitled "Teaching the Virtues," in which she attacked higher education for teaching ethics as social justice rather than as individual decency and honesty. One of Sommers's colleagues chastised her, complaining that she was promoting bourgeois morality and ignoring the real issues, such as the oppression of women, the evils of multinational corporations, and the exploitation of the environment. But at the end of the semester, the same teacher came to Sommers's office, horrified that more than half her students had plagiarized their take-home exam. They had cheated in an ethics course!

"What are you going to do?" Sommers asked. Sheepishly, the woman asked for a copy of Sommers's article on the importance of individual virtue.[14]

The myth of human goodness has led to a massive disconnect between the public and private realms, until many Americans are fractured and compartmentalized, glibly saying, "It doesn't matter what the president does in private." Or, worse, "It doesn't matter what *I* do in private." Americans have embraced a dualism between the body and the "person," which is most obvious in arguments defending abortion (the fetus may be biologically human but not a "person").[15] The same dualism affords the perfect rationalization for libertinism. For if the body is merely a tool for getting us what we want—pleasure or emotional gratification—then its actions are judged by purely utilitarian considerations, not moral ones. Our actions do not reflect the "person," which is a separate entity. Thus we rationalize that a person can behave as a rogue, a liar, or a cheat in private life but can still be trusted in public life.

This runs totally against the grain of the Christian view of human nature. A good tree will produce good fruit, Jesus taught. "Whoever can be trusted with very little can also be trusted with much, and whoever is dishonest with very little will also be dishonest with much" (Luke 16:10). Integrity of character runs through large and small matters, through public and private actions.

INTEGRITY FIRST

I reflected on this principle a few years ago when I lectured on the subject of ethics at Camp Lejeune, North Carolina, the same place where I started out as an infantry platoon commander during the Korean War. With a touch of nostalgia, I returned to address two thousand marine officers and noncommissioned officers. They sat attentively in starched fatigues and spit-shined boots, but when the question-and-answer period began, no one stirred . . . until the general, a rugged, six-foot-six officer, turned around and said in a booming voice, "There will be questions." Suddenly, hands popped up all across the auditorium. (Some things never change.)

The last question was the toughest by far. "Mr. Colson," said a master sergeant, "which is more important—loyalty or integrity?"

Now, a marine lives by the creed *semper fidelis*—"always faithful"—and when I was a marine, I learned that loyalty meant unquestioning obedience. Yet I wish I had pondered the young sergeant's question when I was in the Nixon White House. For now I know the answer.

"Integrity comes first," I said. Loyalty, no matter how admirable, can be dangerous if it is invested in an unworthy cause.

Integrity comes from the verb *to integrate*, which means to become united so as to form a complete or perfect whole.[16] Scripture teaches that spirit, mind, and body all come from the hand of God, and thus they ought to be united, functioning together as a whole. Our actions must be consistent with our thoughts. We must be the same person in private and in public. Only the Christian worldview gives us the basis for this kind of integrity.

Moreover, Christianity gives an absolute moral law that allows us to judge between right and wrong. Try asking your secular friends how they decide what they *ought* to do, what ethical principles to follow. How do they know those principles are right? On what authority do they rely? Without moral absolutes, there is no real basis for ethics.

An absolute moral law doesn't confine people in a straitjacket of Victorian prudery. People will always debate the boundaries of moral law and its varied applications. But the very idea of right and wrong makes sense only if there is a final standard, a measuring rod, by which we can make moral judgments.

REDEMPTION, WILL, AND POWER

Only the Christian worldview offers redemption from sin, giving power to overcome the single most powerful obstacle to becoming virtuous: the rebellious human will. Morality is not just about an intellectual acknowledgment of ultimate standards, of what ought to be; morality is also about developing virtue—that is, the full range of habits and dispositions that constitute good character. We must not merely assent mentally to certain principles; we must *become* people who are just, courageous, patient, kind, loyal, loving, persistent, and devoted to duty. And only the Christian worldview tells us how to develop virtuous character, to become moral persons.

In the movie adaptation of Tolstoy's *War and Peace*, the central character, Pierre, asks dolefully, "Why is it that I know what is right, but do what is wrong?" That is the human dilemma. We may know the right thing, but that is no guarantee that we will do it. As the Old Testament prophet Jeremiah laments, "The heart is deceitful above all things and beyond cure. Who can understand it?" (Jer. 17:9). Or, as the apostle Paul puts it: "I know that nothing good lives in me, that is, in my sinful nature. For I have the desire to do what is good, but I cannot carry it out. For what I do is not the good I want to do; no, the evil I do not want to do— this I keep on doing" (Rom. 7:18-19).

Even if Louis Finkelstein's grand vision had succeeded and a universal code of morality had been agreed upon, would people have been able to live by it? Could they have become moral persons? The optimist says yes, but both Scripture and empirical evidence say otherwise. The secular view of ethics offers no salvation, no power to change the human heart.

I can testify to this from personal experience. I was raised in a good family with almost puritanical standards. My father, whom I idolized, drilled into me the principles of duty, honor, and honesty. I can still remember sitting with him on the back steps of our home on Sunday afternoons, listening to him lecture on the evils of cheating or stealing.

In 1969, when President Nixon asked me to leave my lucrative law practice to serve as his special counsel, I saw it as my duty to do so, even though it meant a drastic pay cut. To guard against temptation, or even the appearance of impropriety, I put my law firm investments and all other assets into a blind trust and vowed never even to see former law partners or clients (who might seek government favors). Any gifts I received, even boxes of candy at Christmas, were immediately turned over to the drivers of my limousine or the operators at the White House switchboard. I was determined: *No one would corrupt me.*

Yet I went to prison for obstruction of justice.

What happened?

My problem was that I didn't understand the deceptiveness of the human heart. In college, I had studied the best of the world's moral philosophy, including Immanuel Kant's famous "categorical imperative," which is really a modified version of the Golden Rule, a near universal moral principle. So I *knew* well enough what was right. The problem was that I lacked the will to *do* it. For we humans have an infinite capacity for self-rationalization; we can justify anything. Which is exactly what I did.

C. S. Lewis explains the dilemma in my favorite of his essays, "Men without Chests." For a person to be moral, the "head," the seat of reason, must rule the "stomach," or the passions. But it can do this only through the "chest," which in Lewis's analogy represents the will, the moral imagination. The problem today, Lewis writes, is that modern rationalism has reduced morality to cognition; it has focused on moral reasoning while ignoring the role of the will and moral imagination; it has robbed us of our "chests." And then we wonder why morality is declining. In Lewis's unforgettable words, "We make men without chests and expect of them virtue and enterprise. We laugh at honour and are shocked to find traitors in our midst. We castrate and bid the geldings be fruitful."[17]

Moral reasoning and intellectual knowledge are not enough. A fallen human being can fulfill the moral law only if the will is transformed. "For what the law was powerless to do in that it was weakened by the sinful nature, God did by sending his own Son in the likeness of sinful man to be a sin offering," writes the apostle Paul. "And so he condemned sin in sinful man, in order that the righteous requirements of the law might be fully met in us" (Rom. 8:3-4). When we turn to God, the Holy Spirit empowers us to do what we cannot do on our own. This is the essence of the term *conversion:* The will is turned around; it is transformed. At the heart of Christianity is a supernatural transforming power that enables us not only to know what is right but also to do it—to become virtuous.

Although only a converted will is capable of virtue in a consistent manner, there is also a natural virtue spoken of in Romans 2 (conscience), which is a consequence of our creation in the image of God. And while Christians must work for the conversion of individuals, we also have a duty to help build a good society by cultivating ethical knowledge even among the unconverted.

THE GOOD LIFE

Our most intractable social problems cannot be solved by public policies but only by the practice of virtuous behavior. Take crime, for example. Sociologists and policy experts endlessly debate the question, What causes crime? But as Michael Novak notes, even if we uncovered the answer to that question, how would it help us? It would merely enable us to produce *more* crime. What we really need to know is how to produce virtue. Society ought to concentrate on finding ways to encourage virtuous behavior, and then crime will begin to fall.[18]

Historically, societies have encouraged virtuous behavior positively through custom and convention, and negatively through social stigmas, taboos, and shame. Admittedly, the latter are difficult to exert in a culture where no moral stigma is permitted for fear of damaging someone's self-esteem. But Christians can cut through this fog and argue for the right of a healthy society to express moral disapproval of socially harmful behavior.

We cannot rely on the law alone, for not all immoral actions should be made illegal. In many instances, right behavior is better enforced by an informal social consensus that defines certain behavior as unacceptable or worthy of contempt. That's why campaigns against drunk driving or drug abuse are often more effective than any law against them. In fact, if we fail to impose social conventions, we invite the imposition of more and more laws, which, in the absence of popular support, have to be enforced with ever increasing severity.

<u>What does it take to create the good life? A firm sense of right and wrong and a determination to order one's life accordingly. Not out of a grim sense of duty, but because it is what fits with our created nature and makes us happiest and most fulfilled.</u> When men and women act in accord with their true nature, they feel a sense of harmony, contentment, and joy. This is happiness, the fruit of virtue. In fact, the ancient philosophers defined happiness as something one achieves only at the end of life, after spending a whole lifetime in character training.[19]

It was this definition that the American Founders had in mind when they declared that we have an inalienable right to life, liberty, and the pursuit of happiness. The last phrase did not mean a right to hedonistic pleasure, as many people believe today, but the pursuit of virtue, a life spent ordering our appetites and desires to the truth of who we are, which produces happy individuals and a harmonious society.[20]

When we know the secret to true happiness, we will seek virtue in every area of life, even those that are typically thought to be purely technical or utilitarian, such as economics. And when that happens, we will make the astonishing discovery that the Christian worldview enhances our economic well-being and gives genuine meaning even to our work.

DISCUSSION QUESTIONS

CHAPTER 6

1 Describe the overall picture you have of Sal's Brooklyn beat when he started this street assignment.

2 Describe Sal's mission and his approach to it. How does the neighborhood change, seemingly in response to Sal's presence?

CHAPTER 7

3 Contrast *(a)* the nonbiblical worldview assumptions underlying the individualistic view of civil liberties and *(b)* the biblical view of God and of creation.

4 Define and discuss *shalom* as it might be played out in your own community. What problems are threatening or depriving your community of its *shalom?*

5   Read aloud Acts 6:1-7, an account of a congregation's solution
    to a community problem. In what ways was this an *economic*
    problem? A *racial* problem?

6   Attempting to solve the problem, who did what? With what
    results? From this passage, what do you learn about working
    toward *shalom* in your own community?

7   There's a fine line between watching out for your neighbors
    in a good sense and being a meddling busybody. Brainstorm
    a list of "do's and don'ts" of good neighbors.

8   We Christians "ought to be in the forefront, helping commu-
    nities take charge of their own neighborhoods." Which of the
    approaches to community peace presented in this chapter
    would address the neighborhood problems you identified in
    question 4? What can—and will—your group do to promote
    shalom in your community?

CHAPTER 8

9   Why doesn't relativism or pragmatism provide a foundation
    for a safe and orderly society?

10 "If we cannot govern ourselves, then we invite others to govern us." In what way is a conscience like a police officer? How will this concept be helpful in your discussions with young people?

11 Why is "the emphasis on social justice at the expense of private virtue . . . not only mistaken but downright dangerous"?

12 What is integrity? Do you agree that it is more important than loyalty? Give examples of integrity as you've seen it lived out in people you've learned to respect. Did integrity for these people come at any evident personal "cost"?

13 How can individual reconciliation with God be a blessing not only to the individual but also to his or her community? Give examples.

14 If "only a converted will is capable of virtue in a consistent manner," why do Christians have a responsibility to "help build a good society by cultivating ethical knowledge even among the unconverted"? How can you individually and as a group cultivate this ethical knowledge?

15 What does your "unalienable right to . . . the pursuit of happiness" mean to you and for you?

ROLE PLAY

Refer to the directions for role play, at the end of session 1 (pp. 52–53).

CONVERSATION STARTERS

a. Assume a business entrepreneur summarizes his or her ethical standards: "I just figure I shouldn't do anything that will get me negative publicity."

b. Assume a college student—not known for his or her virtuous living—summarizes his or her career or life goals: "I just want to somehow change the world."

CLOSING SUMMARY

What is the one thing you want to remember from what you read (or heard or did) in this session?

Consider sharing this with the group.

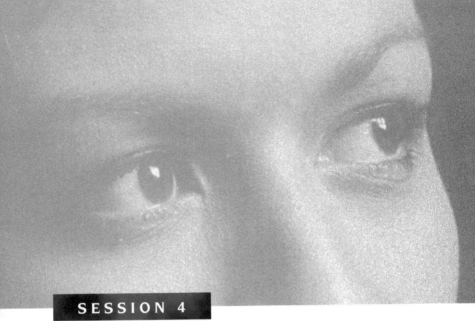

LABOR
AND LAWS

In nothing has the Church so lost
Her hold on reality as in Her
failure to understand and respect
the secular vocation. She has
allowed work and religion to
become separate departments. . . .
She has forgotten that the
secular vocation is sacred.

DOROTHY SAYERS

CHAPTER 9

THE WORK OF OUR HANDS

As you read chapter 9, keep the following questions
in mind:

- How can you see that God intended work to be part of his
  plan for a world filled with *shalom*?
- What basic economic principles are found in the Old
  Testament?
- What problems and abuses become prevalent when capitalism
  and the work ethic is separated from its biblical grounding?

During the 1992 presidential election, a new phrase entered
the American vocabulary: "It's the economy, Stupid." The phrase
turned out to be politically potent. For although there is more
to life than bread alone, we are all concerned about our economic well-being. After all, earning an income and supporting
our families is a prime undertaking in our lives, and we spend
the majority of our waking hours working, whether in the marketplace or at home. Yet how often have you heard a sermon
about the biblical view of work or economics? The church has
largely abandoned these topics, charges British essayist Dorothy
Sayers, and the result is that many believers feel as if their faith
has nothing to do with their work. No wonder, then, that some
people even come to question the relevance of religion to their
daily life. "How can anyone remain interested in a religion which

seems to have no concern with nine-tenths of his life?" Sayers asks.[1]

But the fact is, God's Word has a great deal to say about work. And although the Bible may not endorse any particular economic theory, it does lay out a basic blueprint for a society that is free, prosperous, and just. Indeed, in many ways biblical principles inspired the development of our own system of democratic capitalism, which has triumphed so dramatically in the closing decades of the twentieth century. Around the globe, nations are casting off the chains of socialism and eagerly embracing Western models of economic freedom. And in the West, liberal and leftist political parties are scrambling toward the political center. Even the most fervent socialist sympathizers have finally had to concede that the free-market system is better not only at lifting people out of poverty but also at recognizing human dignity.

Ironically, though, the collapse of the Soviet system and the discrediting of Marxism make it all the more important for us to understand the principles that undergird the Western free-market system. During the past half century, Americans have had before them a clear and menacing contrast between the free world and two regimes of terror: Nazism and Communism. Whatever the failures of our own system, it was obvious to all but the willfully blind that a free-market system was immeasurably superior to the alternatives. Yet today we can no longer simply point to that stark contrast, and as a result we must formulate a positive defense of the principles that undergird a free society.[2] We must articulate the biblical principles that support economic freedom and a sense of vocation.

THE FIRST JOB DESCRIPTION

A Christian worldview perspective on work and economic development clearly follows the basic contours of the categories of *creation, fall,* and *redemption.* In the opening chapters of Genesis, we learn that human beings were made in the image of God, to reflect his character; therefore, we are called to reflect his creative activity through our own creativity—by cultivating the world, drawing out its potential, and giving it shape and form. All work has dignity as an expression of the divine image.

When God placed the first couple in the Garden of Eden, he assigned them the first job description: Work the earth and take care of it (Gen. 2:15). Even in Paradise, then, in the ideal state of innocence, work was the natural activity of human beings. In the words of theologian T. M. Moore, "Labor and economic development, using minds and hands in a communal effort, are thus part of the original mandate from God."[3]

Yet Scripture is never romantic or naïve about the human condition. The world God originally created was soon marred by the Fall, and work is now under a "curse," as theologians put it. In Genesis 3:16-17 the same Hebrew word is used for both the "pain" in childbirth and the "toil" of work—a word that means "labor" or "travail." The implication is that because of the Fall, both of the central tasks of human life—making a living and raising a family—are fraught with pain and difficulty. Understanding this, we can be realistic about the agony and anomie of life in a broken world.

Yet the sorrow that sin injected into creation does not cancel out the way we were originally made or the mandate to work. And redemption enables us to restore the original meaning and purpose of work. It gives us the power to carry out the task we were created for—to develop culture and civilization. Indeed, in our work, we cooperate with God in the task of redemption, helping free the world from the effects of the Fall.

ECONOMIC PRINCIPLES

The Bible also gives the underlying principles of economics, ranging from private property to rules of commerce to economic justice. It speaks clearly to the first requirement of economic liberty: that is, the protection of private ownership of goods and property. One of the traits that makes humans unique, different from animals, is our ability to use our skills and talents to shape material things to reflect our individuality—and when we do this, we create property. Material things in and of themselves are not property; they become property only when humans creatively find ways to use them productively. An example is a sticky, black, smelly substance that was nothing but a nuisance until humans developed technologies for refining it—then, suddenly, oil became a source of wealth. Seen in this light, the defense of the right to property is not a defense of material things per se, but rather of the dignity of human creativity, ingenuity, and inventiveness.[4]

<u>Throughout Scripture we find the right to private property recognized and defended.</u> As a moral principle, this recognition and defense is implicit in the Ten Commandments: in the eighth commandment, which forbids stealing, and in the tenth commandment, which forbids coveting. And in the Mosaic law, those who stole another's property were required to make restitution (Exod. 22).

The accumulation of wealth in itself is not treated as evil in Scripture. Men like Abraham and Solomon were very wealthy. Sometimes wealth is even a reward for spiritual faithfulness, as was the case when God restored Job's property, giving him twice what he had had before disaster struck (Job 42:10-12). Scripture does, however, warn against seeking wealth as an end in itself or using oppression and cruelty as means for amassing it. Paul called "the love of money" (though not money itself) "a root of all kinds of evil" (1 Tim. 6:10), and Old Testament prophets warned that wealth easily leads to spiritual complacency and even disobedience to God (see, for example, Deut. 31:1-21; 2 Kings 20:12-18; Ps. 49; Amos 6:1-7). In other words, the right to private property does not mean we have the right to do whatever we please with our possessions.

Ultimately, of course, we do not own anything; we are only stewards of the things God has entrusted to us. It is God who owns all things: "The earth is the Lord's, and everything in it" (Ps. 24:1). We are to use our economic resources and our labor as he commands, according to his law of justice and mercy. That's why Scripture calls for just scales and balances (Prov. 11:1; 20:23; Amos 8:5) and warns of God's judgment against oppressors who withhold wages or who take advantage of the needy (Lev. 19:13; Amos 5:11-12; 8:5-6). Scripture condemns those who manipulate the economy for their own sinful purposes, whether by hoarding or by other forms of wickedness such as greed, indolence, and deception (Prov. 3:27-28; 11:26; James 5:1-6). Economic justice forbids those who extend credit from taking advantage of those who are in their debt; on the other hand, those who incur a debt must repay it (Exod. 22:14; 2 Kings 4:1-7; Ps. 37:21; Prov. 22:7).[5]

The underlying principle is that private property is a gift from God to be used to establish social justice and to care for the poor and disadvantaged. Repentant thieves were told to steal no more but work with their hands *so that they would "have something to share with those in need"* (Eph. 4:28, emphasis added). Few themes in Scripture are sounded more loudly or clearly than God's commandments to care for the less fortunate. "Learn to do right!" God thunders. "Seek justice, encourage the oppressed. Defend the cause of the fatherless, plead the case of the widow" (Isa. 1:17). Through the prophet Isaiah, God announces that a true fast is not an empty religious ritual but is "to share your food with the hungry and to provide the poor wanderer with shelter—when you see the naked, to clothe him, and not to turn away from your own flesh and blood" (Isa. 58:7). Jesus deepens our sense of responsibility by telling us that in helping the hungry, the naked, the sick, and the imprisoned, we are actually serving him (Matt. 25:31-46).

Yet the poor are never reduced to passive recipients of charity;

the able-bodied are required to work in exchange for benefits. This principle is best embodied in Old Testament laws requiring landowners to leave generous margins unharvested around their fields so the poor would be able to glean enough to live on (Lev. 19:9-10; Deut. 24:19-22). In the New Testament, Paul chastises the able-bodied who refuse to work, urging that they "settle down and earn the bread they eat" (2 Thess. 3:12). The poor are to retain their dignity as competent and responsible people who are capable of helping themselves.

Both the Old and New Testaments were written in societies that practiced slavery, and critics have often attacked the Bible for not challenging the practice. Yet, considering the times in which they were written, the Scriptures are among the most radical documents ever penned. In the Old Testament, God provided a means for slaves to earn their freedom (Deut. 15:12), and in the New Testament, Paul tells slaves that "if you can gain your freedom, do so" (1 Cor. 7:21). More important, the Bible calls both masters and slaves to recognize their primary identity as servants of God: "He who was a slave when he was called by the Lord is the Lord's freedman; similarly, he who was a free man when he was called is Christ's slave" (1 Cor. 7:22). It is not economic conditions that count so much as the condition of the heart—and when the heart is transformed, that will inevitably change the way people structure their external relationships. That's precisely why Christians in the West came to see slavery as incompatible with the God-given dignity of all people, and why many believers became leaders of the abolition movement.

SECULAR WORK IS SACRED

Turning to the testimony of history, we can trace a steady development in the dignity accorded to the individual and to economic vocation. In the first centuries after Christ, the early church was

forced to define a biblical view of work and economic development in contrast to the views inherited from ancient Greek culture, which equated the material world with evil and disorder.
As a result, the Greeks denigrated anything related to material
things—including manual labor. Working with one's hands was
relegated to slaves and artisans, whose labor freed up the intellectual elite for what the Greeks regarded as the "nobler" pursuit of
culture and philosophy.

Against this backdrop, the early church defended a high view of
the material world as God's creation. "There has never been room
in the Hebrew or Christian tradition for the idea that the material
world is something to be escaped from and that work in it is
degrading. Material things are to be *used* to the glory of God and
for the good of men," writes British philosopher Mary Hesse. As
a result, "in western Europe in the Christian era, there was never
the same derogation of manual work. There was no slave class to
do the work, and craftsmen were respected."[6]

Nevertheless, many early theologians were influenced by Greek
philosophy, especially Platonism, with the result that a distinction
came to be drawn between sacred and secular realms. Full-time
religious workers, devoted "to the service of God alone," embody
the "perfect form of the Christian life," wrote Eusebius in the
fourth century, whereas farmers and traders may achieve only "a
kind of secondary grade of piety."[7]

This attitude was challenged by Thomas Aquinas, who stood
against the Platonic stream in Christian thought and stressed the
value of the created world. His philosophy stimulated the Scholas-
tics to explore topics now considered part of economics, such as
property, trade, prices, and wealth creation—culminating in the
work of the sixteenth-century School of Salamanca in Spain,
praised by the great economist Joseph Schumpeter as the "founders" of scientific economics.[8]

The Reformers likewise protested vigorously against the dichotomy between the sacred and the secular and its implicit devaluation of creation. When we carry out our vocation in obedience to God's commands, wrote Martin Luther, then God himself works through us to his purposes. And this partnership with God includes *all* legitimate forms of work, not just spiritual vocations. Luther totally rejected the notion that monks and clergy were engaged in holier work than shopkeepers and housewives. "Seemingly secular works are a worship of God," he wrote, "and an obedience well pleasing to God."[9]

The division into sacred and secular had not only made secular work second-best but also held secular workers to a lower standard of devotion and spirituality. The Reformation challenged that concept, insisting that no believer is exempt from the highest spiritual standards. Looking through the biblical lens, Luther wrote, we see that "the entire world [is] full of service to God, not only the churches but also the home, the kitchen, the cellar, the workshop, and the field of the townsfolk and farmers."[10]

Drawing from passages such as Jesus' parable of the talents in Matthew 25:14-30, the Reformers also cast aside a common medieval belief that making a profit is immoral. "One of the simplest lessons from the parable," writes Father Robert Sirico, "is that it is not immoral to profit from our resources, wit, and labor." After all, the alternative to profit is loss, and loss due to lack of initiative "does not constitute good stewardship."[11] God expects us to use our talents—both our abilities and our money—toward productive ends in order to serve others.

These beliefs about the value of work and entrepreneurial talent shaped what became known as the Protestant work ethic. It, in turn, became the driving force behind the industrial revolution, which has raised the standard of living immeasurably for vast numbers of societies around the globe.[12] The impact of the work ethic is one of the great examples of the way a Christian worldview can revolutionize a culture.

Opposing Views

The Christian view of work, however, has been opposed by a
variety of secular views, which began to emerge after the Enlightenment. The rejection of the biblical doctrine of creation led to
a rejection of its doctrine of human nature (its anthropology).
No longer were human beings seen as the handiwork of God,
living for high moral and spiritual purposes—to love God and
serve their neighbors. Instead, they were seen as merely a part
of nature, driven by self-interest and expediency. As a result, the
Protestant work ethic was separated from its Christian context
of stewardship and service, and degraded into a creed of personal
success.

In the late eighteenth century, for example, Adam Smith, the
founder of capitalism, defined work solely as a means of fulfilling
one's self-interest. No one acts out of benevolence, he argued, but
only out of enlightened concern for personal advancement: "It is
not from the benevolence of the butcher, the brewer, or the baker,
that we expect our dinner, but from their regard to their own
interest. We address ourselves, not to their humanity but to their
self-love."[13] Whereas both classical and Christian ethics had
regarded self-interest as a vice to be overcome for the common
good, Smith contended that self-interest was actually good for
society. His theory of capitalism turned an attitude once thought
to be evil into a virtue. "The paradox," writes theologian Michael
Novak, "consisted in attaining a highly moral outcome [getting
rid of hunger and poverty] by placing *less* stress on moral purposes" and greater stress on rational self-interest.[14]

For Smith, the economy was an amoral, autonomous mechanism, grinding along apart from the moral influence of law or
church or family. Indeed, he urged that the best thing for the
economy is for everyone to stand out of its way and give free reign
to "the invisible hand," which ensures that supply and demand
will always balance. This vision of a self-regulating system of

production and exchange is a secularization of the Christian
doctrine of providence, replacing it with an interlocking order
of nature.

Focusing on self-interest proved very effective, for in a fallen
world, it is one of the strongest forms of motivation. But instead
of raising the moral bar, challenging people to go beyond self-
interest, Smith's system seemed to accommodate our sinful state.
The system demanded the very impulses Christianity had traditionally renounced as immoral: self-interest instead of concern for
the common good, personal ambition instead of altruism, and
drive for personal gain instead of self-sacrifice and charity. Smith's
system seemed to glorify those impulses by treating them as the
driving force for a healthy economy, thus paving the way for a
new ethic of ambition, aggression, and self-advancement.

Moreover, Smith was mistaken in thinking that an autonomous
free market would operate most beneficently. Quite the opposite.
As the early days of industrialism proved, an autonomous, secularized capitalism exploits both workers and the environment, creating new forms of slavery in what poet William Blake called the
"dark Satanic Mills."[15] Capitalism is astonishingly efficient at
generating new wealth, but it operates beneficently only when the
market is shaped by moral forces coming from both the law and
the culture—derived ultimately from religion.

How do we bring these moral forces to bear on today's economy? This is the major issue facing Christians in this area. How
do we transform a secularized, *de*moralized capitalism into a
morally responsible free-market system?

Economic Success Depends On . . .

The most important point we need to make is that an economy
is not an autonomous mechanism. It depends, first of all, on a
juridical framework: on a system of laws to maintain a sound cur-
rency, protect private property, enforce contracts, and clamp down

on corruption. Government acts as a referee, making sure every-one follows the rules and plays fair. Business transactions cannot be carried out in a society where people cannot trust one another, where graft and corruption are the rule, where contracts are made to be broken. We have only to look at the current situation in Russia to see what happens when capitalism is introduced without the rule of law and the judicial infrastructure to maintain order in commerce: Ruthless businessmen, like the "Russian Mafia," pillage the country. Similar examples of "crony capitalism" abound in the Third World, where those in power steal from the people with impunity.

Humane capitalism also depends on a sound moral culture, for a free market readily caters to the moral choices we make, supplying whatever consumers want—from Bibles to pornography. Only a virtuous citizenry will refuse to manufacture or buy products that are immoral and destructive. Interestingly, the idea of a command economy was concocted to bypass this very requirement: It was thought that the only way to guarantee the production of socially beneficial products was by taking economic decisions out of the hands of private citizens and placing them in the hands of the state. But state-run economies didn't work. And we now know there are simply no shortcuts: Morality in the marketplace depends on the decisions made by each individual economic agent. This is why the Christian's role is indispensable, for we alone have the spiritual resources to help create a healthy moral climate.

Even entrepreneurship itself requires the practice of moral virtues. Those who invest their time and money in enterprises in which the rewards are not immediate must practice hard work, self-sacrifice, and delayed gratification, says Michael Novak.[16] They must also cultivate sensitivity and courtesy to others, because if you don't please the customer, you're out of business. It is said that when McDonald's first set up shop in the Soviet Union, the company had to teach cashiers to smile and say thank you—

courtesies not required back when all stores were government monopolies.

All this can be summed up by saying that economic success depends on morality—strange as that may sound to some economic conservatives. I am sometimes told by Republican members of Congress that they struggle to hold together religious conservatives and corporate interests in the same party. For example, religious conservatives have pushed for sanctions against nations that practice religious persecution, while business interests oppose sanctions for fear they would hurt trade. My response is always that these two groups are not enemies but allies, who in fact need each other. For "businesses are plants that do not grow in just any soil," Novak writes. As we have shown, they thrive best in a culture that is both politically free and morally virtuous. Novak uses the image of a three-legged stool: A healthy democracy comprises political liberty, economic freedom, and moral responsibility. Weaken any leg, and the stool topples over.[17]

As societies around the world shake off the chains of communism and socialism, it is more imperative than ever that Christians make a case for the moral and spiritual basis of a free economy. For if a thoroughly secularized capitalism is adopted, it will surely lead not to freedom but to new forms of slavery, just as early capitalism created its "dark Satanic Mills." Capitalism provides the best opportunity for economic growth and human freedom only if it is tempered by compassion and regard for social justice.

HOW NOW SHALL WE WORK?

The modern tendency to regard economics as an arena of amoral forces and mechanisms has had a profound effect on the way ordinary people order their work lives. Torn out of a Christian context, the meaning of work has been distorted. Bereft of a vision of eternity and driven by an ever more acquisitive culture, many people have become obsessed with success in the here and now, resulting in a major shift in social priorities.

Workplace as Social Environment

For many Americans, weakened ties to family and church mean the workplace has become the primary social environment. Coworkers have become the new family, the tribe, the social world. "We become almost citizens of our companies," says *Time* correspondent Lance Morrow, "living under the protection of salaries, pensions, and health insurance."[18] Many corporations consciously seek to become the center of employees' lives, offering child care, health centers, drug and alcohol counseling, and an array of social services. As sociologist Robert Schrank notes, "The workplace performs the function of community."[19]

Indeed, some people even *prefer* it to real community. In her provocative book *The Time Bind,* sociologist Arlie Hochschild suggests that many parents are actually choosing to overwork as an escape from family life. Back in the nineteenth century, home was pictured as a haven from the stress and pressure of the workplace. But for many of the parents Hochschild interviewed, home is a place filled with the incessant demands of noisy children, endless piles of laundry, and few tangible rewards—while at work they enjoy adult sociability and feel that their hard work is appreciated. One mother of three told Hochschild, "I usually come to work early just to get away from the house."[20]

Yet at the same time, evidence is mounting that institutional child care has negative effects on children, both in terms of frequent illnesses and unruly behavior.[21] As a result, many Americans feel a gnawing unease about the trade-offs they are making for work—a concern the popular press has been quick to pick up on: "The Myth of Quality Time," blazed a headline in *Newsweek,* and *U.S. News and World Report* titled a recent article "Lies Parents Tell Themselves about Why They Work."[22]

Fulfilling Work

All this is symptomatic, however, of a more fundamental problem—which is that Americans have lost a sense of a higher purpose for work. In our materialistic culture, work is reduced to a utilitarian function: a means of attaining benefits for *this* world, *this* life—whether material gain or self-fulfillment. Work no longer has a transcendent purpose as a means of serving and loving God. No wonder, then, that many are questioning the very meaning of work. As Morrow writes, people today are asking, "Is there some inherent worth in work?"[23]

This offers Christians a rich opportunity to make the case that work is truly fulfilling only when it is firmly tied to its moral and spiritual moorings. It is time for the church to reclaim this crucial part of life, restoring a biblical understanding of work and economics. A biblical theology of work should be a frequent subject for sermons, just as it was during the Reformation, when establishing one's vocation was considered a crucial element in discipleship.[24] Churches should organize classes on business ethics and biblical work principles for those in the workplace.[25] Finally, they should set up programs to help the able-bodied poor become self-sufficient instead of dependent on government welfare.

The record shows that only the church can impart the work ethic and sense of purpose that lifts people out of poverty. When Allen-Edmonds Shoe Corporation set up a new factory in inner-city Milwaukee, company president John Stollenwerk contacted pastors at several neighborhood churches. When asked why he had not contacted local, state, and federal job-training programs to recruit new employees, Stollenwerk replied, "It just never occurred to us." Government training programs may impart specific skills, he explained, but they cannot provide the moral habits of reliability, hard work, and commitment to family that make good workers. Churches, on the other hand, impart precisely these fundamental values.[26]

Faith-Based Programs

Beyond that, many churches are providing outstanding models of programs that spur economic self-sufficiency. They are establishing job-training programs to help the poor become employable; they are setting up credit unions, job banks, and business fairs. In Brooklyn, New York, for example, Father Ronald Marino set up a program called Resources, Inc. to train immigrants in work and management skills. Then he started his own companies to employ them.[27]

In Portland, Oregon, the Union Gospel Mission started Life Change, a job-training program for convicted felons and drug addicts. One twenty-four-year-old man who was homeless and on drugs is now a college student in electrical engineering with a 3.8 grade-point average. A thirty-eight-year-old woman who was a prostitute is now the manager of a local Subway sandwich shop.[28]

Voice of Hope, a Christian community-development program in West Dallas (mentioned in chapter 7), uses its housing-rehabilitation project as a way to teach job skills to ghetto teens. The young people learn carpentry, painting, roofing, landscaping, and practical money management.[29] Mississippi Boulevard Christian Church in Memphis, Tennessee, encourages economic development in the surrounding low-income neighborhood by holding weekly mini-malls on the church parking lot. Minority businesses and entrepreneurs sell their products and network with one another. The church also runs an annual Trade Expo.[30]

West Los Angeles Church of God in Christ operates a community-development corporation that aims at "economic empowerment" of the poor in its neighborhood. Its programs include job training and entrepreneurial development, and it also partners with major corporations and businesses to provide employment for neighborhood residents.[31]

As welfare reform reduces the government's role in helping the poor, the church has a great opportunity to step into the gap.

Many Christians are already mobilizing to help welfare recipients make the shift from dependence to work, as the following success stories illustrate.[32]

In Mississippi, the Faith and Families program, which matches families on welfare with church members, has reached 350 families. More than half are now off cash welfare, and the program is being copied in other states.

In Texas, 219 churches have joined Pathfinder Families, helping 230 welfare recipients who are trying to find work under the state's strict time limits.

In Michigan, nearly 60 churches in Ottawa County have helped 60 families leave welfare in just over a year. The county is the first locality in the United States to move every able-bodied welfare recipient into a job—an astonishing success.

In Maryland, 21 congregations in Anne Arundel County have helped 30 families obtain jobs and leave public assistance.

And in Florida, a coalition of 70 churches has helped 700 elderly and disabled legal immigrants adversely affected by welfare reform.

Similar principles of economic development are being applied by Christians around the world to combat Third-World poverty. In Manila, the capital of the Philippines, one section of the city houses more than 65,000 people in shacks that are nothing more than wood and corrugated metal lean-tos. With no sewers, no plumbing, and no city water, the stench is sickening. Children run naked in the streets while adults sit on the sidewalk, staring vacantly.

In the midst of these desperate conditions, Prison Fellowship International has started a microenterprise project that takes people out of the nearby Mantalupa Prison, mentors them in a church, and then loans them $120 to buy a pedicab (a bicycle with a cab on the side, used for ferrying passengers and packages through crowded streets). The loan program has become a stunning success: 95 percent of those who receive loans repay them within nine months.

I visited the program and saw the parking lot where thirty brightly painted pedicabs, all bearing the Prison Fellowship logo on the front, were lined up like automobiles in a showroom, polished and gleaming in the sun. Greeting us were the proud pedicab owners (all former inmates) and their families, along with the pastors who mentored them.

The former inmates had put together a concert, and as they stood on the stage singing, one little girl, perhaps four years old, with brown button eyes, pulled herself up onto the platform and walked toward her father, who was standing in the front row. She clutched his legs and looked up with an adoring expression; he looked down and began to caress her hair. That picture is frozen in my mind's eye; everything I have done in the ministry over twenty-five years was worth that one moment—to see an ex-prisoner, ex-gang member with a loving family, a job, and hope.

The church's goal in all these programs is to meet a need far deeper than the need to make a living: The programs are addressing the need to be creative, a need imprinted in every human heart by the Creator. Alexander Solzhenitsyn captured this truth brilliantly in *One Day in the Life of Ivan Denisovich,* his classic novel describing life in the Gulag. There, despite the starvation rations, the brutality of the guards, and the backbreaking labor, the main character, Shukhov, discovers that the truly human elements of life can still break through: friendship, generosity, faith . . . and work. Even with his body abused and aching, Shukhov feels a stab of pride in his ability to build a wall of bricks with a fine, even line. As the guards muster the prisoners to march back to camp, Shukhov takes one final look at his work. "Not so bad!" he thinks. Then "he ran up and looked the wall over from right to left. He had an eye like a mason's level. It was straight. His hands had skill in them yet."[33] Even in the harshest of circumstances, work is still a gift of God that imparts a sense of personal fulfillment and useful service.

A FAITHFUL ROAD MAP

Contemporary concerns over economic issues reflect a profound confusion in secular society—whether it is welfare reform, tensions over work and family commitments, or the relationship of morality to economic policy. Only Christianity holds the key to this dilemma. <u>For only the Christian worldview provides the moral foundation essential to preserving free economic systems; only the Christian worldview provides a high view of work that gives meaning and dignity to human labor.</u> Once again we see that Christianity offers the truth about reality, providing a road map to find our way amidst the confusions and perplexities of everyday life.

Christianity even gives us the basic presuppositions needed to run a nation through just and fair-minded laws and to foster a political system that is both free and well ordered. In fact, Christianity played a definitive role in shaping the character of our own government, as we will see in the following chapter.

CHAPTER 10

THE ULTIMATE APPEAL

As you read chapter 10, keep the following questions in mind:

- What is the difference between a just law and an unjust law?
- In what ways does the American system of government and law, as designed by the Founders, reflect biblical principles?
- What have been the effects of pragmatism and deconstructionism on transcendent law?
- What are the consequences of the loss of moral authority?

The place was Birmingham, Alabama. The year, 1963. The date, just days before Easter weekend.

It was nine years since Rosa Parks had refused to sit in the back of the bus in Selma, Alabama, and nearly as long since the Freedom Riders made their harrowing journeys on Greyhound and Trailways buses to challenge segregated seating. A group of civil rights leaders—Martin Luther King Jr., Ralph Abernathy, Andrew Young, and others in the Southern Christian Leadership Conference (SCLC)—had gathered downtown in the "war room" suite in the Gaston Hotel to make their most significant strategy decision yet.

The group had launched a civil rights campaign in Birmingham, and it was taking off, with thousands of young people joining their elders in peaceful marches. A boycott of downtown stores was making an impact. And the strategy of nonviolent resistance was working: They were filling the jails to overflowing, making it impossible to suppress the movement by sheer force.

This much progress in Birmingham was remarkable. Birmingham—a city so racist that the authorities had shut down parks and city baseball leagues rather than integrate them. A city whose leaders had declared that blood would flow in the streets before they complied with the Supreme Court's decision to integrate schools. A city where serving food to whites and blacks at the same lunch counter was still illegal. A city that in the past six years had seen seventeen bombings—all unsolved—of black churches and homes of civil rights leaders. A city where racist terrorists had castrated a man and left his body on a deserted road.

Perhaps it was no surprise, then, that Birmingham officials had decided to fight the civil rights movement, adopting tactics that had already been used all too successfully a year earlier in Albany, Georgia. They had found a federal judge to issue a restraining order against King and other leaders of the movement who had announced plans to march on Good Friday. If the leaders obeyed the restraining order, as they had in Albany, they would miss the march—and they had seen what happened then. Without leadership, the movement had lost momentum and fizzled. Yet if they disobeyed the order, they would be defying a federal court, taking civil disobedience to new levels. Was that morally justifiable?

King's advisers urged him to forgo the march so he could raise the money to bail the other marchers out of jail. But how could he ask others to sit in prison unless he was willing to join them? Besides, his pledge to march on Good Friday had been made repeatedly in public rallies. If he didn't show up, supporters would be demoralized and enemies would think he had backed down.

What to do? King went into one of the suite's bedrooms to pray through his decision. When he reemerged after more than an hour, he was wearing a new pair of overalls he had bought to wear to jail.

"I'm going to march," he said. "We can't know what lies ahead. We just have to fulfill our promises as best we can. We're in God's hands now."

"Son," said his father, Dr. Martin Luther King Sr., "I've never gone against any of your decisions. But this time I think you'd better stay home. I wouldn't disobey that injunction."

For a moment the agony of the decision seized King once more. He thought for a moment, then said, "No. I'm determined."

"All right then," his father said, nodding.[1]

■   ■   ■

A photographer caught the moment of King's arrest in a photograph that became famous—the great civil rights leader in handcuffs, glancing back toward his supporters, his face haunted. Inside the Birmingham jail, he was locked in solitary confinement in a room the size of a monk's cell, narrow and windowless. Imprisonment was made even more bitter when his lawyers brought in a copy of the Birmingham *News* containing a statement signed by eight white clergymen criticizing his strategy of civil disobedience.

But suddenly King had an inspiration. He was going to compose a rebuttal to those clergy in the form of an open letter—a defense of the civil rights movement that would appeal to the conscience of all America. On scraps of toilet paper and writing paper later smuggled out page by page, King wrote a lyrical epistle on why it is sometimes justifiable to break the law.

The civil rights movement, he acknowledged, had gained much of its leverage from urging people to obey the Supreme Court's 1954 decision outlawing segregation in the public schools. Thus, "at first glance it may seem rather paradoxical for us consciously to break laws. One may well ask: 'How can you advocate breaking

some laws and obeying others?' The answer lies in the fact that
there are two types of laws: just and unjust. One has not only a
legal but a moral responsibility to obey just laws. Conversely, one
has a moral responsibility to disobey unjust laws. I would agree
with St. Augustine that 'an unjust law is no law at all.'

   "Now, what is the difference between the two? . . . A just law
is a man-made code that squares with the moral law or the law of
God. An unjust law is out of harmony with the moral law. To put
it in the terms of St. Thomas Aquinas: An unjust law is a human
law that is not rooted in eternal law and natural law."[2]

   The tradition of civil disobedience, King noted, goes back to
Old Testament times—to Shadrach, Meshach, and Abednego,
three young Jewish men who for the sake of conscience disobeyed
the laws of the Babylonian monarch Nebuchadnezzar. It goes
back to the reformer Martin Luther, who declared, "Here I stand;
I can do no other. God help me." Back to John Bunyan, who was
imprisoned for his beliefs: "I will stay in jail to the end of my days
before I make a butchery of my conscience." And Thomas Jefferson, who justified the American Revolution with these ringing
words: "We hold these truths to be self-evident, that all men are
created equal."

   King would always remember this incarceration as the moment
when his beliefs were put to the severest test. His "Letter from
Birmingham Jail" became one of his greatest testaments of faith.

   A great burden was lifted from his mind when he learned that
the money had been quickly raised to secure the release of all
civil rights workers. He was surprised and relieved, and at that
moment, as he later wrote, he became "aware of a feeling that had
been present all along below the surface of consciousness," a feeling that "I had never been truly in solitary confinement; God's
companionship does not stop at the door of a jail cell. I don't
know whether the sun was shining at that moment. But I know
that once again I could see the light."[3]

A LAW ABOVE THE LAW

Martin Luther King Jr. secured his place in American history
when the populist movement he led finally convinced the nation
to affirm that the principles of the Declaration of Independence
truly apply to all Americans. But just as important as the success
of his crusade is the principle on which it rested, for that principle
is the most fundamental basis for our republican form of government: that government is not simply a social contract between the
people and those who govern, but a social contract made under
the authority of a higher law.

The greatest moral struggle in our nation's history—the campaign to end slavery—turned on the same principle. Abolitionists
denounced the fugitive-slave bill (by which Congress required
people to return escaped slaves) as contrary to a "higher law," even
though it carried out an express provision of the Constitution.[4]
Lincoln employed the same argument in opposing the Supreme
Court decision condoning slavery.[5] He wrote passionately about
"the duty of nations as well as of men to own their dependence
upon the overruling power of God."[6] Only a deep conviction
about our obligation to submit to a higher authority could have
steeled this humble country lawyer to oppose slavery when it was
a legally established institution.

The most significant moral debate of our own day—the debate
over abortion, euthanasia, and related life issues—is fueled by the
same conviction. The pro-life movement refuses to accept current
abortion law on the grounds that no human law is valid as long as
it is contrary to a higher law.

Transcendent Law

This understanding of a transcendent law above human law (or
positive law) is critical to the preservation of liberty and justice.
As the Declaration of Independence puts it, there exist certain
"unalienable rights" that are beyond the authority of government

either to grant or to deny; it can only recognize them as preexisting. For if the government confers these rights, then they are *not*
unalienable, for the government can also take them away—and
any group out of favor can be crushed by the self-interest of the
majority or the naked force of the state.

Professor Robert George of Princeton University made the
point in a colorful way in a civil-liberties course by reading to
his students the opening words of the Declaration of Independence: "We hold these truths to be self-evident, that all men are
created equal, that they are endowed by their Creator with certain
unalienable rights." Then he looked out at the sea of students in
the packed lecture hall and said: "These are the foundational
words of the American doctrine of civil liberties, and in light of
the content of that doctrine as expressed in the Declaration, perhaps it wouldn't be inappropriate to begin our deliberations by
offering thanksgiving to the Creator who endowed us with these
rights. So let us in silence, each according to his own tradition and
in his own way, give thanks to the Creator for our precious rights
and liberties." And then he added, impishly, "Those of you who
are not believers might take this opportunity to reflect in silence
upon the source of our most important rights and liberties, which
I believe you too cherish." When he looked up again, he saw two
hundred fifty undergraduates with their heads bowed (and to the
side, a handful of teaching assistants looking pale and horrified).[7]

The idea of a transcendent law has deep historical roots, as
even a cursory survey makes clear. In ancient Jewish culture, the
law (Torah) was revered as divine revelation. Among the ancient
Greeks, Plato and Aristotle contended that human justice is
defined by higher truths, or ideals, accessible to human reason
and knowable through natural law—the moral principles that are
in tune with our nature as human beings. The Romans likewise
appealed to an eternal source of law, as reflected in Cicero's statement that "law is not the product of human thought, nor is it any

enactment of peoples, but something eternal which rules the whole universe."[8] By A.D. 380 Christianity was the official religion of the Roman Empire, and from then on, Western law was largely shaped by the Christian conception of law, based on the doctrine of creation. Theologians like Augustine and Aquinas contended that human law must reflect the moral order created by God—knowable by believer and nonbeliever alike, since it is the "law written on the heart." A law that does not reflect this natural law, as King was to write from the Birmingham jail, is an unjust law—which is no law at all.

Thus the Western political tradition has generally assumed that in order to be valid, human laws must be grounded in the natural law by which God orders his creation, which is in turn a participation in his eternal law.[9] This assumption was expressed in the Magna Carta of 1215, a groundbreaking charter guaranteeing certain rights and privileges to the nobles against the king. It was also the foundation of English common law.

"The law of nature dictated by God Himself . . . is binding in all countries and at all times," wrote the great eighteenth-century jurist Sir William Blackstone. "No human laws are of any validity, if contrary to this; and such of them as are valid derive all their force and all their authority mediately or immediately, from this original." Blackstone understood that the genius of Western common law was that it reflected the customs, beliefs, and traditions of the people as written by "men infused with the Spirit of Christ."[10]

King Limited by Law

But then, with the rise of nationalism, there arose ideas of national sovereignty and political absolutism, such as the doctrine of the divine right of kings, which states that the king reigns with direct authority from God—that the law is whatever the king decrees. Many Christians rose up to oppose these ideas and to reassert the primacy of natural law. In the late 1500s, Jesuit theologian Robert Bellarmine published several pamphlets arguing against the divine right of kings and in favor of natural rights and popular sovereignty. His writings were so influential that King James I felt forced to respond in a series of pamphlets of his own.[11] In the 1600s, Scottish cleric Samuel Rutherford wrote a book titled *Lex Rex* ("the law is king"), asserting that the law stands above the king and that he is subject to it like all other citizens. The book was banned in Scotland and publicly burned in England, and Rutherford was arrested. But his ideas lived on and profoundly influenced the American Founding Fathers through the work of John Witherspoon and John Locke.[12] In the new republic, citizens would be ruled not by men but by law.

Limited by Scope of Authority

Yet the government was to be limited not only by the rule of law but also by the scope of its authority over society. In Catholic social thought the idea of limited government was developed through the concept of *subsidiarity,* and in Reformed thought through the concept of *sphere sovereignty.*

Subsidiarity (the Latin *subsidium* means "help, support, assistance") holds that the higher social institutions, like the state, exist only to help subordinate institutions, like the family. The implication is that if the state goes beyond helping them—if it destroys them or absorbs their functions—then it is acting illegitimately and disturbing the social order.[13]

Sphere sovereignty grew out of the rallying cry of the Reformation—*coram deo* ("in the face of God")—meaning that the individual is accountable to God directly, no longer approaching him only through the mediating structure of the church. The consequence is that all spheres of society—including the state, family, school, corporation, as well as professional and voluntary associations—stand not under the church but directly under God's authority. This understanding was greatly liberating because it meant that no sphere may properly dominate the others; all are responsible to God directly, through the conscience of the individuals involved. Moreover, the power of each sphere is limited by the power of the others. As Dutch theologian Abraham Kuyper explained in the nineteenth century, the sovereignty of the state is limited "by another sovereignty, which is equally divine in origin"—namely, the sovereignty of the other spheres of society.[14]

Thus the Reformation heritage passed on a balanced view of the state as ordained by God yet limited by the other divinely ordained social institutions. The function of the state is to restrain the force of sin unleashed by the Fall. Genesis 3:24 tells us that God stationed angels with a flaming sword to guard the tree of life—the first cops on the beat. By thus preserving social order, the state allows liberty to flourish. But the liberty of the other spheres in turn limits the state. Their liberty is, as Kuyper wrote, "the God-ordained means to bridle the authority" of the state, which could otherwise degenerate into despotism.[15] In this balanced conception we see the roots of what the American Founders called "ordered liberty."

Separation of Powers

Another contribution of Christianity was the notion of separation of powers, based on the doctrine of the Fall. The Founders realized that since everyone is prone to sin, it is a fatal mistake to entrust too much power to any individual or group. As a result they established three branches of government—the judicial, legislative, and executive—based on the biblical teaching that God is our judge, lawgiver, and king (Isa. 33:22). The Founders also established a federal system in which state governments were to keep a check on the national government. This is why the Constitution originally reserved to the states the right to appoint senators, and even the election of the president was made the task of electors from the states (the electoral college). The states were to have real power, not function merely as administrative units of the national government.

Republican System

Finally, the Founders built a system that would protect against direct democracy—against any system where "the voice of the people is the voice of God." Such democracies, James Madison warned, "have ever been spectacles of turbulence and contention."[16] Hence the Founders built a republican system, where the will of the people is sifted through elected representatives, intended to be persons of virtue and concern for the common good, capable of rising above the passions of the moment. At the same time, the representatives remain accountable to the people, achieving a marvelous balance.

What an ingenious plan! I never cease to marvel at it and to be grateful for this historical expression of a Christian worldview. For more than two centuries, the American experiment has provided a dramatic illustration of the way biblical principles successfully sustain both order and liberty.[17] Yet in recent decades, those principles have come under withering assault from increasingly aggressive forces of modern secularism—so much so that the rule of law and the very character of our political order is now threatened.

JUDICIAL IMPERIALISM

The idea that human (or positive) law must reflect a higher law was seriously challenged in the latter part of the nineteenth century—especially after the work of Charles Darwin. His theory of evolution implied that there is no created moral order that functions as the basis for law; rather, life is the result of a process of trial and error, with new structures being preserved if they help the organism get what it needs to survive. This new view, appearing with the imprimatur of science, seemed to suggest that truth itself is found by a process of trial and error—the "true" idea being the one that works best at getting the results desired. Thus was born the philosophy of *pragmatism.*

Blows of Pragmatism and Deconstructionism

Pragmatism was formulated when several prominent university professors organized a group oddly named the Cambridge Metaphysical Club. These leading intellectuals—among them Oliver Wendell Holmes, Charles Pierce, and William James—defined truth as the hypothesis that works best. Or, as James succinctly put it, "Truth is the cash value of an idea."[18]

What pragmatism meant for law was stated baldly by Holmes in 1897 when he advised an audience of law school students to put aside notions of morality and look instead at the law as a science—the science of state coercion.[19] His crassest summary of what this means is captured in his famous dictum that law is the "majority vote of that nation that can lick all others."[20] In other words, without divine law as the final moral authority, the law is reduced to sheer force.

More recently, the authority of the law received another blow at the hands of *deconstructionism,* which began as a method of literary criticism but is now applied to all types of texts, including legal texts. According to deconstructionism, language does not reveal meaning (which would imply that there is a transcendent realm of truth); rather, language is a social construction. Any text reflects several (often conflicting) social and cultural forces, aimed ultimately at enhancing some social group's power. Interpretation does not mean identifying what the author meant but "unmasking" the underlying power relationships.[21]

Filter-Down Effect

In recent years, these radical views of the law have begun to filter down to shape actual court decisions—initially, in cases involving religious rights. There was no anti-Christian conspiracy at work here, contrary to what many Christians have believed; rather, religious cases were the most obvious target because they most clearly relied on what now had to be discredited—the authority of a higher law.

The courts moved swiftly and dramatically. As recently as 1952, Justice William O. Douglas had described America as a "religious people whose institutions presuppose a Supreme Being" and urged that the state should therefore "accommodate the public service to their spiritual needs."[22] Douglas was not defending any particular religion but simply stating that religion is good for people and that the state ought to respect it. But only two decades later, in 1973, the Court breezed right past the people's deepest religious and moral concerns, claiming to discover in the Constitution an implied right to "privacy" protecting a woman's right to abortion (*Roe v. Wade*). In one swoop, the Court sought to extinguish a political debate then being carried out in fifty state legislatures regarding a sensitive moral question—the legal status of the early stages of human life. It was an act of judicial hubris that could only call into question the law's authority, thereby assuring that the abortion debate would continue and grow ever more rancorous. Which, of course, it has done.

But *Roe* was only the most influential in a swelling stream of cases—involving prayer, religious displays, and sexual rights—in which judges cavalierly usurped the legislative process and showed an increasing hostility to the religious and moral traditions that have historically informed American law. Indeed, in some cases judges actually ruled that religious motivation behind a law serves to disqualify it. For example, in 1987 the Supreme Court struck down a Louisiana statute mandating the teaching of creation alongside evolution.[23] Why? Because the Court decided that the legislature's claimed secular purpose (namely, academic freedom) was a "sham," covering over what was really an attempt to promote biblical religion. This represents a stunning turnaround: Whereas biblical principles were once considered the authority that undergirds the law, now they disqualify a law.

One of the most destructive decisions in recent years was the 1992 case *Planned Parenthood v. Casey*.[24] While upholding some modest state restrictions on abortion, the Court sought to place the right to abortion created in *Roe* on firmer constitutional ground. It abandoned the old tactic of justifying abortion by an implied right to "privacy" lurking in the "penumbras" of the Fourteenth Amendment and instead went straight for the explicit right of "liberty."[25] The Court then chastised pro-life supporters for having the effrontery to challenge their decisions, and in essence admonished them to be quiet and go home. So after having summarily overridden the democratic debate about abortion in 1973, twenty years later the Court decreed that even to challenge abortion is an affront to the rule of law.[26]

The majority then defined the "liberty" of the Fourteenth Amendment in breathtakingly sweeping terms: "At the heart of liberty," wrote Justice Anthony Kennedy, "is the right to define one's own concept of existence, of meaning, of the universe, and of the mystery of human life." In short, the Court placed the isolated individual, constructing his or her own sense of meaning, at the center of gravity for constitutional law. Collective self-government by the people according to a common moral code was rejected as "majoritarian intolerance."[27]

Indeed, the Court has rejected *any* belief in a transcendent ethic as "intolerance," thereby rejecting the idea of a higher law above the Court. In 1992 in *Lee v. Weisman*, the Court decreed that even an innocuous, to-whom-it-may-concern prayer offered by a rabbi at a junior high school commencement was unconstitutional because it infringed on a fifteen-year-old's right not to have to listen respectfully to religious expression with which she disagreed.[28] What would have been considered a mark of civility a mere generation ago was transformed into a constitutional grievance. More disturbing, however, the religious expression disallowed by the Court covered not just the traditional faiths but any "shared conviction that there is an ethic and a morality which transcend human invention."[29] In other words, the Court was saying that no transcendent morality is to be permitted in the public square, only the postmodernist view that regards morality as a "human invention."

And if no appeal to transcendent authority is permitted, then the justices themselves become the supreme authority. In the 1995 case *Romer v. Evans,* the justices struck down a referendum, democratically enacted by the citizens of Colorado, barring special civil rights protections and preferences based on "sexual orientation." Admittedly the referendum was not carefully drafted, but Justice Kennedy, writing for the majority, completely discounted the voters' stated purpose, presuming to have an uncanny ability to know their minds better than they did. "Laws of the kind before us," he wrote, "raise the inevitable inference that the disadvantage imposed is born of animosity toward the class of persons affected."[30] In a single disdainful sentence, a basic moral position long shared by Christians, Jews, Muslims, and people of other faiths—and, moreover, a position democratically enacted into law—was reduced to nothing more than personal "animosity." The justices no longer merely disagreed with the biblical ethic; they didn't even recognize it as an ethic but dismissed it as bigotry.

The same attitude soon filtered down to lower levels of the judiciary. Writing for the Ninth Circuit Court of Appeals in 1996, overturning a state referendum banning assisted suicide, Judge Stephen Reinhardt slammed the courthouse door on people "with strong moral or religious convictions." He wrote: "They are not free to force their views, their religious convictions, or their philosophies on all other members of a democratic society."[31] Yet what is the democratic process but an attempt by like-minded citizens to join together and pass laws in conformity with their best judgment of right and wrong? And on what basis can a judge say that all citizens are free to participate in this process *except* those "with strong moral and religious convictions"?

This judicial coup d'état culminated in the 1997 decision *Boerne v. Flores,* the first challenge to the Religious Freedom Restoration Act (RFRA) of 1993. The purpose of RFRA was to reestablish a strict standard for protecting free religious exercise, which had been struck down by the Court three years earlier. Significantly, RFRA was passed unanimously in the House, had only three dissenting votes in the Senate, and was enthusiastically signed by President Clinton. If ever a piece of legislation reflected the will of the people, it was RFRA.[32] Nevertheless, in *Boerne* the Supreme Court declared RFRA unconstitutional on the grounds that the express authority of Congress to enforce the basic civil rights guaranteed by the Fourteenth Amendment is not "substantive" but merely "remedial." In other words, Congress cannot use its power to expand constitutional protections except for the sake of rectifying violations of rights that the Supreme Court itself has deigned to recognize. Thus two major trends by activist courts converged in this single case: one against the transcendent right of religious liberty and the other against self-government. Not only was the free exercise clause emasculated, but also a vote reflecting the nearly unanimous will of the American people was overruled.

Furthermore, the Court decreed that it has the supreme authority to define constitutional liberties and establish their scope, an arrogant grab for power that would have horrified the Founders. The right of judicial review is not in the Constitution, and Jefferson actually warned against "judicial oligarchy," while his frequent adversary, Alexander Hamilton, was equally resistant to unrestrained judicial power.[33]

Tragically, conservative judges seem unable to stand against the juggernaut of judicial imperialism. Prominent conservatives such as Robert Bork, Edwin Meese, and Supreme Court Justice Antonin Scalia have sought to resist judicial activism with various forms of legal positivism (for example, original intent jurisprudence) that reject appeals to natural law. Scalia goes so far as to insist that judges must not consider morality, custom, or even legislative intent in making decisions, but only the literal meaning of the text. For example, Scalia has argued that it is not up to judges to consider morality; rather, it is up to the people to enact their moral convictions into law. But of course those are exactly the kinds of laws that liberal judges are striking down as illegitimate. Thus we are caught in a catch-22, where conservative judges say the courts may not consult morality, that it's up to the people to encode morality into the law—while at the same time liberal judges are striking down democratically enacted laws that express the people's moral convictions, even disqualifying those convictions as mere personal "animosity."[34]

The result of these trends is that today the courts, unrestrained by higher law and disdainful of majority will, are the dominant force in American politics. As law professor Russell Hittinger writes, in *Casey* the Court has laid down a "new covenant" by which it agrees to give citizens the right to decide for themselves the meaning of life, to decide what is right and wrong, to do as they please. In exchange for this guarantee, the Court asks only that the people accept the Court's assumption of ultimate power.[35] Or as Notre Dame's Gerard Bradley puts it, the Court has said: "We will be your Court, and you will be our people."[36]

But this new covenant with the Court is inherently unstable and will give way in time to either anarchy or sheer power. Imbalance of power among the three branches of government has always been the great vulnerability of the American system. From time to time, the scales have tilted precariously; but providentially, we may say, each time the balance has been restored.

Until today. Judicial imperialism now threatens to destroy the delicate balance that guarantees our liberty. The late historian Russell Kirk once warned that <u>the Supreme Court's "power to do mischief would become almost infinite" were it to become the dominant force in American public life, for it would "abolish America's democracy."</u>[37] Precisely. This is why it is so urgent for Christians with a biblical worldview of law and justice to alert our neighbors to the serious threat facing our system of government.

TAKING DOWN THE TEN COMMANDMENTS

The Christian understanding of law as based on a higher moral law has parallels in most civilizations throughout history. As C. S. Lewis pointed out, all major religions and moral systems assume the existence of an objective morality (which he called the Way or the Tao).[38] We all, whether Christians or not, intuitively sense that there must be some ultimate moral justification for the law, something that makes it right. Otherwise, any law can be shot down with the defiant barroom expression "sez who?" So argued the late Arthur Leff of Yale Law School in a celebrated 1979 speech. Unless there is a God who is himself Goodness and Justice, Leff said, there can be no ultimate moral basis for the law. For if there is no God, nothing can take his place. No human standard—no person, no group of people, no document—is immune to challenge.[39]

Leff deftly captured the consequences of a secular worldview. Once the Enlightenment began to deny the reality of divine creation and revelation, the basis of law was eroded. Enlightenment thinkers optimistically assumed they would find an alternative basis in human reason and experience. But as Leff so colorfully points out, the moral beliefs of any group or individual are open to challenge. And the logical conclusion of all efforts to ground the

law in something less than God's transcendent law is moral
skepticism—the great "sez who?"

The consequences of this are shaking the very foundations
of our government and society today.

Removes Constraints

*First, the loss of moral authority in the law removes restraints on
individual behavior.* Americans seem strangely oblivious to the
connection between the loss of moral authority in the law and the
social chaos that results: crime, corruption, the loss of civility. I
discovered just how oblivious they are when I was invited to talk
about criminal-justice issues with a group of community leaders
some years ago.

In get-acquainted conversation over lunch, one tall, distinguished man assured me of his company's commitment to religious liberty. "We led the campaign in our city to take the Ten
Commandments off classroom walls," he boasted.

"Why did you do that?" I asked.

"We must be sensitive to all faiths," he said confidently.

"But Christians, Jews, and Muslims all believe in the Ten
Commandments. Even Buddhists and Hindus don't object to
them," I responded.

"Separation of church and state," he said.

"Of course." I nodded. "But the Decalogue and the *Lex Divina*
are the historical roots of our legal system. That's why Moses is
included among the great lawgivers whose faces are represented in
the fresco that adorns the walls of the House of Representatives
chamber."

"Tolerance, sir. Times have changed. We must recognize that."
He drew himself up in his chair, a solid pillar of the community.

After our meal, as I began speaking on the subject of justice
reform, many took notes as I reeled off the chilling statistics.

The same man then interrupted me, asking whether I had seen

some of the latest surveys regarding crime in the schools. "Two-thirds of our kids cheat in school," he said. "And a third admit that they steal. What can we do about it?"

I couldn't help smiling. This was the same man who insisted we take the Ten Commandments off the classroom walls. And this is precisely the postmodernist impasse: We want freedom from rules and transcendent moral principles, but we hate the moral chaos that ensues.

Reduces Government to Utilitarian Procedures

Second, the loss of moral authority in the law means government is reduced to utilitarian procedures. Aristotle said that at the heart of politics is the question How shall we order our lives together? The question presupposes that there is some common good around which we should order our lives, a moral imperative proper to government. But today, as the logic of *Casey* suggests, the task of government is simply to protect individual autonomy—people's right to do whatever they choose. In the Court's new vision, writes Gerard Bradley, good government is secured by the liberation of the atomistic individual from the constraints of the common morality held by traditional religions.[40] As a result, the government has no positive moral task; rather, it functions as little more than a traffic cop, keeping people from bumping into each other as they do their own thing. The government has become what Harvard professor Michael Sandel calls a "procedural republic," its laws nothing more than procedures for helping people get what they want.[41]

Means Loss of Moral Debate

Third, the loss of a moral basis for law means we can no longer engage in moral debate. If politics is only about who gets what, then politics becomes an interminable shouting match, with endless bickering over competing demands for rights—settled ultimately by whoever has the loudest voice or the most votes. Issues are settled not by principle but by power. In these circumstances, individuals feel increasingly helpless and eventually give up on the political system—a particularly dangerous trend in a democratic society, which depends on the participation of an informed and active citizenry.[42]

Reverts to Arbitrary Human Rule

Finally, the loss of moral authority in the law means we have forfeited the rule of law and reverted to arbitrary human rule. The rule of law cannot survive unless there is an unchanging and transcendent standard against which we can measure human laws. Otherwise, the law is whatever the lawmakers or judges say it is—which can only result, eventually, in the collapse of free government.[43] The postmodernist assault on objective moral truth has put us on the road to tyranny.

Yet we must not give up hope, for Christian truth still offers us a way out of the postmodernist impasse. Christians everywhere can help revitalize our political culture and reestablish the rule of law by advancing a biblical view of law and politics.

THE ART OF PERSUASION

How should Christians work to renew our political and legal structures? If we have learned anything in recent decades, it is that we should not roll out heavy-handed political movements that recklessly toss around God-and-country clichés and scare off our secular neighbors. Our goal is not to grab power and impose our views. Instead, we should act through principled persuasion and responsible participation.

Principled Persuasion

The rule of law. Persuasion means our first task is apologetics—striving to convince our neighbors that the Christian worldview

provides the best way to order society. We can assume most of
our neighbors do not understand the necessity of something even
so basic as the rule of law. When I was in school, that was covered
in the first civics lesson; today, civics courses are more likely to
address the exploitation of Native Americans by European settlers.

The public good. We also need to press home the importance
of the idea of the common or public good. Take the illustration
of a stoplight: For the public good, all people are required to stop
at stoplights; otherwise, there would be chaos and death on the
streets. This law applies to Christians, agnostics, Hindus, and New
Age proponents alike; whether or not they are offended by the law,
they must obey it for the public good.

We need to apply the same reasoning to other laws, such as
those recognizing marriage only between two persons of the opposite sex. There are important reasons why protecting heterosexual
marriage is in the interest of society: It recognizes a social pattern
that every civilized society has adopted in order to propagate the
human race and raise children. Christians need to argue that such
laws do not "impose" a religious belief but are based on rational
moral principles and historical evidence showing that protection of
the family promotes the public interest. This is why decisions like
Casey and *Romer* are so disastrous, for they make determination of
the public good impossible. Finally, we can argue that the Christian worldview provides the most reliable standard for determining
the public good and encouraging responsible personal behavior.

Perhaps the toughest sell today is persuading people that they
ought to govern their personal behavior for the sake of the public
good. Individualism has grown so rampant that most people think
society exists to serve them, and they do not feel they owe anything
to society. We need to argue that unless individuals voluntarily
restrain their own behavior for the common good, government
will have to restrain them by coercive measures—at the cost of our
liberty.

Witness the coercion that already characterizes efforts to maintain political correctness. As people disregard the voluntary restraints of civility and social convention (the outdated customs of courtesy), the state begins to micromanage behavior by passing increasingly oppressive laws. For example, witness the often ridiculous attempts to define what is or what is not sexual harassment. Antioch College has published a code requiring students who are dating to give and get verbal consent from one another at each stage of escalating physical involvement.[44] Even more absurd, a six-year-old child was penalized by his public-school teacher for planting a friendly kiss on the cheek of another six-year-old, and the principal handed the miscreant's mother a copy of the school's sexual harassment policy.[45] And a Kansas bank was fined because it did not have Braille instructions on the ATM in its *drive-through* banking lanes![46]

We may dismiss such things as signs of temporary national insanity, but they are not illogical. They are the inevitable consequence of the loss of voluntary restraints. At one time, hurling a racial epithet would have been considered a lack of civility and would have been suppressed through social disapproval and ostracism; today, in the absence of such informal sanctions, it has to be an actionable hate crime. At one time, well-behaved young men did not "take advantage" of the "fairer sex"; today, in the absence of such social conventions, women must be protected by laws against sexual harassment. We have been "freed" from the older rules of courtesy and morality only to be hemmed in by new rules imposed by law. To reverse this erosion of freedom, we must make the case that self-government in the political sense depends on self-government in the personal sense—that is, governing our own speech and behavior by the norms of civility and respect.

The defense of liberty. The Bible is not a political document, yet it has profound political implications that are important to the general welfare of all citizens. Those who say Jesus and the apostles ignored politics miss the political implications of the maxim "Give to Caesar what is Caesar's, and to God what is God's" (Matt. 22:21). The first-century Christians knew exactly what Jesus' words meant—and it was because of a political act (they would not say, "Caesar is Lord") that they were crucified, tortured, and thrown to the lions.

What is the fundamental scriptural teaching on the state? On one hand, we are to live in submission to the state. For our benefit God has appointed kings and rulers to carry out the ordained duties of the state: to restrain evil, to preserve order, and to promote justice. Thus, we are to "honor the king" and to submit ourselves "to the governing authorities, for . . . the authorities that exist have been established by God" (Rom. 13:1; see also Dan. 2:21; Rom. 13:1-7; Titus 3:1; 1 Pet. 2:13-14, 17).

Some people have interpreted these passages as an absolute grant of authority, meaning that government is to be obeyed at all times and in all circumstances. But the injunction to obey is conditioned on the assumption that officials and magistrates are carrying out the purposes for which God has ordained government (in Romans 13:4 the ruler is called "God's servant"). Thus if rulers act contrary to their delegation of authority, if they do not act as God's servants, then Christians are not bound to obey them; indeed, believers may be morally obligated to resist. For example, if the state prohibits the preaching of the gospel, it is clearly acting contrary to the commandments of the One who granted government its authority in the first place. If the state practices injustice, like massacring Jews or engaging in systematic tyranny, it loses its claim to divine authority.

Through the ages, this principle has been affirmed by people such as Augustine, Aquinas, Calvin, Knox, and, as we have seen, Martin Luther King Jr. The church must hold the state morally accountable before the transcendent judgment of God, though this principle must be exercised with solemn judiciousness as the body of Christ collectively seeks the leading of the Holy Spirit.[47]

Deciding *which* actions result in a loss of state's legitimacy is a difficult and sensitive issue. In the early days of Hitler's regime, Christians in Germany struggled with this question, which led, in 1934, to the publication of the Barmen Declaration, a document protesting the Nazis' attempt to control the church and insisting on the church's independence. Those who agreed with the declaration called themselves the "Confessing Church" and engaged in escalating resistance to Hitler's oppressive policies; its most prominent leaders were jailed or even executed.

Christianity has historically proven to be the most dependable defender of human liberty. The commitment to a higher law means that Christians have been on the front lines in resisting laws or actions contrary to that law. The biblical view was argued eloquently by the British statesman Edmund Burke during a famous 1788 debate in the House of Lords over the impeachment of the governor general of India. The governor general had claimed a right to arbitrary authority over the unruly nationals, arguing that they were, after all, used to despotism. Burke replied with these wonderful words: "My lords, the East India Company have not arbitrary power to give him [the governor general]. The king has no arbitrary power to give. Neither your lordships, nor the Commons, nor the whole legislature, have arbitrary power to give. Arbitrary power is a thing which no man can give. . . . We are all born, high as well as low, governors as well as governed, in subjection to one great, immutable, preexisting law. . . . This great law does not arise from our combinations and compacts; on the contrary, it gives to them all the sanction they can have."[48]

Precisely. Neither king nor parliament holds absolute authority over even the lowliest subject of the British Empire. That bedrock Christian conviction gives us a basis for resistance to earthly authority when that authority is unjust, which is why the great roll call of those who have given their lives to defend liberty features predominantly believers.

Tyrants recognize this all too clearly, which explains why the Chinese government persecutes religious believers so fiercely, jailing pastors, burning churches, outlawing home meetings. It's not simply that communists are atheists and want to stamp out religion; it's that they cannot tolerate anyone who worships a King who stands above the kings of this world. For that higher allegiance gives a basis for demanding freedom and rights from the earthly king.[49]

The rule of law, the promotion of the public good, and the defense of liberty—these are the principles we must learn to articulate in making the case for a Christian view of politics, engaging in "backyard apologetics" over the barbecue grill with friends. But though our beliefs derive ultimately from Scripture, in a pluralistic society we must also translate them into terms nonbelievers can understand. For example, when we work to change abortion laws, we must not only appeal to divine revelation but also point out that the most fundamental duty of government is to defend the defenseless. When we oppose the legalization of assisted suicide and eugenics, we can note that the very purpose of government is to prevent the private use of lethal force. (Government wields the power of the sword precisely so individuals *won't*.) We must advance public and persuasive arguments that appeal to reason and evidence.[50]

Responsible Participation

We must also make the case by the way we live. Others will see the truth of what we believe most clearly if we live out our convictions as responsible citizens in our communities.

First, Christians must be good citizens. The most elementary requirement of any society is that its citizens behave responsibly, obey the law, and carry out their civic duties. Christians should be

the best of citizens, as Augustine said, because we do out of love
for God what others do only because they are forced to by law.
This means that we vote, pay taxes, care for our neighborhood,
and live peaceably with others. We honor and obey our leaders
and civil magistrates, and we pray for those in authority. We can
also support groups that seek to protect religious liberty, such
as the Beckett Fund, the American Center for Law and Justice
(ACLJ), the Center for Law and Religious Freedom, the Rutherford Institute, and the Alliance Defense Fund.[51]

*Second, Christians must carry out their civic duty in every walk of
life.* When Alexis de Tocqueville came to this country in the early
nineteenth century, he was startled by the extent to which citizens
helped their neighbors, organizing all manner of voluntary associations to meet social needs and carry out projects for the common
good. He commented that he did not know ten men in all of
France who would do what ordinary Americans do every day as a
matter of course.[52] Most of the associations that so impressed the
French statesman were founded and run by Christians, following
the command to love our neighbors.

The same remains true today. People may make light of the
"Jesus Saves" banner across the door of the mission shelters and
soup kitchens, but they can't deny that these places are dispensing
mercy and compassion to the destitute. Visit our inner cities, and
you will discover that the Salvation Army, gospel missions, and
Catholic charities provide the vast majority of private relief services.
In poverty-stricken areas, volunteer organizations like Habitat for
Humanity are building homes and providing other relief for the
poor. Through Prison Fellowship, thousands of volunteers minister
to the outcasts of society—those behind bars. And through Prison
Fellowship's Project Angel Tree, hundreds of thousands purchase
and deliver gifts to the children of inmates every Christmas.

Just doing our duty within our own sphere of influence can produce surprising results. In early 1998, Barbara Vogel told her

fourth grade class at Highline Community School in Aurora, Colorado, about the civil war in Sudan, where Christians in the south are being rounded up by Muslim slavers and sold into slavery in the north. Mrs. Vogel's kids began to cry. "We thought slavery didn't happen anymore," they said.

The children decided to do something about it. They formed a group called Slavery That Oppresses People, known as STOP. They learned about Christian Solidarity, an organization that redeems slaves—literally buys them back and returns them to their families. Though many of Vogel's pupils live in public housing, they saved their allowances and sold lemonade, T-shirts, and old toys. Soon they had enough money to free one hundred and fifty slaves!

But the students didn't stop there. They then launched a letter-writing campaign, sending fifteen hundred letters to newspapers and public officials. The story spread. A homeless man living out of his car sent his last $100. A class of handicapped children raised money through a bake sale. A truck driver told people all across the country about the kids and collected funds. Within nine months, more than $50,000 in donations had poured in, and more than five thousand slaves had been set free.

The U.S. Congress recognized Barbara Vogel's kids as America's "Little Abolitionists" and hung a flag over the Capitol in their honor. "As a public-school teacher, I cannot say [in class] that Christ is the most important thing in my life," says Vogel, "but that doesn't mean that I can't model my faith."[53]

As we engage in civic affairs, we are making an eloquent witness for the faith. And in the process, we are strengthening self-government and limiting the state, for when intermediate structures are vibrant, government finds less occasion to become intrusive.

Third, Christians must be engaged directly in politics. As already noted, this begins with voting; beyond that, it includes joining civic groups and political organizations, and perhaps even running for public office. As we do so, we must be ever vigilant to keep our priorities in order, not compromising our commitment to Christ or putting partisan agendas first. Christian organizations active in politics need to set distinctively Christian goals and be uncompromising in biblical fidelity, never allowing themselves to be in the hip pocket of any political party. This is a narrow line to walk, but it can be done.

A good example is Justice Fellowship (JF), the public-policy arm of Prison Fellowship, which organizes task forces to work for biblically based reforms in the criminal-justice system. JF's approach follows the outlines of a Christian worldview. On the basis of *creation*, it says that because there is a holy God, there is a transcendent standard of justice; therefore, to qualify as just, all human law must be based on divine law. This is why JF works to defend religious liberty and protect transcendent principles expressed in the law. On the basis of the *fall*, it says that because we are morally responsible beings, justice must address our conscience. We must define crime as a moral problem, requiring a moral and spiritual solution. This is why Prison Fellowship goes behind bars to hold Bible studies and other faith-based programs. On the basis of *redemption*, it says that criminals are called to repent of their crimes and, as far as possible, to restore what they have damaged. Society, for its part, is called to restore both the criminal and the victim to the community. And how do we restore the civil order that has been damaged by crime? JF advocates what is known as *restorative justice*, which includes principles such as promoting the rights of victims in the legal process, encouraging offenders to reconcile with their victims, and requiring offenders to work and pay restitution to their victims. The object of restorative justice is to repair the moral and social order God has called us to live in. JF's agenda often cuts across party lines, and the organization has had remarkable success without compromising biblical principles.

Christians also can and should seek political office—and the best strategy is to shatter the common stereotypes. I know scores of men and women who do this successfully on both state and national levels. For example, Mark Earley is a former missionary and unapologetic evangelical, who as a state senator in Virginia was uncompromising on moral issues yet also won respect for his careful work on a variety of issues. When he announced that he would run for state attorney general in 1997, the chattering class in adjacent Washington, D.C., predicted that voters would turn against this "religious zealot." But Earley waged a strong campaign on the issues, and he not only won, but he also won with the biggest victory margin for any Republican in the state's history.

Fourth, the church must act as the conscience of society, as a restraint against the misuse of governing authority. Corporately, the church must zealously guard its independence, keep its prophetic voice sharp, and resist the allure of worldly power. It should hold government morally accountable to live up to its delegated authority from God (along with holding all other spheres of society accountable to fulfill the functions ordained to them by God).

This is not to say that Christians go about "imposing" their beliefs on an unwilling populace. Whenever the church speaks to public issues, some secularists will mutter darkly that what Christians really want is a theocracy, where they are in charge. That is not true. Historically, it was Christians who first formulated the principle of separation of church and state, starting with Augustine's distinction between the City of God and the City of Man. Christians recognize that God has ordained government as a separate institution with its own distinctive purposes. Government is a civil function, not a church function. That's why Christians have often been the staunchest defenders of religious liberty—for all faiths. One need only compare the Western polity, shaped historically by Christianity, with, for example, an Islamic polity, which recognizes no distinction between church and state and which often mercilessly oppresses and persecutes religious minorities.[54]

In addressing the state, we must do so not on the basis of power, as special interests do, but on the basis of principle. This is a crucial distinction, yet it is one that secular politicians and journalists frequently miss. For example, in early 1998 James Dobson of Focus on the Family met with Republican congressional leaders in Washington to confront them for failing to promote the social issues they had promised to support. For Dobson, this was a matter of principle—and a valid one. Yet journalists interpreted Dobson's action as a power play, warning in apocalyptic tones that religious conservatives were "marching on Washington" and demanding their due. Newspaper articles described Christians as a powerful voting bloc that had delivered 45 percent of the vote in the 1994 Republican sweep of Congress and warned that they were now demanding "their place at the table." Christians were depicted in the same terms as those applied to a labor union or any other special-interest group.[55]

Of course, we do have a right to a place at the table, just as any other citizens do. And yes, we do have political clout, but only because millions of Americans share our moral concerns. Yet these facts are not the basis of our political stance. We contend for certain truths in the political arena because they are crucial to liberty and public justice—and we would do so whether we had 45 percent of the vote or 5 percent.

So our message is not, We put you in office, now pay up. Rather, we are saying, This should be done because it is right, because it is a principle that undergirds any well-ordered civil society, and because it is a proper duty of the state as ordained by God.

SUMMARY

All this can be summed up by saying we should exhibit the best of Christian patriotism, always holding dear our own land and yet holding it up against the standard of divine justice. The United

States, for all her faults and flaws, remains history's best hope for achieving morally ordered liberty. It is still the great beacon of hope for emerging nations as they witness the remarkable blessings brought forth by religious, political, and economic freedom. But if it is to remain so, we must be at our posts, "the king's good citizens but the Lord's first," as Thomas More said as he went to his death for opposing Henry VIII.[56] <u>We must always be ready to show our fellow citizens the way to restore truth and moral authority to American law and politics.</u>

And we must begin by returning to the foundation of the Christian worldview—the principle of creation. For as we have seen, it was the rejection of the idea of creation that led to the loss of the concept of an eternal law above the law. And this, in turn, was the result of a new view of science that turned the very definition of knowledge on its head.

DISCUSSION QUESTIONS

CHAPTER 9

1　Genesis 2 indicates that work, in itself good and valuable, has been marred because of the Fall (Genesis 3). Quickly brainstorm perceived benefits and liabilities of work. (For this question, define work to include tasks that receive no financial compensation.) Make a mental note: Here, at the beginning of this discussion, for you personally, do the negatives of work outweigh the positives, or vice versa?

2　Noting the Scripture verses cited in the "Economic Principles" section (pp. 161–64), discuss the positive purpose or effects of these scriptural economic principles:

private property

wealth

stewardship

economic justice

economic responsibility

human dignity

3　At heart, do you feel that "secular" work is on equal footing with work that is typically called "ministry"? What influences your feelings one way or the other? Do you see a biblical basis for your feelings?

4 Help one another identify the "productive ends" of your work time and abilities. If you cannot identify any productive ends, brainstorm options: What small or large steps could you make (in occupation, attitude, or location) to effect more "faithful" outcomes?

5 If self-interest replaces biblical principle as the framework of the work ethic, what abuses can be expected?

6 What evidence do you see of Robert Schrank's comment that often "the workplace performs the function of community"? Do you think this is a positive or a negative trend? What role can or does the church have in meeting this need for community?

7 What can your church do to prepare its young people to enter the workforce with a biblical view of work as their goal?

8 In what ways can your group or church help people (whether

employees, employers, unemployed, homemakers, or retired)
reclaim a redemptive view of work and of economic stewardship?

9 How has your view of your own work changed as a result of
this study?

CHAPTER 10

10 On what basis did Martin Luther King Jr. disobey the law in
Birmingham? On what basis do you agree or disagree with
King's reasoning? His actions?

11 In what ways does the American system of government and
law as designed by the Founders reflect biblical principles?

12 How did the rejection of the idea of creation lead to the loss of
the concept of an eternal law above the law?

13 Give examples of how you are already suffering from the four consequences of the loss of moral authority.

14 Summarize what you've learned in this chapter about the three "principles we must learn to articulate in making the case for a Christian view of politics":

the rule of law

the promotion of the public good

the defense of liberty

15 In your particular community, with its strengths and weaknesses, what does it mean for you to responsibly participate in the public life:

being a good citizen?

carrying out your civic duty?

engaging in political activity?

participating with the church in its role as the conscience of society and in providing restraint against governmental misuse of authority?

16 Suppose you were running for political office. As a group, create a list of decision-making guidelines for use in that office.

ROLE PLAY

Refer to the directions for role play, at the end of session 1 (pp. 52–53).

CONVERSATION STARTERS

a. Assume a young person admits to having one goal in life: "Big money. That's all I want, just money to buy anything I want."

b. Assume a neighbor says, "There should be a law against children sassing their teachers (or parents)." How could you turn this offhand remark into a conversation about the role of law, the public good, and the loss of voluntary restraints? (Have we "been 'freed' from the older rules of courtesy and morality only to be hemmed in by new rules imposed by law"?)

c. Assume a neighbor says, "Politicians are all crooks. We'd be better off without them."

d. Assume someone says, "I don't care what the law says, I'm going to drive down the wrong side of the road. It's my right."

CLOSING SUMMARY

What is the one thing you want to remember from what you read (or heard or did) in this session?

Consider sharing this with the group.

SCIENCE
AND THE ARTS

CHAPTER 11

THE BASIS FOR TRUE SCIENCE

As you read chapter 11, keep the following questions in mind:

- What are the basic contradictions of scientific naturalism?
- What elements of the Christian worldview provide the underpinnings of modern science?
- In what ways should we respond to proponents of the philosophy of scientific naturalism?

D*arwin's Dangerous Idea,* the title of a recent book, could easily fool an unsuspecting browser at the local bookstore. One might expect that the author, Tufts University professor Daniel Dennett, wants to warn readers of the dangers of Darwinism. But in reality, Dennett hopes to persuade readers to *embrace* the "dangerous" implications of Darwin's theory. He argues that Darwinism, rightly understood, is a "universal acid" that dissolves away all traditional moral, metaphysical, and religious beliefs. For if human beings have evolved by material, purposeless causes, then there is no basis for believing in a God who created us and revealed moral truths. Dennett even suggests that traditional churches and rituals be relegated to "cultural zoos" for the amusement of onlookers.[1]

The book is one of the more colorful examples of a common tactic—using science as a weapon to shoot down religious faith.

The standard assumption is that science constitutes objective knowledge while religion is an expression of subjective need. Religion, therefore, must accommodate its claims about the world to whatever science decrees. In this way, science is elevated to an overall philosophy—often called *scientism* or *scientific naturalism*—which assumes that the only things that are real are those that can be known and measured by experience and observation. Everything else is unreal, a product of subjective fantasy, including things like love and beauty, good and evil, God and conscience.

David Hume, an eighteenth-century Scottish philosopher and critic of Christianity, exposed the real agenda of scientism in dramatic prose. He recommended that library shelves be purged of any book dealing with religion, ethics, metaphysics—anything that cannot be reduced to empirical facts. Take the book in hand, he urged, and ask, Does it contain reasoning based on mathematics? Does it contain reasoning based on facts and experiments? If the answer is no, then "commit it to the flames." If any book does not deal with mathematics or empirical facts—that is, with science—then "it can contain nothing but sophistry and illusion."[2]

Like Hume, many intellectuals today assume that science is the source of all genuine knowledge. Whether it travels under the banner of scientism, positivism, materialism, or naturalism, this is the dominant worldview of Western culture. Science, which originally simply meant the study of the natural world, has been conflated with scientific naturalism, the philosophy that the natural world is all that exists. As early as 1922, G. K. Chesterton warned that scientism had become a "creed" taking over our institutions, a "system of thought which began with Evolution and has ended in Eugenics."[3] And in 1955, one educator warned that while America's public schools are ostensibly neutral, they are "propagating a particular dogmatic faith, namely, scientific naturalism."[4]

That "dogmatic faith" aggressively seeks to subsume everything else under naturalistic categories. Even human beings are reduced to "objects" or "things" that can be inspected, experimented on, and ultimately controlled. Philosopher Arthur Koestler denounced this as "the ratomorphic fallacy," arguing that it treats humans as though they were a species of laboratory rat.[5] Similarly, the great Christian apologist C. S. Lewis warned that the rise of scientific naturalism would lead to "the abolition of man," for it denies the reality of those things central to our humanity: our sense of right and wrong, of purpose, of beauty, of God.

And if we deny the things that make us truly human, then we will create a culture that is, by definition, *in*human. If we treat morality as subjective feeling, then moral ideals will be relegated to the private realm, and the public realm will be stripped of all morality. If we deny the reality of the virtues that make us superior to the beasts, then those virtues wither away, reducing us to the level of beasts. Thus while science has created technological advances that make life easier and healthier, when science is confused with the philosophy of scientific naturalism, it destroys the very things that make life worth living. We gain control over the natural world at the cost of our own souls.

Lewis foresaw this predicament clearly. "For the wise men of old," he wrote, "the cardinal problem had been how to conform the soul to reality, and the solution had been knowledge, self-discipline, and virtue." The purpose of life was defined in terms of the growth of the soul, and there was an abiding moral standard to which to conform. But for the contemporary technical mind-set, "the problem is how to subdue reality to the wishes of men: the solution is a technique." This mind-set acknowledges no abiding standards, so there is nothing to check the human desire for control and domination.[6]

Watch a good TV interviewer interact with today's scientists, and you quickly realize that ethical subjectivism has stripped many scientists of the ability to evaluate the implications of even their own work. Their ethical understanding has not kept pace with their brilliant discoveries. As a result, science and technology blunder on without clear moral guidance, creating more sophisticated gadgets but also creating confusion as to what purposes, goals, or values they should serve.[7]

Yet despite these ominous weaknesses, it is no easy task to dislodge scientific naturalism from its position of intellectual dominance, for it has invested scientists with enormous power. If science is the only source of knowledge, then their own discipline trumps all others, and they alone speak with authority to the culture at large. Therefore, if we are to stand against attacks on Christian faith made in the name of science, our first target should not be specific theories, such as Darwinian evolution, but the underlying philosophy of scientific naturalism.

BASIC CONTRADICTIONS

Christians ought to argue that scientific naturalism is incoherent and self-contradictory, for scientists must exempt themselves from the very framework they prescribe for everyone else. All human beings are reduced to mechanisms operating by natural causes—*except* scientists themselves. Why? Because to carry out their experiments, they must assume that *they*, at least, are capable of transcending the network of material causes, capable of rational thought, of free deliberation, of formulating theories, of recognizing objective truth. They themselves must form the single glaring exception to their own theory. This is the fatal self-contradiction of naturalism.

Lewis pointed out another contradiction that is equally devastating. The naturalist assumes that everything that exists can be explained in terms of natural forces. But that assumption itself cannot be the result of natural forces or it would not qualify as a genuine truth claim. For if an idea is simply the product of parti-

cles bumping around in our brains, then it is neither true nor false
but merely a natural phenomenon. If, for example, a man tells us
his room is on fire but we know that he just swallowed a halluci-
nogenic drug, then we probably will not call the fire department.
If we think an idea is the result of physical, chemical causes in the
brain, then we discount it and don't even credit it as a rational
thought.

Now, scientific naturalism necessitates the conclusion that *all*
ideas are products of natural causes in the brain—*including the
idea of scientific naturalism itself.* Thus, if it is true, then it is not
a rational thought and ought to be discounted. "Every theory of
the universe which makes the human mind a result of irrational
causes is inadmissible," Lewis wrote. For "in order to think, we
must claim for our reasoning a validity which is not credible if
our own thought is merely a function of our brain and our brain
a byproduct of irrational physical process."[8]

The task for Christians, then, is clear: *to expose the flaws in scientific naturalism, which has invested science with ultimate intellectual
authority.* We must do this not because we are against science but
because we want to restore science to its proper role as a means
of investigating God's world and alleviating suffering. And Christians are the ones to lead the way because the original conception
of science was developed in the context of the biblical worldview,
and only in that context can it function properly. In fact, surprising as it may be to many people, without Christianity there would
be no science.

THE NATURE OF NATURE

The method of investigation that we now know as modern science
first emerged in Christianized Europe, a culture steeped in biblical
faith, and most of the key figures in the scientific revolution were
believers, working from a basis of faith. In fact, contemporary

historians of science, both Christians and non-Christians, agree that Christianity provided the underlying attitudes and intellectual presuppositions that made modern science possible in the first place.[9] Consider some of the most important elements of the Christian worldview, contrasting it to alternate worldviews:

The physical world is real, not an illusion. Most Eastern cultures embrace pantheism, which teaches that the physical world is an illusion (maya). But the Bible teaches that God created the material world; it is real and can be known. This assumption primed Western thinkers to value the physical world and to consider it worthy of study.

Nature is good but not divine. Many pagan cultures hold to *animism,* which teaches that the world is the abode of the divine or an emanation of God's own essence. Consequently, they believe that nature is alive with sun gods, river goddesses, and astral deities. This ancient belief is being revived in our own day. For example, in Disney's film *Pocahontas,* the young Indian maiden scolds the white man for thinking the earth "is just a dead thing," admonishing him that "every rock and tree and creature has a life, has a spirit, has a name." This is a startlingly clear expression of animism.[10]

But Genesis 1 stands in stark contrast to all this. It teaches that nature is not divine; it is God's handiwork. The sun and moon are not gods; they are lights placed in the sky to serve God's purposes. Historians describe the effect of this doctrine as the "de-deification" of nature, and it was a crucial precondition to science. For when nature commanded religious worship, then digging too closely into her secrets was thought to be irreverent. By "de-deifying" nature, Christianity turned it from an object of fear and worship into a possible object of scientific study.

Nature is orderly and predictable. Another unique contribution of Christianity was the idea of laws of nature. No other religion or culture, Eastern or Western, has ever used the word *law* in relation to nature. In fact, before modern times, most people regarded nature as mysterious, dangerous, and chaotic. As a result, notes historian Carl Becker, the idea of natural law did not arise from ordinary experience but only from the biblical teaching that God is both Creator and Lawgiver.[11] The early scientists had to act on *faith* that nature is orderly, long before they had amassed enough scientific evidence to prove it.

Humans can discover nature's order. Moreover, early scientists had to act on faith that the order in nature can be discovered by the human mind—a conviction grounded in the biblical teaching that we are created in the image of God. Again, a cross-cultural comparison shows how unique this conviction is. The ancient Chinese believed in some kind of order in nature, but they conceived of it as an inherent necessity, inscrutable to the human mind. That's why the Chinese, despite their great technical achievements, never developed science as a self-correcting, experimental enterprise (as we know it). By contrast, the biblical teaching of the image of God was taken to mean that human rationality reflects in some manner the rationality of God himself—the rationality by which he made the world. Therefore, we can "think God's thoughts after him" (to use a phrase popular with the early scientists) and discover the order he built into creation.

We need to experiment. But *how* do we think God's thoughts? The answer to that question was crucial for science. The ancient Greeks had defined science as intuition into the rational structure inherent in things, which implies that the world is the way it is because it is rationally necessary. Therefore, true knowledge of the world is gained primarily by logical analysis.

But near the end of the Middle Ages there emerged a form of Christian theology known as *voluntarism*, which taught that rational order is not something inherent *in* nature but is imposed *on* nature by God's will and design. Voluntarism helped inspire experimental methodology in science, for if the world is not structured by rational necessity but is a creation of God's free

choice, then we cannot gain knowledge by sitting in an ivory
tower and conducting logical analysis, as the Greeks had taught.
Instead, we have to go out and see what God has actually done.
We have to observe and experiment.

Many of the early scientists drew an explicit connection
between voluntarist theology and scientific method. For example,
Roger Cotes, a friend of Isaac Newton, wrote that the world
arose from "the perfectly free will of God," and "therefore" we
must investigate the world by "observations and experiments."[12]

Galileo made similar arguments and then gave a memorable
example of what they meant. When he wanted to find out
whether a ten-pound weight falls to the ground faster than a
one-pound weight, he didn't ask philosophical questions (in his
day he was much criticized for not cogitating on the "nature of
weight"). Instead, he dropped two balls from the leaning tower
of Pisa and watched what happened.

The order in nature is mathematically precise. Modern science
depends on the idea that the order in nature is precise and can be
expressed in mathematical formulas. This, too, was a contribution
of Christianity. In all other religions, the creation of the world
begins with some preexisting material, which the gods cannot
fully control. For example, in the West, the Greeks believed that
matter existed from eternity and that it was capable of resisting
the rational order imposed by the creator (who was an inferior
deity—a demiurge). As a result, the Greeks expected to find a
certain lack of precision in nature, a fuzziness around the edges,
frequent anomalies and irregularities.

By contrast, the Bible teaches that God alone is eternal, that
there is no preexisting "stuff" that is either beyond his control
or capable of resisting him. The world comes completely from
God's hand (creation *ex nihilo,* from nothing) and is completely at
his command. As a result, Christians expected the order in nature
to be precisely what God wanted it to be—mathematically precise.

For example, when Copernicus proposed that the planets go around the sun instead of the earth, he actually had no empirical evidence for the new hypothesis. Before the invention of telescopes, observations of the planets fit an earth-centered system just as well as a sun-centered system. The sole factor favoring a heliocentric system was that it was mathematically simpler; it didn't require as many adjustments in the equations. And since Copernicus was convinced that God had made the world mathematically precise, getting better formulas was good enough for him. Of course, when telescopes were invented, it turned out that Copernicus was right. But standing at the threshold of the scientific revolution, Copernicus was inspired not by the scientific facts available to him but by his Christian faith.

The same faith inspired Johannes Kepler, the man famous for discovering that the orbits of the planets are not circles, as people thought at the time, but ellipses. Kepler noticed a slight mismatch between mathematical calculations of the orbit of Mars and actual observations of the orbit. The difference was so tiny that other scientists shrugged it off, but Kepler was convinced that everything in creation is precisely the way God wants it to be. If God had wanted the orbits to be circular, they would have been *exactly* circular; since they were not, then they must be *exactly* something else. Kepler struggled for years to reconcile the equations with the observations until he finally hit on the discovery that the orbits are ellipses. Through those difficult years, it was his Christian faith that spurred him on—his conviction that the biblical God has complete control over matter and, therefore, it will be mathematically precise.[13]

"The possibility of an applied mathematics," writes historian R. G. Collingwood, "is an expression, in terms of natural science, of the Christian belief that nature is the creation of an omnipotent God."[14]

SCIENCE AS APOLOGETICS

We hear from all sides that science has disproved Christianity, but today the historical evidence gives us a clear response: On the contrary, it was Christianity that made science possible. <u>Instead of being intimidated by attacks made in the name of science, we can show that the very existence of the scientific method, and all it has accomplished, is a great apologetic argument for the truth of Christianity.</u>

Historically, many believers have done just that. Isaac Newton, often considered the greatest of the early scientists, was a devout Christian whose pursuit of science was strongly motivated by his desire to defend the faith.[15] He firmly believed that scientific study of the world would lead straight to the God who created that world. Science shows us "what is the first cause, what power he has over us, and what benefits we receive from him," Newton wrote, so that "our duty towards him, as well as that towards one another, will appear to us by the light of nature." And why does science show us all this? Because the business of science is to "deduce causes from effects, till we come to the very first cause, which certainly is not mechanical." In other words, the world may operate by mechanical causes, but as we trace them back, we deduce that the first cause must be an intelligent and rational Being.[16]

"This most beautiful system of sun, planets, and comets could only proceed from the counsel and dominion of an intelligent and powerful Being," wrote Newton.[17] Small wonder that his friend Roger Cotes proclaimed that Newton's work "will be the safest protection against the attacks of atheists, and nowhere more surely than from this quiver can one draw forth missiles against the band of godless men."[18] This is precisely the approach we must recover today.

Standard school textbooks still treat the rise of science as the cause of the demise of religion, which puts Christian young people on the defensive in the classroom. This stereotype is the legacy of the first modern historians such as Voltaire and Gibbon, who were Enlightenment rationalists eager to discredit Christianity. As a result, they composed histories of Western civilization that cast religion as an enemy of science and progress.[19] This is now so thoroughly ingrained in conventional wisdom that even Christians who are not trained scientists must be aware of the arguments in this chapter, learn to see through the stereotypes, and be able to make a defense of our faith.

I will confess that though I achieved moderate academic honors in college, I nearly flunked physics, so I cannot hold myself out as an expert in science (though Nancy has written extensively on the subject). But I can follow the reasoning of scientific apologetics, and I submit that most ordinary Christians can as well. Our case is strong and gives us the tools to challenge the reigning naturalistic orthodoxy and present a persuasive apologetic.

Ordinary Christians Speaking Out

Many Christians are doing just that. Consider the story of Phillip Johnson, a professor on the law faculty at the University of California at Berkeley, a hotbed of 1960s radicalism. During a 1987 sabbatical in England, Johnson bought several books about Darwinian evolution. Reading them with his sharp lawyer's eye, he was astonished to discover how flawed the reasoning was, how flimsy the evidence. It dawned on him that Darwinism is dominant today not because of the strength of the scientific evidence but because Darwinism bolsters a worldview—one that rejects God and depicts humans as morally autonomous. He realized that the question of design versus Darwinism is at heart a battle between contrasting worldviews.

So today, dressed in baggy tweeds and peering through rimless glasses, Johnson breaks up his teaching schedule by accepting frequent invitations to present the case for design to lecture halls jammed with the world's most illustrious scientists. His books are best-sellers, and he's mentoring a cadre of bright young scholars who are working out the scientific details of the design argument.[20]

One doesn't have to be a professor to take up the case. In Colorado in 1996, fifteen-year-old Danny Phillips protested a classroom video on human reproduction from the PBS series *NOVA*, which opened with the sweeping statement that life originated billions of years ago when "powerful winds gathered random molecules from the atmosphere." Danny approached school authorities, arguing that the video violated a local school policy requiring teachers to present evolution as theory, not fact. He presented his case respectfully and persuasively, pointing out that the video's opening statement was unnecessary and doctrinaire—that it asserted without any evidence that life on earth is the outcome of natural laws operating purely by chance. A review committee from the school board agreed to discontinue using the video. Immediately, like vultures swooping down for the kill, representatives from the ACLU descended on the board, breathing threats of lawsuits, and school authorities reversed their decision.[21]

Danny was one young student alone against stiff opposition, so perhaps the reversal was predictable. Yet just raising the issue responsibly is an important starting point. And the way he went about it provides a good model for approaching public school officials. Danny acted completely on his own, so critics could not dismiss him as a pawn of outside groups. He limited his complaint to a clear case of naturalistic philosophy presented as scientific fact. And he politely offered for classroom use an educational video called *Darwinism: Science or Naturalistic Philosophy?* featuring debaters with impeccable academic credentials in an event held at Stanford University.[22]

Shifting the Balance
If Christians intelligently raise issues in the classroom and the media, using reason and evidence, eventually we can shift the bal-

ance. Already there are signs that the scientific establishment is becoming nervous. The *Washington Post* reported on recent school controversies in an article titled "Creationism Makes a Come-back."[23] What's worse, warned *Science* magazine, it's coming back armed with a "shrewd new strategy."[24] That new strategy involves promoting critical thinking skills and helping people distinguish genuine science from naturalistic philosophy taught under the guise of science—as in the video Danny protested.

We need to communicate that what is at issue is not the specif-ics of evolution versus the specifics of Genesis. Rather, at issue is the worldview claim that life is the product of impersonal forces versus the claim that life was designed by an intelligent agent. We must fight worldview with worldview.

Consider the stark, dogmatic assertions made by typical school textbooks: "You are an animal, and share a common heritage with earthworms."[25] "Evolution is random and undirected . . . without either plan or purpose."[26] Our public schools are supposed to be neutral with regard to religion, but these statements are clearly not neutral; they are antagonistic to any and all theistic religions. They go far beyond any empirical evidence (how could anyone prove that evolution has no purpose?) and therefore are more philosoph-ical than scientific.

Dealing with Schools

Our first goal in dealing with schools, then, should be to get edu-cators to separate philosophical claims from scientific theories. In other words, we must get them to stop treating philosophical statements as if they were science. Most teachers are fair-minded and are responsive if the issue is raised intelligently and respect-fully.

Second, we should press for teaching science honestly. That is, educators should teach not only the examples that confirm evolu-tion but also those that contradict it, the anomalies and unsolved

questions. In *Education or Indoctrination?* science educator Norris
Anderson illustrates how dogmatically naturalism is presented in
textbooks. For example, "Darwin gave biology a sound scientific
basis by attributing the diversity of life to natural causes rather
than supernatural creation."[27] Or again, "Today, the evidence for
evolution is overwhelming. . . . Evolution is no longer merely a
theory." The same text takes a preemptive strike against trouble-
some critics by denouncing them as know-nothings: "There have
always been those who resisted the appeal of evolution and every
now and then declare 'Darwin was wrong,' in the hope of some
profitable publicity, usually revealing that they do not understand
Darwinism."[28]

Yet Anderson himself understands Darwinism better than
most. Formerly a textbook writer, he helped prepare the infamous
BSCS series (Biological Sciences Curriculum Study), which inau-
gurated the current dogmatic approach to teaching evolution. "I
was practically an evangelist for evolution," Anderson says wryly.
But he experienced a turnabout when a colleague told him privately, "I believe human evolution happened, but there's absolutely
no evidence for it." Anderson was appalled and suggested that the
textbooks be rewritten to reflect the real state of the evidence. His
proposal was vehemently rejected.

"That's when my idealism began to crumble," Anderson says.
"I saw that scientists close ranks to present a false image of scientific certainty."[29] His response was to spearhead a successful
campaign in his home state of Alabama to paste an insert on
the inside front cover of biology textbooks listing some of the
anomalies and ambiguities in evolutionary theory. Several other
states are now considering similar inserts.

This is a good start, for we must help people see that the deck
has been stacked, that the presentations are completely one-
sided. We need to press for an honest approach that shatters
that "false image of scientific certainty" and openly weighs the

evidence for and against any completely naturalistic account of
life and the universe.

Encouraging Youth

Perhaps the most important thing we can do is encourage Christian young people to go into science as a profession and to demonstrate in practice the viability of a biblical framework for science.
Most Christians don't think of science as a mission field, as I discovered when a friendly young man introduced himself to me on
a cross-country plane flight. He told me how much my books
meant to him in his spiritual growth and then explained that he
was studying molecular biology; as soon as he had his degree,
however, he was planning to go to the mission field in South
America.

"In that case, I see that my books have fallen short in guiding
your spiritual growth," I responded.

The young man looked startled.

"Why do you feel you have to go to South America to serve
God?" I asked. "How many Christian molecular biologists do you
suppose there are?"

"Not many," he admitted.

Before the plane landed, he came by my seat one more time.
"I've been thinking," he said, "I can be a missionary as a molecular
biologist."

Precisely. If we are going to craft a winning strategy for extend-
ing Christ's lordship over all of life, we need missionaries in
science and in every other discipline and vocation.

And the time is right. Though scientific naturalism has separated religion and science into antagonistic categories, the human
urge for a unified vision of the world is spilling over those artificial
boundaries. The Center for the Renewal of Science & Culture at
the Discovery Institute in Seattle funds and publicizes research
uncovering evidence for design in fields such as physics, cosmology,

and biology. The Templeton Foundation has encouraged research into the relationship between science and religion, building bridges between them. As a result, religious issues are being hotly debated at scientific meetings.

What Kind of Religion?

The critical question is this: *What kind* of religion will receive the official approval of science? At the 1993 annual meeting of the American Association for the Advancement of Science (AAAS), participating scientists were somewhat startled to hear a clear, sweet voice rising above the group in a hymn as they assembled on Sunday morning. The singer was Nancy Abrams, wife of cosmologist Joel Primack, and the hymn was "The Handwriting of God," which celebrated the residual cosmic background radiation from the big bang. "God's secrets are written in the first light," announced the refrain. "Soon we'll be reading God's journal of the first day."

The performance highlighted a session on the relationship between science and religion, where participants flocked to discuss such topics as "The Religious Significance of Big Bang Cosmology" and "Scientific Resources for a Global Religious Myth." Not surprisingly, given that this is the age of do-it-yourself "god kits," many speakers argued that traditional faiths must give way to "a science-based myth." They urged their listeners to elevate cosmic evolution into a "compelling 'religious' narrative" with "the power to bind humans together in a new world order."[30]

What these priestly pronouncements miss is that Western science grew out of, and presupposes, not some "science-based myth" but Christianity, as we have seen in this chapter. As scientists grow more interested in these questions, it is crucial for Christians to seize the opportunity to demonstrate what the true basis of science is.

God calls us to "demolish arguments and every pretension that sets itself up against the knowledge of God" and to "take captive every thought to make it obedient to Christ" (2 Cor. 10:5). We must not fail to heed this call when it comes to modern science, for otherwise there's no telling what "compelling" but false new myths scientists may concoct to feed our society's deep spiritual hunger.

The reformation of science—and the way we think about reality—is not just a matter for ivory-tower academicians. It affects our entire worldview—not only ideas about religion and ethics but also about the arts, music, and popular culture, as we will see in the following chapters.

BLESSED IS THE MAN

As you read chapter 12, keep the following
questions in mind:
- What positive character traits do you see in Henryk Górecki?
- As portrayed in this chapter, what seems to have motivated his work?
- What evidence do you see of a Christian worldview?

Headed to his mother's house north of Malibu, the young movie producer was driving along Pacific Coast Highway when the low buzzy ring of his car phone sounded. He snatched it up and listened to the panicky voice at the other end.

"No," he said. "No . . . no . . . I told them. . . . Look, if we're ever going to get this picture made, we have to have a star who can open it. . . . No, it's not something we can talk about. The script is just not that strong. If it doesn't open big here and do well internationally, we could find ourselves on the streets. . . . Yes, yes, that we can do. We're prepared to talk power numbers. No, I don't want just her agent. I want her at that meeting personally. I want her to feel . . . Okay . . . Okay . . . but just do it *now*, all right? . . . Okay, talk to you."

After the success of *Pretty Woman*, every Hollywood studio was hot to recycle the hooker-with-a-heart-of-gold scenario. They were preparing to roll out screens full of the stuff, "sanitized" by

the woman's point of view: brutal men, the lonely struggles of
single moms, and a woman's hallowed right to choose her own
lifestyle. Meanwhile, men could overlook the "message" for the
obvious titillating attractions, feeding their own fantasies. This
was sexual politics, Hollywood style.

How did I end up here? the young producer wondered. He had
started out with such high ideals, thinking he would write and
produce serious films for adults, not adult-only schlock.

He tuned the radio to his favorite classical station, as he often
did when his own life grew dissonant, and heard a faint, distant
throbbing of double basses. Outside the window, the houses
screening his view of the Pacific began to be spaced farther apart,
and between them he glimpsed turquoise sea-foamed bays within
surrounding arms of brown cliffs.

The theme started by the double basses grew stronger and more
intense as other strings joined, pitting long, low strains against
one another in a dirgelike progression. Somehow the music kept
drawing his attention toward the cradling bays on the left. It
seemed to speak with the power of the sea rumbling against the
land and climbed in a steady progression that lifted his eyes to the
blue, cloud-gauzed heavens. It made him long for . . . for what?

Suddenly a soprano began to sing, and her voice made him think
of his mother, who was waiting for him. He was late and knew he
might find her testy. But then again, he had waited for her his
entire childhood. Waited for her to come back from the studio.
Back from location. Back from his father's funeral after the plane
crash—which, he had been told, he was "too young to understand."

But he had understood the loss of his father only too well.
What he still did not understand was why his mother had pushed
him away from her at that moment. Or in the following years,
while she conducted numerous affairs and he was shunted off to
boarding school.

Now both of them were trying to recapture something, and yet

he went to their weekly dinners together with a guardedness he
had not been able to shake off.

He didn't recognize the language in which the soprano was
singing, but as the music ascended, he was gripped by her magnificent, yearning song. Suddenly, at its height, when the music
turned bright and bittersweet, he found himself in tears, longing
for something he couldn't even name.

People used to speak of being "ravished" by music. That must
be what was happening to him. The music was releasing such an
enormous store of emotions that he felt utterly at its mercy. He
pulled over to the side of the road and gave in to the mourning
and ecstasy that the music evoked, resting his head against the
steering wheel. In the background, he heard traffic passing, but
the music's strange hold on him kept him motionless as he cried
his heart out for every loss he had ever suffered.

The strains began to subside into the patterns out of which
they had emerged, easing the sorrow. He looked up at the sandy,
pumpkin-brown cliff to his right, then to the ocean across the
highway, where a group of coral-prickly boulders marched out to
meet the waves. He knew he would remember this roadside spot,
this holy ground of nowhere. He would never be able to pass those
sea-marching boulders without remembering the first time he had
heard this powerful piece of music.

As the music quieted to a point where he thought it must end,
he turned up the volume to hear the name of the piece and its
composer. Instead, another movement began.

He wasn't going anywhere, he decided, until he knew what he
was listening to, for this music expressed exactly what the real artist in him had always wanted to create in film. Fidelity to contemporary experience yet with an unabashed capacity to address the
deepest human sentiments. Before the second movement ended,
he picked up his cellular phone and dialed information. Then he
called KMCB.

"What are you playing?" he asked. "What's the piece on right now?"

"Górecki's Third."

"What? How do you spell that?"

"Not like it's pronounced. He's Polish. Henryk Górecki. You say 'Goo-*rets*-kee,' but it's spelled G-O-R-E-C-K-I."

"Is it available? Can you get it on CD?"

"Is this the first time you've heard it?"

"Yes, I'm calling from my car. I've never heard anything like this."

"You and everybody else. It's at the top of *Billboard* magazine's chart. The classical chart. It's even at number seven on the pop chart. It's a phenomenon."

■   ■   ■

In 1993 the world discovered Henryk Górecki and his Symphony no. 3, *Symphony of Sorrowful Songs*, a work composed more than fifteen years earlier. Though the movie producer in our story is fictional, his reaction is based on news accounts of radio station managers who say they were inundated by calls from listeners— many of whom did pull over to the side of the road to weep, overwhelmed by the music.

In a world where serious contemporary music often has been dominated by the jarring dissonance of experimental music, how does this composition manage to be truly contemporary and yet so full of pathos? Why does the *Symphony of Sorrowful Songs* communicate to such a vast audience? And perhaps most mysteriously, to what unnamable reaches of the human spirit is Górecki speaking? Who is this composer, and how does he do it?

Henryk Mikolaj Górecki was born in Poland in 1933.[1] His mother, Otylia, played the piano, and his father, a railroad employee, was an amateur musician. Henryk's mother died when he was two years old, and after his father remarried, Górecki received no musical encouragement and was even forbidden to play his mother's piano. He taught himself to play in secret and eventually insisted on being allowed to study. But his musical progress had been set back so much that he was turned down the first time he applied to the Intermediate School of Music in Rybnik—a type of performing-arts high school.

Yet by 1955, when Górecki entered the Higher School of Music conservatory in Katowice, he was already an accomplished composer, and before he graduated, his music was being featured at national festivals. He went on to win international music festival awards in Paris in the early 1960s and became head of the Higher School of Music in Katowice. But what best explains Henryk Górecki's genius was the part he played in one of the late twentieth century's defining moments.

In 1977 the cardinal of Krakow, Karol Wojtyla, commissioned Górecki to compose a work for the upcoming anniversary of St. Stanislaw's martyrdom nine hundred years earlier. From the beginning, this commission carried grave risks for a musician in Communist Poland, for St. Stanislaw represented the moral authority of the Christian faith over secular rulers. Back in 1079, St. Stanislaw was a bishop who incurred the wrath of King Boleslaus II by opposing the king's adulteries and unjust wars. At first the king repented, but later he returned to his old ways and ordered his henchmen to kill the bishop. When they refused, the king did the job himself. While Bishop Stanislaw was celebrating Mass in the cathedral one day, the king split the holy man's skull with a sword.

The martyred Stanislaw became the patron saint of Poland, an emblem of the moral authority of the church and a rebuke to all the tyrants who have ruled Poland through its long, sad history. To compose a work in honor of St. Stanislaw in Communist Poland was to declare oneself in open opposition to the government.

Yet Górecki's acceptance of the commission cannot have surprised the authorities. As head of one of Poland's most respected educational institutions, Górecki had for several years conducted a running battle with the "yapping little dogs"—as he referred to Communist Party officials—who constantly tried to interfere in the workings of the school. In the West, the arts are often seen as a nonpolitical force, but the Communists always understood that the arts can have political implications—and they strongly "preferred" that their artists express an allegiance to Marxist-Leninism.

Górecki was also known as a devoted Roman Catholic. He taught his students the great canon of sacred music not merely as a historical artifact but as a living, vital tradition. His own compositions reflected the same conviction, with much of his work based on traditional sacred chant melodies. Official Communist ideology insisted that Christianity was a thing of the past—a religion for old people, soon to die out. Yet here was Górecki, the head of a state institution and already one of Poland's most celebrated composers, drawing his inspiration from this supposedly dry well. His work served as a rebuke, just as St. Stanislaw's work had done nine hundred years earlier. Now he was poised to create what would surely be a magnificent choral tribute to this saint—and just at the time when Solidarity had begun to shake the foundations of Communist Poland. A rumbling to which the Kremlin's political seismographers were exquisitely attuned.

Then, in the midst of Górecki's work on the new composition, something amazing happened. In 1978, a year after commissioning the piece, Karol Wojtyla, cardinal of Krakow, became Pope John Paul II. The following year, the pope was scheduled to visit his homeland to commemorate the anniversary of St. Stanislaw, and Communist Party officials knew that his visit would be watched by the entire world. As a result, they began pressuring Górecki to stop work on his commission.

A running battle ensued. Górecki's phone was tapped, his mail intercepted, his meetings secretly taped. Students he had nurtured were denied positions, and he was prevented from appointing the best of the younger composers to teaching positions. Communist Party members on the faculty were encouraged to plot against him. At an important anniversary of the conservatory, he was airbrushed out of all the photographs. Television news programs about the anniversary omitted any footage of him. Górecki became a non-person. Officially, he ceased to exist. How long would it be until he was arrested . . . or worse?

Eventually, the party made it impossible for Górecki to continue as head of the Higher School of Music in Katowice, and in 1979 he resigned from this position. He would take his chances living by his music alone.

When John Paul II arrived on June 2 of that year, the Polish government did its best to suppress all news of the event. Officials put up checkpoints along all roads leading to papal appearances, blacked out television coverage in adjoining districts, made sure no television shots of the event revealed the massive crowds in attendance, sent jets streaking low overhead to intimidate the crowds, and in every other conceivable way tried to minimize the impact of the pope's visit. Yet everywhere in Poland, even in districts far removed from John Paul's personal appearances, people placed posters of their champion in their windows and even laid floral tributes at newsstands showing his picture. The essential freedom of the human spirit had not been eliminated by Gulags, secret police, or economic deprivation during the long, dark years of the Cold War; it had been harbored and nurtured by an ever living Christian faith. Now that faith reemerged—vigorous, joyous, hopeful.

Plans also went forward for Górecki's composition, now completed and titled *Beatus Vir* (Blessed Is the Man), and it was scheduled to be played several days later at John Paul II's final appearance in Poland. The Communist Party brought increasing pressure to bear on Górecki, even pressuring other musicians not to participate in the performance. As a result, no one was available to conduct *Beatus Vir.*

All right, said Górecki, he would conduct the choral work himself.

As a last resort, the Communists turned to physical intimidation. They hired a gang of thugs to "demonstrate" outside Górecki's house. The "demonstrators" marched back and forth, waving placards protesting Górecki's "antiproletarian compositions." When Górecki gave no sign of caving in to this pressure, the goons broke into his house and looted it.

Undaunted, Górecki and his family journeyed to Krakow. There, on the evening of June 9, *Beatus Vir* was premiered in the Franciscan Basilica before John Paul II and a packed congregation—with the composer conducting a magnificent orchestra and choir.

"Dominus!" the choir sang. *"Dominus! Dominus! Dominus!"* ("Lord! Lord! Lord! Lord!")

Through the opening bars, the choir called on God again and again in unison, voicing the earnest plea of the millions praying on this occasion. They echoed the prayer that must have been stilled in St. Stanislaw's throat nine hundred years earlier, as the king's sword split his skull.

"Lord! Lord! Lord!" the choir sang yet again, each call stealing into the silence, for the voices sang without accompaniment at this point.

Where is God? the silence asked. *Where was he when the saint cried out? Where is he now that all of Poland is crying out?*

"Lord!" the choir sang, with all the urgency of Poland's suffering millions and their compatriots in other Eastern European countries—and beyond, to every cry of human desperation for divine mercy.

A longer silence followed, and then the orchestra began to play long, low strains, strangely reminiscent of the events of that week. On Wednesday, John Paul had visited the concentration camps of Auschwitz and Birkenau. There he commemorated the deaths of two Christians—Father Maximilian Kolbe and Edith Stein—whose martyrdom spoke in a representative way of all those who have been slaughtered at totalitarian hands in the twentieth century.

A baritone voice began singing, "O Lord, listen to my prayer. Listen. Listen."

A rocking, cradling rhythm suggested a repetitive, even monotonous plea for help. "O Lord," sang the choir, "hear my prayer. In your justice, hear me."

The choir and the baritone joined together and rose toward the midpoint climax of the piece. "O Lord! You are my God."

Here the trudging tones suddenly swung up, as if the world itself were turned right side up once more, and the swinging movement of history became no longer a monotonous death knell but the pealing of church bells ringing out the joy of "Christ with us."

> *Make me quick to heed your mercy,*
> *Teach me to do your will,*
> *For you are my God.*
> *May your spirit lead me into the land of righteousness.*

After this splendor came a pause, and then the baritone returned to the low strains of the beginning, but with the certain knowledge that . . .

> *O Lord, you are my God.*
> *My fate is in your hands.*
> *Lord God, you are my salvation.*

For what, after all, had changed? Political power had merely switched hands: The Nazis had been succeeded by the Soviets and their Polish collaborators. Salvation would have to be inspired by something other than the will to power. Our fate remains in God's hands, the music insisted, in spite of those who hold the weapons of violence in theirs.

Then the music became surpassingly lovely.

"O taste and see that the Lord is good."

After all, was not John Paul II beyond the authority of all state power, free to articulate the hopes of oppressed peoples everywhere? Free and willing to remind the world that truth cannot be changed, that beyond the weapons of violence is a much more significant struggle waged in the hearts of men and women, the struggle between good and evil?

The orchestral bells rang out, recognizing that throughout history Christ has raised up champions for the truth. The bells pealed that Christ would always raise up champions to remind the world where ultimate authority lies.

"Blessed is the man who trusts in him."

This day of spiritual triumph would pass, giving way to many difficult days. But the hope that Henryk Górecki had conveyed in his powerful musical witness would not be forgotten.

■   ■   ■

After that historic moment, Górecki retreated into private life and might have escaped the world's notice—had it not been for his *Symphony of Sorrowful Songs.* Composed in 1976, his Symphony no. 3 was recorded three times but with little impact. Then, in 1993, the London Sinfonietta recorded the *Symphony of Sorrowful Songs* once more, this time with soprano Dawn Upshaw. The recording became an international phenomenon. Perhaps the Lord wanted to reward this musician who showed such dedication and courage.

The movie producer who pulled over to the side of the road was thinking of his mother and their alienated relationship.

Henryk Górecki may well have been thinking of his own mother when he composed Symphony no. 3. The text sung by the soprano consists of three songs, the first of which is a fifteenth-century monastic lamentation of Mary at the foot of the cross. The second is a prayer found scratched on the wall of a cell in a gestapo headquarters in Poland; the prayer is signed by an eighteen-year-old girl, urging her mother not to weep for her and asking Christ's mother to remember her. The third sorrowful song borrows the words of a Polish folk song, in which a mother bewails the loss of her soldier son. Since Górecki lost his own mother at an early age, we can imagine that long before he expressed the sorrow of the human condition in his compositions, he had himself turned to the One who could assuage his grief and longing.

From the personal to the universal, Henryk Górecki shows what the courage of one man can do against massive evil. He shows us the incredible power of music to reach into the soul of a jaded world. And through Górecki's music, Christ teaches us to sing despite our tears.

CHAPTER 13

SOLI DEO GLORIA

As you read chapter 13, keep the following
questions in mind:
- What is the classical understanding of the arts?
- Through the centuries, what role have Christians played
  in the arts?
- What are the consequences of art being viewed as a religion?
- How can Christians today encourage good art?

Henryk Górecki's Symphony no. 3 may be the first music ever
to top both classical and pop charts. Solemn clerks in classical
music stores were startled to see punk rockers with spiky orange
hair coming in to ask for the piece. People of all ages and back-
grounds are drawn to Górecki's hauntingly beautiful, near liturgical sound, which borrows from both medieval music and folk
melodies.

But the primary significance of Górecki's work is that it represents a return to tonal music—music based on the major and
minor scales. In most classical music composed in the latter half
of the twentieth century, those scales have been tossed aside, and
composers are producing atonal music (based on the twelve-tone
scale of Arnold Schoenberg or the "chance music" of John Cage).

The trouble is, atonal music was rejected by the public from the very beginning for its sheer unpleasantness. For example, Sir Harrison Birtwistle's dissonant style has been described by reviewers as "extremely violent," capable of inflicting "an almost physical pain."[1]

Why are contemporary composers producing music with such harsh dissonance? The answer reveals a shift in the very definition of art. The musical language of tonality was traditionally thought to represent the natural law of sounds (based on the overtones that accompany any naturally produced sound). It goes back to the ancient Greeks, who discovered that if you divide a string into pure mathematical lengths in simple ratios such as 2:1, 3:2, or 4:3, you get "pure"-sounding intervals (consonance).[2] But contemporary composers view tonality as an arbitrary construct that can be discarded so that new musical languages can be invented. In parallel fashion, artists in other fields have given up the traditional notion that art reflects nature or objective reality in some way, and they have substituted the idea that artists create their own autonomous, abstract, and artificial world from which they can cast down thunderbolts on the world of ordinary folk. Indeed, much contemporary art seems intended primarily to shock, to destroy traditions and conventions.

A few years ago on CBS's *60 Minutes,* Morley Safer engaged in a blistering critique of contemporary art. The program highlighted Robert Gober, who creates sculptures shaped like urinals; Robert Ryman, who paints entire canvases plain white; and Jeff Koons, whose work is exemplified by two basketballs floating in a fish tank. "Is this art?" Safer asked.[3]

It is an important question, for the way we define art has the power to shape our culture. As we saw in the work of Górecki, art affects us at the deepest level of the soul. It can shape our thoughts, move our emotions, enlarge our imaginations. The music we listen to, the images we plant in our minds, the stories we tell—all have enormous power over the kind of people we are. They both express and shape our beliefs and values.

Just think of the effective way Jesus used images and stories. He could have just said, "Take care of people who are hurt and victimized." Instead, he spun the story of the Good Samaritan. He could have just said, "God forgives your sins." Instead, he told the parable of the Prodigal Son. Why? Because a story gets at aspects of the truth that are beyond the power of didactic teaching. Symbols, metaphors, allegories, and images move the whole person—the emotions and senses as well as the intellect. The rich, evocative words of literature are far more powerful than factual description.

For the Christian, the arts are also an important way to understand God and his creation. The arts give us ears to hear and eyes to see more clearly. We know from Scripture that creation is God's handiwork and that it reveals his glory; but often our ears are deaf, and our eyes are blind to that revelation. Artists are gifted with a special sensitivity to the glories of creation, and through their work, they can bring these glories into sharper focus for others.[4] Think of the music of Bach, the paintings of Rembrandt, the sculpture of Michelangelo.

Why, then, has art been so degraded in our own day? How have we moved from Bach to Birtwistle's dissonances? From Rembrandt to Ryman's blank canvases? From Michelangelo to Gober's urinals? How have we lost a sense of art's high dignity and purpose?

THE HARMONY OF THE SPHERES

The answer is an underlying philosophical shift from objectivism to subjectivism, and as we examine the history of ideas about art, we will see how this change in worldviews has led to disastrous consequences.

The classical understanding is that the arts are a powerful

means of communicating something significant about reality, a means of representing truth. Not that a work of art has to capture events in a photographic manner. After all, a painting may depict invisible things, such as angels, or abstract ideals, such as justice portrayed as a blindfolded woman with a scale; yet these images still convey something that is real. A novel is fictitious, yet it may represent profound realities about the human condition. Music is the most abstract of the arts, yet as we have seen, the traditional musical scale is rooted in an objective reality, based on mathematical relationships among sound frequencies found in nature.

From the time of the ancient Greeks, music was thought to reflect an orderly, mathematical structure built into the universe itself. With the rise of Christianity, these ideas were absorbed into a biblical worldview. Art was seen as rooted in the orderly structure and harmony of the universe God had created. Therefore, the basic justification for art is in the doctrine of creation.

Moreover, when God created the world, he cared enough to make it beautiful. There is no more convincing argument that God himself is pleased with beauty than to gaze at the delicate hues of a wildflower against dark green moss, the blue expanse of a Montana sky, the sharp outlines of the Swiss Alps. What's more, when God communicated his Word to us, he did so in a variety of literary styles: history, poetry, liturgical formulas, ethical principles, hymns, letters, maxims and proverbs, and even a love song.

Since God made human beings in his image, our capacity for aesthetic enjoyment is part of the way he created us—one of his good gifts to us. An engaging story, a majestic symphony, a beautiful landscape painting—these works of art give us aesthetic pleasure and cause us to contemplate not only the beauty of the world God created but also the eternal beauty of God himself. "One thing I ask of the Lord," says the psalmist, ". . . that I may . . . gaze upon the beauty of the Lord" (Ps. 27:4). In Scripture we find commands to make the temple beautiful and to make it ring with music. God wants us to use our best artistic skills in the worship of him.

Throughout history, believers have done just that, using the arts to glorify God and edify one another. The early church raised its voice in praise in a variety of chant styles (some of which have recently been turned into best-selling CDs). The medieval period gave us awe-inspiring cathedrals, designed to lift the mind to divine truth and to give "delight in the beauty of the house of God," in the words of twelfth-century Abbot Suger, architect of the great cathedral of St. Denis in France.[5] Indeed, in every period of Western history, many of the enduring artistic treasures have been produced by Christians.

Music

In music, the Renaissance produced the sublime treasure of sacred polyphony: the serene harmonies of Palestrina, the seamless textures of John Taverner, Thomas Tallis, and William Byrd. This is music that creates a sense that one is standing in a cathedral, the sound rising like high vaults towering overhead.

The baroque period gave us Antonio Vivaldi, a man of the cloth, nicknamed "The Red Priest" because of his wild red hair. Johann Sebastian Bach was a Lutheran, with an intense evangelical commitment, and signed most of his works "Soli Deo Gloria"—to God alone be the glory. When Bach was composing the majestic *St. Matthew Passion,* which depicts the suffering and death of Christ, he was so deeply moved that tears rolled down his face. The work is punctuated with devotional arias in which the composer pours out his intense sorrow and gratitude over Christ's suffering.

George Frideric Handel, also a Lutheran, was fifty-six years old when, at a time of crisis in his life, he closeted himself in his room to compose his famous *Messiah*. During that time, he reportedly underwent such an overwhelming spiritual experience that he sobbed with emotion, later telling his startled servant, "I did think I did see all Heaven before me, and the great God Himself."[6]

In the classical period, Franz Joseph Haydn, a Catholic, used prayer to break through writer's block. If a piece "does not make progress," he said, "I try to find out if I have erred in some way or other, thereby forfeiting grace; and I pray for mercy until I feel that I am forgiven."[7]

Among the Romantic composers, Felix Mendelssohn was a Lutheran of profound personal faith (his father converted from Judaism). Mendelssohn wrote many works celebrating the Christian faith, including his 1830 "Reformation" symphony, which ends with a ringing rendition of Martin Luther's hymn "A Mighty Fortress Is Our God."[8] Antonín Dvořák, with his lively Slavic melodies, was a sturdy believer who penned invocations in his manuscripts: They begin with the phrase "With God," and end with "God be thanked."[9]

Literature

Many of the greatest masters in Western literature have been Christian poets. Think of Dante, whose *Divine Comedy* paints a rich mural of the soul's encounter with sin (hell), suffering (purgatory), and glory (heaven). Think of John Donne, with his memorable lines "Death be not proud," "No man is an island," and "Never send to know for whom the bell tolls; it tolls for thee." Or think of John Milton, who composed the magnificent epic *Paradise Lost* to "justify the ways of God to men."

There are others we might not immediately think of, such as Samuel Taylor Coleridge, who was elevated to an icon in the drug culture of the 1960s because he composed some of his visionary poems under the influence of opium. What literature textbooks rarely mention is that Coleridge sought freedom from his opium addiction by turning to Jesus Christ.[10]

Many of the traditional stories and fairy tales of Western culture were either written by Christians or at least reflect the ethos of a Christian culture, as Vigen Guroian shows in *Tending the Heart of Virtue*. For example, the well-known story of *Pinocchio* (the original, not the Disney version) features a wooden puppet that becomes a real boy by overcoming his proclivity for lying and self-indulgence. The story expresses the profound Christian truth that those whose hearts are "wooden" with sin can become "flesh" through a process of moral regeneration.[11]

Likewise, many of the classic works of literature clearly reflect a Christian worldview. *The Count of Monte Cristo* by Alexandre Dumas traces complex themes of revenge and forgiveness. *The Swiss Family Robinson* by Johann D. Wyss, the adventures of a Swiss clergyman and his family, is rich in Christian piety. Robert Louis Stevenson's novels such as *Kidnapped* and *Treasure Island* reveal a biblical worldview. And few people raised Christian themes and the great moral questions of life more brilliantly than Fyodor Dostoyevsky.

Visual Arts

Moving to the visual arts, we can trace throughout history a variety of styles that have been used to express a Christian vision. Many medieval paintings are lovely but symbolic, composed of two-dimensional images and stylized figures against a flat gold background. Beginning with the Renaissance, painting became more natural. In the thirteenth century, theologian Thomas Aquinas rejected the otherworldliness of the Middle Ages and stressed the importance of the natural world as God's creation, arguing that "grace does not deny nature but perfects it." Aquinas's philosophy was quickly felt in the arts, exemplified by Cimabue and Giotto, who began to paint more realistically, transforming the stiff medieval icons into living individuals. [12]

The Reformation brought a greater appreciation of everyday life and work. Artists began to paint ordinary people—farmers and housewives—plying their trades against real landscapes. Painters like Albrecht Dürer, Jacob van Ruisdael, and the incomparable Rembrandt wove spiritual themes deeply into the fabric of their masterpieces of everyday life.

The Counter-Reformation produced ornate, grandiose baroque art, inspired by a new appreciation of the Incarnation—that in Christ, God was manifest in the flesh. This led to a greater appreciation for creation, especially the physical body, as a revelation of God. Artists like the Flemish painter Peter Paul Rubens depicted heavy, fleshy, solid figures to convey the idea that God reveals himself in the physical world—that it carries a weight of spiritual glory.

Among more recent artists, nearly everyone is familiar with the Dutch painter Vincent van Gogh and the intense, swirling lines of his trees, starry skies, and sunflowers. But few know that van Gogh, son of a Protestant pastor, at first believed he had a religious vocation. He worked as a missionary in the slums of London and then in the mining districts of Belgium. It was only as he began to show signs of mental instability and lost the financial support of his mission society that he turned to painting. In one fascinating work, he paints himself as Lazarus raised from the dead—a clear testimony of his faith.

·   ■   ■

From even this sketchy historical survey, we can see that Christians have played an important role in creating and sustaining the great art of our culture. Yet you would never guess it from most secular books, for they often scrub out references to the artists' religious faith. This makes it easy for secular critics to belittle Christians wrongly as artistic know-nothings.

Indeed, some historians have even accused the church of being opposed to the arts. To answer that charge, we must look again at the testimony of history. It's true that at various points through the centuries Christians have had to stand against art in various forms—not because they were against art itself, but because they opposed its misuse. For example, the church has always condemned lewd, vulgar, coarse, or immoral content in art; it has also disapproved of grandiose art projects used for display and status.

The use of images within the church has also sparked recurring controversies.[13] During the Reformation, for example, Protestant extremists rampaged through cathedrals, knocking over statues and smashing stained-glass windows. As a result, some historians have criticized the Reformation; Kenneth Clark, in his influential television series *Civilisation*, denounced it as "an unmitigated disaster" to art.[14] But even the iconoclasts must be understood within their historical context. The medieval mind attributed great spiritual power to images. Icons were venerated, kissed, and addressed in prayer. Statues of the saints were said to bleed, weep, perform miracles, and even grant indulgences, exempting sinners from the pains of purgatory.[15] Eager to fight what they saw as idolatry, the iconoclasts mistakenly thought the way to end worship of the saints was to smash statues of the saints.

But this was not the true spirit of the Reformation. Its true spirit was exemplified by Martin Luther, who, after being condemned by the emperor, risked his life by coming out of hiding to *stop* the riots that burned images and smashed statues. Luther's own favorite art form was music, and he composed many hymns, including the much-loved "A Mighty Fortress Is Our God." Luther said that "the gift of language combined with the gift of song was given to man that he should proclaim the Word of God through music."[16] John Calvin, likewise, held a high view of some of the arts: "Because sculpture and paintings are gifts of God, I seek a pure and legitimate use of each."[17]

Throughout history, believers have pursued the same search for a "pure and legitimate use" of art. How, then, was this tradition eventually pushed out of the mainstream? How did art become so secularized that today it is sometimes pursued for little more than shock value?

FROM ART TO ANTI-ART

To understand why art has lost its high purpose, we must place it in the context of a broader worldview shift (noted in chapter 11), when modern science was elevated to an idol, the sole source of knowledge. The assumption took hold that anything science cannot detect and measure must not be real, leading to an assault not only on religion but also on the realm of the imagination and intuition expressed in the arts.

It began with rationalist critics looking with disdain on all the mythological creatures so beloved of poets and painters, saying, in essence, "Come now. Science proves there are no such things as unicorns and centaurs, witches and fairies, dragons and cyclopes. Away with these myths and superstitions!" Eventually, rationalists concluded that art, by its very nature, is a falsification of reality. Isn't literature comprised of imaginary stories? Doesn't poetry employ metaphor and hyperbole? The artist might paint a sunset in all its glorious hues, but the scientist knows that a sunset is "really" nothing but the refraction of white light through dust particles in layers of air of variable density.[18] To many people it began to seem that if science is true, then art must be false, or at best merely an expression of personal emotion.

Not surprisingly, this all-out attack put artists on the defensive, and they began to question the meaning and purpose of what they did. If art did not express the truth in some way, what *did* it do? Some artists capitulated to the imperialism of science and tried to signify in their work the generalized principles that were said by science to underlie what we see and hear. This produced a trend toward ever more abstract art. Cubism, for example, with its geometrical shapes and angles, can be understood as an attempt to portray the mathematical structures underlying the physical world. In architecture, movements like the Bauhaus in Germany and de Stijl in Holland produced stark, boxlike buildings in an effort to base their art on "numbers, measurements, and abstract line."[19]

But the more typical response by artists was to concede the physical world to science and relegate art to a wholly separate world—one that it would create for itself. In fact, this was when artists first began to speak of their work in terms of "creating." Today this usage is so familiar that we do not realize that only four centuries ago it would have been shocking to speak of a poet or painter as "creating" something new. Such language seemed to equate the artist with God in his unique role as the Creator.

Understood in a biblical context, of course, there is nothing wrong with claiming that human creativity reflects the creativity of God, in whose image we are made. But torn out of that context, the notion quickly became idolatrous. In defending their work, artists began to overcompensate by claiming that art is actually *superior* to science. They contended that it is the imagination, not scientific reason, that is most godlike. And they insisted that art finds its highest form not in representing reality but in creating something completely new and imaginary. In every poem, every painting, the artist was conceived as the creator of a new universe, a microcosm in which his or her decisions were absolute. The artist's creativity, says literary scholar M. H. Abrams, was modeled on the "absolute fiat of Jehovah in the book of Genesis."[20]

Beginning in the nineteenth-century Romantic movement, the artist became idolized, and art itself became a surrogate for religion. In George Bernard Shaw's 1908 play *The Doctor's Dilemma*, a painter on his deathbed recites this credo: "I believe in Michelangelo, Velásquez, and Rembrandt, in the might of design, the mystery of color, the redemption of all things by Beauty everlasting. . . . Amen. Amen."[21] And if art was a religion, then the artist's work was beyond criticism, for "the appropriate attitude to Divinity, of course, is one of adoration," writes Abrams.[22] Ordinary people were no longer qualified to hold an opinion on whether works of art were good or bad, and art became the realm of an elite.

Thus "art inherit[ed] all the duties of the church," writes historian Jacques Barzun.[23] Artists were elevated to prophetic status in both senses of the word: as people gifted with unique insight, offering a vision of an ideal world, and as people who denounced the sins of the real world. In the first function, artists were heralded as the avant-garde of society, those who see farther than the rest of us. This attitude produced styles such as symbolism, abstraction, and expressionism—all attempts to free art from contamination by the everyday world and to construct an ideal, autonomous, quasi-spiritual world. In the second prophetic function, artists took it upon themselves to denounce the ugliness of the bourgeois, materialistic, industrialized society that had made the artists' own role so precarious. This attitude produced naturalism in art: the attempt to portray the ills of society with stark, ruthless accuracy.

Yet both prophetic functions—the vision of the ideal and the denunciation of the real—were united by a common theme: hostility toward the real world.[24] And in the end that hostility became the dominant theme as both approaches collapsed into protest, criticism, and attacks on established morality and social structures. For the autonomous world that the idealist artists were attempting to create was quite beyond their power. "It takes an omniscient God" to bring good out of evil, to make the last into the first, to bring down rulers and lift up the humble, writes Barzun. Therefore, "to a godless age, the negative part of the inversion alone remains potent."[25] All that was left was to attack and destroy, to subvert and "transgress"—or, in the poet Baudelaire's phrase, to "shock the bourgeoisie."

But art that attacks all standards ends up destroying itself—
because eventually even artistic standards are attacked and cast
aside. Which is why in the twentieth century Marcel Duchamp
could exhibit a commercially produced urinal and call it art.
Jackson Pollock dripped paint randomly on a canvas. Andy
Warhol reproduced Campbell's soup cans, and Roy Lichtenstein
painted images from comic strips. Today, artists exhibit "junk art"
or "found art," consisting of bricks, broken glass, and crushed
aluminum cans stuck on canvas or stacked into a sculpture. The
common theme in all these examples is that there is no special
standard distinguishing art from objects in the everyday world.

A parallel development in music is John Cage's "chance music,"
composed by tossing dice or some other chance mechanism. Cage
has even offered "musical" pieces with no sound. In a performance
of his work "4-33," the pianist sits at the piano, gazing at an
open score, his hands suspended above the keyboard as if ready
to begin. He does this for 4 minutes and 33 seconds, then shuts
the score and leaves the stage.

The musical parallel to "found art" is "noise music," recordings
of the background noise of the city. For example, Luigi Russolo
recorded "the palpitations of valves, the coming and going of pis-
tons, the howl of mechanical saws, the jolting of the tram on its
rails" and then signed his name to the racket.[26]

The very concept of quality, of standards, is rejected by many
of today's artists as a "paternalistic fiction," says art critic Robert
Hughes.[27] The wholesale rejection of standards has led to the
anti-art movement, exemplified by a 1993 exhibit titled "Abject
Art" at the Whitney Art Museum in New York City. The exhibit
featured what its catalog described as "abject materials such as dirt,
hair, excrement, dead animals, menstrual blood, and rotting food."
The display included a three-foot mound of synthetic excrement,
a dismembered sculpture of two women engaged in sexual acts,
and a film depicting Jesus Christ as a naked woman.

What was the point of all this? "To confront taboo issues of gender and sexuality" and other subject matter "deemed inappropriate by a conservative dominant culture," explained the catalog.[28] The show also included works that had sparked public controversy earlier: Andres Serrano's photo of a crucifix in a jar of urine, a homoerotic photograph by Robert Mapplethorpe, and a film by porn star Annie Sprinkle called *Sluts and Goddesses: How to Be a Sex Goddess in 101 Easy Steps.* In other words, the artists had no higher aim than denouncing the beliefs and standards of ordinary people, especially those who had had the audacity to voice moral protest in the past. Thus an influential branch of late-twentieth-century art has degenerated into expressions of rebellion on a par with eight-year-olds who giggle at bathroom jokes.

When even prestigious art museums display anti-art, it is clear that no one can say what art is any longer. And if art cannot be defined, then it will be destroyed. A few years ago the Manchester Academy of Fine Arts held a competition where an award was given to a watercolor entitled *Rhythm of the Trees.* The work displayed "a certain quality of color balance, composition, and technical skill," the judges decided. To their chagrin, the artist turned out to be a four-year-old child whose mother had submitted the work as a joke.[29] Artistic standards have been so thoroughly debunked that art critics honestly cannot tell the difference between the work of a trained artist and the dabbling of a small child.

And so we return to Morley Safer's question, "Is this art?" For the secular world today the answer is, "Who knows?" There are no standards by which art can even be defined.

The decline of the arts illustrates the staggering impact of a false view of *creation, fall,* and *redemption.* As we have seen, the process began when artists accepted the dogma of scientific naturalism, which set up science as the only source of genuine knowledge and relegated beauty to the subjective realm. In defense, artists claimed that realm itself as an arena where they could reign godlike in their capacity for creativity. <u>Art became a surrogate religion, with artists hurling prophetic denunciations at "sinners."</u> But it is a religion with no power of redemption, and so in the end it has degenerated into little more than assaults on mainstream society's beliefs and values.

FOR GLORY AND FOR BEAUTY

Christianity alone has the resources to restore the arts to their proper place, for Christianity is a worldview that supports human creativity yet does so with appropriate humility. Made in the image of the Creator, humans find fulfillment in being creative in their own sphere. Yet unlike God, the human artist does not create out of nothing. "Human creativity is derivative and reflective, working within the bounds of what God has formed," writes Os Guinness.[30] As C. S. Lewis put it, "an author should never conceive of himself as bringing into existence beauty or wisdom which did not exist before, but simply and solely as trying to embody in terms of his own art some reflection of that eternal Beauty and Wisdom."[31] Because of the Fall, we do not have a clear glimpse of Beauty or Wisdom; we see only a poor reflection. But because of Christ's redemption, the arts can be restored.

Scripture treats the arts as a divine calling. In his book *State of the Arts: From Bezalel to Mapplethorpe,* Gene Edward Veith tells of a great Old Testament artist named Bezalel. God chose Bezalel and "filled him with the Spirit of God, with skill, ability and knowledge in all kinds of crafts" (Exod. 31:3). Typically when we think of people being chosen by God and filled with the Spirit, we think of people sent into the ministry or to the mission field. But Bezalel was called to work as an artist, filled with the Spirit "to make artistic designs for work in gold, silver and bronze, . . . in all kinds of craftsmanship," in order to beautify the tabernacle, the early Hebrew tent of worship (Exod. 31:4-5). And Bezalel was not alone. Repeatedly in Exodus we find references to people to whom "the Lord had given skill" as craftspeople.[32]

Similarly, the Lord tells Moses to make garments for the priests "for glory and for beauty" (Exod. 28:2, 40, NASB). <u>This ought to be the slogan of every Christian artist, musician, or writer: to work for the glory of God and the creation of beauty.</u>

Given these scriptural principles, Christians have a responsibility to support artists and promote the arts. Sadly, many believers never think much about the arts until they discover that their taxes are being used by the National Endowment for the Arts to fund some blasphemous or indecent project. Even then, our response tends to be economic or political (boycotts and protests) rather than aesthetic. This makes it easy for critics to paint us as anti-intellectual, anticultural reactionaries.[33]

But God does not call his people simply to run around putting out fires after the secular world has lighted them. He calls us to light our own fires, to renew culture. And the best way to drive out bad art is to encourage good art. "If you do not read good books, you will read bad ones," said Lewis. "If you reject aesthetic satisfactions, you will fall into sensual satisfactions."[34] Since human beings are created in the image of God, they *will* create culture of one kind or another. The only question is whether it will be a decadent culture or a godly one.

To make it a godly culture, we must start by finding ways to reconnect with our own literary and artistic heritage. Go to concerts, read classic literature, visit art museums. Get to know the composers, writers, and painters who have been inspired by Christian faith. Enjoy the arts not only as art but also as media that speak to us spiritually. Louise Cowan, coeditor of *Invitation to the Classics,* tells how she lost her childhood faith in university courses on religion—only to regain it later in courses on literature. Tracing the Christian themes in Shakespeare spoke to her heart in a way that discursive theological treatises had failed to do.[35]

If the classics seem remote, begin with more recent or contemporary artists who have faced the challenge of standing against the tide of a secular culture and who give a powerful witness to Christian truth in our own century. For example, among twentieth-century composers who have created musical masterpieces reflecting their Christian faith is Francis Poulenc, who was a witty playboy of French music until a friend's death plunged him into despair and then a profound religious experience, which inspired his music from then on. Igor Stravinsky shocked the world with his strange, discordant music, but later in life he experienced a religious conversion and wrote compositions such as *Credo,* the Nicene Creed put to music. Among contemporary composers, acquaint yourself with John Tavener (not to be confused with the Renaissance composer Taverner mentioned on page 249) and Arvo Pärt, Orthodox believers who express the church's ancient musical heritage in a modern idiom. Sample the new renditions of ancient and medieval sacred music that have become a widespread fad today. What an irony that while many churches are striving to be relevant by imitating secular styles, the church's own musical heritage has taken the secular world by storm.[36]

In literature, the twentieth century has given us T. S. Eliot, often celebrated in literature textbooks as the first modernist poet. But few books mention that Eliot became a Christian in middle age, after which he wrote such significant works as "Ash Wednesday" and *Four Quartets.* The spangled language of the Jesuit priest and poet Gerard Manley Hopkins calls us to worship: "The world is charged with the grandeur of God. It will flame out, like shining from shook foil."[37] Christians should also be familiar with contemporary poets such as Luci Shaw, John Leax, Paul Mariani, and Irina Ratushinskaya.[38]

Among fiction writers, Christians should explore the riches of C. S. Lewis, especially his space trilogy and Narnia stories; the romances of George Macdonald (Lewis's mentor); the detective

fiction of Dorothy Sayers; the supernatural novels of Charles
Williams; and the fantasy of J. R. R. Tolkien, especially his
incomparable *Lord of the Rings* trilogy. On this side of the Atlan-
tic, the works of Walker Percy, Flannery O'Connor, and Allen
Tate represent the Catholic literary renaissance of the 1940s.
Among contemporary writers, Christians should get to know
Larry Woiwode, Frederick Buechner, Ron Hanson, Annie
Dillard, Walter Wangerin Jr., and Stephen Lawhead, to name a
few. And we must not ignore the powerful novels of Alexander
Solzhenitsyn—works that not only expose the horrors of the
Soviet prison camp system but also reveal the response of the
human heart to unspeakable suffering.

Visual artists have likewise expressed the classic Christian faith
in modern forms. Among twentieth-century painters, some of the
most beautiful and tender works have been rendered by Georges
Rouault, who as an adult became an evangelical Catholic. He used
the language of modern art to paint images that are reminiscent of
stained-glass windows, with stark black lines and luminous colors,
an exceptional balance of tradition and innovation. Contemporary
artists who express the drama of divine grace in powerful images
include Sandra Bowden, Ted Prescott, and William Congdon.

Corporately, the church can take a role in supporting the arts
by involving artists in their services: They can invite musicians
to write and play music; ask poets and writers to create dramatic
presentations for religious holidays; encourage artists to design
banners and bulletins and other works of beauty for the sanctu-
ary. One Christmas, my colleague T. M. Moore, president of
Chesapeake Theological Seminary, organized a powerful drama-
tization of John Milton's ode "On the Morning of Christ's
Nativity." The production involved the choir and other musicians, painters (who prepared backdrops and staging), a stage
crew, dancers, and actors.

Some churches focus on the arts by holding annual arts festivals that feature workshops, displays, readings, and concerts. Other churches designate a room or hallway as an art gallery, where they display the work of congregation members or of traveling art shows. We should also make a point of supporting organizations of Christian artists such as the Lamb's Players and the Washington Performing Arts Group.

Finally, every Christian family can make the home a place where art and culture are nurtured. When children are surrounded by the best in music, art, and literature, they grow up learning to appreciate the best. Play classical music in your home. Hang reproductions of historic works of art on your walls. Involve your children in reading literature that inspires their moral imagination. Good stories do what scolding or lecturing can never do: They make us *want* to be good. As child psychologist Bruno Bettelheim notes, children's moral choices are based not on abstract standards of right and wrong but on the people they admire and want to emulate. "The question for the child is not, 'Do I want to be good?'" Bettelheim writes, "but 'Who do I want to be like?'"[39] As children read, they encounter characters they can admire and identify with, and as children vicariously make choices along with the characters, their own character is shaped.

No one should grow up without the arts, for they move us as whole persons, not just our cognitive faculties. I discovered the joys of classical literature only after becoming a Christian, when my conversion gave me a hunger for truth in all its forms. My all-time favorite novel is *The Brothers Karamazov* by Fyodor Dostoyevsky, which raises the great moral dilemmas debated by philosophers through the ages and boils them down to one unforgettable dictum: "If there is no God, then everything is permitted." Recently I also determined to educate myself on classical music, and as a start, purchased a set of CDs of famous masterpieces. Although I have always had something of a tin ear, these recordings have opened a new world to me.

Music, literature, and art offer us a window through which we can appreciate God's truth more fully.

∎   ∎   ∎

Several years ago, a nun in a black habit appeared on television talking about famous works of art. At first, viewers were taken aback, but today *Sister Wendy's Odyssey* is an immensely popular series. And why *shouldn't* a nun be an art critic? Who more than Christians have good reason to appreciate and create works of art?

It's time for the church to reclaim its artistic heritage and to offer the spiritual direction that contemporary artists need if they are to create works "for glory and for beauty," works that inspire and ennoble a culture. <u>For what happens in high culture soon filters down to shape popular culture.</u> The degradation of classical art and music has caused a parallel degradation of television and popular music—but even here, in what seems to be a moral wasteland, Christians can bring renewal and redemption.

One Christian is doing just that, with surprising results.

DISCUSSION QUESTIONS

CHAPTER 11

1 Has the "dogmatic faith" of a naturalistic worldview colored or adversely affected your faith? When, how, and why?

2 How can the reign of scientific naturalism lead to the "abolition of man" or to an inhuman culture?

3 Succinctly summarize the basic contradictions of scientific naturalism.

4 What six elements of a Christian view of nature made modern science possible (see "The Nature of Nature")? Why are these points important for you to know if you're talking with a skeptic who dabbles in science?

5 How can you go about reforming science as presented in your schools or community?

6 How and why would you encourage Christian young people to pursue a career in science?

CHAPTER 12

7 Tell of a time when the arts (music, painting, poetry, . . .) touched you deeply. Try to articulate the message and power of the piece for you. What "truth" did it speak to your spirit?

8 Chapter 13 notes that art "can shape our thoughts, move our emotions, enlarge our imaginations." If possible, play a portion of Górecki's *Symphony of Sorrowful Songs*. How does it speak to you? How does it touch or change your thoughts, emotions, or imagination? (If you cannot provide the Górecki piece, play another musical selection, written by a Christian, that you find very powerful. Suggestions: the ending of *The Messiah* by George Frideric Handel; portions of Beethoven's *Ninth Symphony*; in a contemporary vein, Michael Card's *Job Suite*).

CHAPTER 13

9 Compare the classical understanding of the arts with the contemporary understanding that results in dissonant music and abstract art.

10 Why should the arts be important to Christians? Do you find that the arts indeed *are* important to most Christians? If you see a disparity, what do you think is behind it?

11 What caused the arts to veer off the path marked out by many exemplary Christian artists of earlier centuries?

12 What are the consequences of art being viewed as a religion?

13 Read aloud Exodus 35:20-21; 35:30–36:7. (The unread verses list gifts and materials brought by the people.) Who was involved in this artistic endeavor? Who did what, and for what purpose?

14 Do you see in this passage any guidelines or principles that might help you *(a)* encourage artists or *(b)* hone and use your own talents?

15 Brainstorm ways you can use the arts in your home, your church, and your community "to glorify God and edify one another." This might include sharing lists of favorite books, authors, composers, musicians, and artists, or starting a lending library.

ROLE PLAY
Refer to the directions for role play, at the end of session 1 (pp. 52–53).

CONVERSATION STARTERS

a. Assume a schoolteacher says, "Christianity and science are like oil and water. They don't mix—never have, never will."

b. Assume a skeptic says, "You Christians, you're always tearing down—censor this, ban that—and so negative all the time. Don't you have any appreciation for creativity?"

CLOSING SUMMARY
What is the one thing you want to remember from what you read (or heard or did) in this session?

Consider sharing this with the group.

MEN AND WOMEN OF A DIFFERENT TYPE

TOUCHED BY A MIRACLE

As you read chapter 14, keep the following
questions in mind:
- To what mission did Martha feel called? How and why?
- What did Martha's success require of her?

Martha first came to the immortal hosts' attention one night
when I was assigned to *In Extremis* (At the Point of Death)
Watch. The galleries opened up to a view of a suburban California
kitchen where a young woman was actually prostrating herself on
her Mexican tile floor, her face to the ground, her arms spread
wide in humility and penitence, as she gave her career over to
God. Acting out of spiritual yearnings so deep that they overcame
her self-consciousness about making dramatic gestures, the young
woman was expressing her desire with her whole body—her entire
being. She definitely wanted God to see, hear, and answer.

"This one is serious," the Glory announced. "Pay attention."

That single moment in eternity marked the beginning of a
miracle. Or perhaps it was the miracle itself. I still can't decide.

Before I tell you about this miracle, I should probably tell you
who *I* am. Imagine me as a guardian angel. A trustworthy guide.
A means of viewing Martha's experience with both the telescopic
wide-angle lens of eternity and the telephoto close-ups of life on
earth.

What confuses me about miracles is the human factor. Otherwise, I know well enough what they are. Miracles occur when God acts in human history, crossing the boundary from eternity into time, bringing about what can't be caused in any other way. Across the millennia, I've seen my share of such events, often in times and places so dark that only a divine light could reach them. But how God enfolds the human will into these actions confounds and puzzles me. Perhaps that's why I was told to pay attention to Martha: to learn more about how God chooses to work through men and women.

Martha made this gesture of total surrender relatively early in her Christian life, only three years after her conversion. Perhaps her desperation stemmed from the fact that she works in Hollywood, where God's voice sounds very much like a voice crying in the wilderness. Perhaps she was crumbling under the pressure of a life lived on the free-fall terms of "the industry," where there's no guarantee of work, no regular paycheck, no company benefits, no health plan, no nothing. It's an industry like no other.

So Martha needed a peace like no other, a confidence with no illusions. Realizing that only the God who hung the world could lift her up, she surrendered herself that night to a God who can make even Hollywood holy ground.

■   ■   ■

Martha Williamson came to Hollywood straight out of college. She paid her dues and plenty of them, working as a personal assistant to various producers. She did everything from making coffee to picking up the producer's laundry, from tracking down talent to fending off wanna-bes. Long after most of the industry had discovered computers, Martha was still typing multiple scripts on an ancient typewriter for a highly successful weekly variety show.[1]

By the time she became a Christian in 1981, she was a trusted associate producer, helping to make real production decisions—

and her change of heart immediately declared itself in the workplace. The company head who had taken her under his wing
began calling her "the Jesus girl."

During the early 1980s, Martha joined a professional association of Hollywood directors and writers who met regularly for
Christian fellowship and encouragement. The association prayed
regularly that God would perform a miracle in Hollywood, that
he would empower a clear Christian witness out of the heart of
the entertainment industry itself.

People actually stood up in these prayer meetings, scripts in
hand. They had acquired the rights to C. S. Lewis's *The Magician's Nephew* or some other piece of Christian allegory and
wanted the group to pray that they would get a movie produced
and help change the direction of the entire motion-picture industry. The group would then pray specifically for the success of the
project.

Although Martha muttered "amen" to these prayers, she was
really thinking, *Fat chance.* She doubted that these dreams would
ever come true. She was already a Hollywood insider, taking
"pitch-meetings" so fast she could hardly remember their content.
She knew the people who ran the studios, and she knew they
didn't work the way her well-intentioned friends hoped. A project
conveying a Christian message would have to succeed in the larger
culture *before* any Hollywood movers and shakers would consider
doing it. Maybe someone would produce a story on, say, the civil
rights movement, highlighting the faith dimension, but never *The
Magician's Nephew.* The powers that be had no sense of mission.
They were there to make money.

And frankly, so was Martha. While others talked of transforming the Hollywood culture, she had to admit that most of the time
she just wanted to get paid. That was hard enough in this town.

Yet she did have her own dreams. She believed she had the talent to write funny, ironic comedy and drama. She also believed

she could produce scripts for network television. She did not want to go to work for a Christian film company. She did not want to write about biblical characters, creating celluloid to fill up dead TV hours on Sunday mornings. She wanted to write prime-time shows from a Christian perspective.

She determined that she would give it a try, and she made the move from associate producer to writer. And it was shortly after becoming a writer that she lay facedown on her floor, acknowledging her utter dependence on God. She had quickly come to understand that planning her own career would prove maddening, and she vowed to God that she would not make any extraordinary efforts to hustle after work. She would not plan complicated strategies. She would do what God put before her and let him take her where she was meant to go. She believed that he knew the deepest desires of her heart and that he knew what he wanted for her. She would entrust everything to God's care.

·   ·   ·

As we in the heavenly hosts see things, the miracle was Martha's inner transformation. But what most humans would see as the miracle began when the CBS television network offered Martha a chance to be the executive producer of a show called *Angel's Attic*. She turned them down—primarily because CBS had just turned her down on another project and she was angry about it.

Martha had spent the past weeks working as a "fixer" for a television pilot called *Under One Roof*. The show had great potential. It starred the illustrious James Earl Jones and dealt with the realistic issues of one family living in Seattle. Just the type of dramatic series Martha had always wanted to work on. The pilot had turned out well, and it was just the quality programming that network executives always say they're looking for.

Yet, incredibly, CBS had turned it down. Then, only four hours later, they sent Martha the pilot for *Angel's Attic*.

The network was determined to do "an angel show." Polls showed that 70 percent of the American public believe in angels and that almost any product about angels could be marketed successfully. But when Martha watched the tape CBS had sent over, she discovered that it featured angels who quarreled among themselves and complained about the Almighty. The show was patterned after a cop show as much as anything, with God as the thickheaded superior and the angels as renegades who got the job done only by breaking bureaucratic rules. The old formula was to be bolstered, supposedly, with special effects showing the angels hovering in the air—wings and all. Even worse, the angels weren't even real angels. They were recently deceased people sent to earth for unknown reasons.

Martha respected the executives at CBS. They had nurtured her career for many years, challenging her to write from her heart, supporting her work on *Jack's Place* starring Hal Linden. So she couldn't fathom how they could turn down high quality like *Under One Roof* yet be determined to pick up a trite, formulaic show like *Angel's Attic*.

That night on her way to a dinner appointment, Martha carried on a furious mental debate with herself. Clearly, she would have to rethink her working relationship with CBS. Another network had already offered her a job, which represented a bird in the hand. Yet she had been hanging on to hopes that *Under One Roof* would be picked up so that she could continue on with CBS, doing her own kind of show.

Martha grabbed her car phone and dialed the vice president who had sent her the *Angel's Attic* tape. The network's offer was making her crazy, she told him, and she just wanted to get the issue out of the way. Then she could sort out whether she had a future at CBS (which she probably didn't) or whether she would write for the other network (which she probably would).

"I'm sorry," she told the vice president. "I know you've invested a lot in this show, and you've got a promising cast. But it's just not the kind of thing I want to do."

"But that's why we sent it to you, Martha. It needs to be turned into the type of program you and other talented people *will* want to do."

"No. I'm sorry, but no. We can have lunch next week, and I'll give you whatever advice I can to pass along to the person you hire."

The following week Martha talked with her agent, who reassured her that the writing job for the other network looked like a done deal, although in her business nothing was really nailed down until the electronic transfer rolled the digits into your account. To bring closure to her working relationship with CBS, she had lunch with the executives there. She felt somewhat dejected at ending such a good working relationship, and right up until the last moment, even as she was stepping into her car and saying good-bye to her CBS colleagues, she found herself giving them advice about their angel show.

That afternoon her agent called to say that the details for the job at the other network were being worked out, although the producers wanted to change her title, signaling that they were bargaining away some of the creative control they had promised. But it was the same money. Maybe even more money. All this was business as usual.

The next morning everything changed.

■   ■   ■

If I were a TV angel instead of a real one, right at this point in the story I would make a dramatic entrance. I would say to Martha, "I am an angel, sent by God," and tell her what God wanted her to do. But as it was, she had no idea I was watching over her. She only knew, with a sudden but absolutely certain conviction, that God wanted her to work on that angel show.

During the twelve years of her Christian experience, Martha had grown more and more attentive to the Lord's voice, to the point where she thought she could usually distinguish God's leading from her own wishes. For her, a word from God did not announce itself gradually. It did not rise up over time like an intuition or insight. For her, a word from God came all at once . . . and then it kept demanding obedience. Unless she obeyed at once, she knew she would be miserable. If Martha had made any progress at all in her spiritual life, it was learning to minimize the time between hearing God's direction and acting on it.

That's what happened on this crucial morning. At some point during the time she got out of bed, drank her morning coffee, and brushed her teeth, she simply *knew* that God wanted her to do *Angel's Attic*. She even suspected that the angel show was the lifetime opportunity for which God had been preparing her.

She realized that she hadn't prayed about it before turning it down. Always a mistake. With that, she confessed to God that she had been wrong and told him that she heard him now.

Was this a genuine miracle? With so little fanfare? No sound and light show? No special effects? Yet what else can explain the perfect alignment of the public's angel craze, the clumsy pilot, the network's enthusiasm, Martha's relationship with the network, and her relationship with God?

Martha called her agent but was informed that she would now have to "candidate" for the CBS job, which only yesterday had been hers for the asking.

"Okay," she said. "Set up the meeting."

Her agent called back. "Martha, the CBS people can't see you until next Wednesday. The agreement with the other network is buttoned up, but you have to sign it tomorrow. It's good for only twenty-four hours. You're going to have to take this now."

"I can't."

"Are you crazy? You're turning down a great show and a

whopping paycheck for a chance at producing what everyone agrees is a turkey? This isn't like you. This isn't smart."

"Set up the meeting with CBS. I'm sure I'm going to get the job with them."

"Martha, you threw that show back in their face. Why would they give it to you now?"

"I know this all sounds crazy, but it's a God thing. Just set up the meeting."

Martha didn't scribble down her notes about how to fix *Angel's Attic* until the morning of her CBS meeting. Still, she went into the meeting supremely confident. If God had told her to candidate for the show, she reasoned, he was going to give her the job.

At the meeting, the executives sat at a semicircular table, including the then president of entertainment, Peter Tortorici. These were not people who had any affinity for spiritual things. How would they take to what she had to say?

"We're surprised, Martha," Tortorici said, after introductions, "but we're glad you decided to rethink your decision about being involved in the project. What would you do with the show?"

"Every successful show has its own dramatic rules," she began, "but the pilot doesn't demonstrate what those rules are. Or if it does, the rules aren't working. For example, you can't have angels who disagree with God's orders. Angels are messengers of God. They do only what he says."

She sensed the executives bracing at her confident tone, her assumption that she knew what angels do.

"Will we see God giving the angels their orders?" one executive asked tentatively.

"No," Martha said. "No one sees God. That's why, if God wants someone to see a celestial being, he sends angels. And angels aren't people who have recently died. They're angels from the beginning of time."

"But why would people want to watch a show about angels if

they can't imagine becoming one?" The men and women around the table looked troubled by this thought.

"Because the show shouldn't be about the angels. That's the whole problem. The show has to be about whether the people they appear to are willing to do what God wants. That's where the drama is," she said firmly. "And we have to confront all the big questions. Why did God let my baby die? Where is God in the midst of terminal illness? Why doesn't God take care of the poor? Why doesn't God stop evil people from victimizing the defenseless?"

"You think we can take on issues like that?" they asked, surprised.

"We have to," she said. "And we have to do it from the standpoint that God loves everyone and wants the best for them. That he's intervening through his angelic messengers so that our characters, who are in critical situations, will know he loves them and will then do the right thing. You know I'm a Christian, but I'm not proposing we make this a Christian show. What I am proposing is that the dramatic rules of the show follow what all the major religions believe about God—that he loves us and cares for us."

She was on a roll now. "And there's no doubt that there's an audience for this," she said. "Religious people are tired of seeing themselves portrayed as fanatics, hucksters, serial killers, or just plain stupid. The audience for this show could use some real *inspiration* for a change."

The executives suddenly turned to specifics. *A good sign or a bad one?* Martha wondered.

"Can you reshoot some scenes and adapt the original pilot?"

"No."

She watched their faces as they tried to swallow a two-million-dollar loss.

"What about the cast?"

"That's your strongest point. Roma Downey and Della Reese

are great, but you've got to take Roma's sincerity and Della's authority and give it a chance to brew its own kind of chemistry. There's got to be a tough sympathy there, a mentoring relationship. They can't be antagonists."

"Martha, why don't you wait in the office next door for a few minutes," said Peter Tortorici. "We need to discuss a few things here."

When he called Martha back to the meeting, he said, "We want you to do everything you just said. But we need a first episode in three weeks. As of right now, you've got an office and a parking space, and you'd better get started. Deal?"

·   ■   ■

Whether or not the CBS executives were subject to divine influence, not even an angelic voice can say. Martha chalked up their openness to desperation. They needed the show, but they knew it wouldn't work without someone who had a real vision for it. Yet Martha could not have known this beforehand. So perhaps the real miracle here was her determined obedience even in the face of losing her immediate prospects for employment, along with her willingness to play a divine long shot. I would like to claim credit myself for Martha's being *Touched by an Angel,* as her show came to be titled, but to be honest, God sent me only to be an observer in this case.

For more than a year, *Touched by an Angel* remained a long shot. The terrible original pilot had produced a media "buzz" that nearly sealed the show's death warrant before Martha's efforts saw the light of a cathode-ray tube. Even then, CBS couldn't find the right time slot for the show. For an entire season they moved it around the television schedule, with the result that its ratings were dismal.

When the show finally went on hiatus (the seasonal break in production), it looked as if *Touched by an Angel* would be canceled after only one season. Martha was dead tired from pulling together scripts, cast, and crew, and she only wanted to rest and regather her energies. But she received another word from the Lord: She needed to campaign for the show's renewal with every bit of energy she could muster.

With the help of coworkers and Hollywood friends, Martha jetted around the country, conducting a media blitz to raise the show's viewership for the final two episodes, which had not yet aired. The viewer ratings didn't rise significantly for those two episodes, but they didn't slip either. Television people would recognize that as a positive sign: The show's viewership was loyal, hunting out the show whenever and wherever it appeared on the schedule.

Still, at its best *Touched by an Angel* attracted only a twelve share in the Nielsen television ratings. No one except Martha and her loyal supporters believed it would be picked up for another season.

Finally, Martha went to New York and trolled the halls of the network, grabbing anyone who would talk to her about the show's fate. Eventually she gained access to the network president, and while her appeals in other venues had been to the bottom line, here she spoke to the man's soul.

"When you are lying on your deathbed," she ventured to say, "you won't be thinking how glad you were that you renewed *Walker, Texas Ranger.* But you'll never forget renewing *Touched by an Angel,* and you'll always be glad."

The president made no promises, and to this day Martha does not know what finally tipped the balance. That part of the miracle remains hidden in someone else's heart. But the network's unexpected decision to renew *Touched by an Angel* for a second season gave it the chance it needed to become the enormously popular show it is today.

Martha Williamson's life was touched by a miracle. And so are the millions of people who watch the results of her work every week.

.   .   .

What has this celestial observer learned from all this? God's unending determination to make his love known to human beings. What strange cultural forces God will use—even an angel fad to bring about his will. And what unlikely opportunities he will seize—even an ill-conceived TV show—to proclaim his love.

Every generation of Christians faces unique challenges. . . . The challenge of living with popular culture may well be as serious for modern Christians as persecution and plagues were for the saints of earlier centuries.

KENNETH A. MYERS

CHAPTER 15

DOES THE DEVIL HAVE ALL THE GOOD MUSIC?

As you read chapter 15, keep the following questions in mind:

- What is, and is not, the harm of popular culture?
- What is so frighteningly real about the scenario of Aldous Huxley's *Brave New World*?
- How did a shift in worldview contribute to a decline in popular culture?
- What can we do to link ourselves and our lifestyles to truth, goodness, and beauty?

Several years ago I was the speaker at a prayer breakfast held during the National Association of Broadcasters Convention. The young woman seated next to me at the table was pleasant and engaging—a writer, she told me—determined to produce a successful prime-time television show boldly expressing Christian themes. I smiled, thinking, *How noble . . . but how naïve.* And I wondered how many bright, young, open-faced midwesterners have had their idealism smashed on the rocks of Hollywood.

"Well, you hang in there," I said, intending to bolster her hopes a bit before she gave up and retreated to some safe Christian publishing house.

"Oh, I will," she replied cheerily. "In fact, I had one trial run for my show, and then the network bumped it. But I'm pounding on doors to get it back on the air. I know God is in this."

Suddenly she had my attention. "What did you say your name was?"

"Martha Williamson," she smiled. "And I'm going to do it. Really."

Oh me of little faith.

Many Christians grumble about television trash and the lack of wholesome fare for families, but Martha Williamson rolled up her sleeves and did something about it. Her story is all the more remarkable for the fact that there is nothing to set her apart from the many talented, creative people in Hollywood—nothing except her dogged faith. She is a great example of how Christians are called to use their gifts to make a difference in shaping American popular culture.

THE MEDIUM IS THE MESSAGE

The call to redeem popular culture is surely one of the most difficult challenges Christians face today. For, thanks to modern communications technology, popular culture has become intrusively pervasive. It is virtually impossible to avoid the culture's influence through advertisements, tapes, CDs, television, radio, movies, magazines, computer games, video arcades, and the Internet. Popular culture is everywhere, shaping our tastes, our language, our values.

When I was a kid, my exposure to popular culture was limited—the occasional Saturday afternoon Western at the local movie theater, the Green Hornet radio serials, the Hardy Boys adventure series, and the *Saturday Evening Post*. That was it. But today popular culture beckons from every billboard, blares from the television on countless channels around the clock, pops up on our PCs, blasts from the car radio, and bedecks our T-shirts and tennis shoes. None of us can escape it.

As popular culture has spread, its content has coarsened shockingly. No one needs to be told that over the past three or four decades the level of sex and violence has risen sharply in movies, music, television, and even comic books. Of course, Christians have always had to deal with things that were vulgar, lewd, or coarse, but for the most part, we could simply avoid them. Today that is virtually impossible.

But while most of us realize how dangerous it is to expose ourselves to immoral *content*, we often fail to realize that the *form* of popular culture affects us just as much—not only *what* is said but also *how* it is said. This is what educator Marshall McLuhan meant by his famous adage, "The medium is the message."[1] The best way to grasp this is by a comparison to high culture. A sonnet or a symphony has a complex structure that takes some effort to understand. It challenges us; we have to work to appreciate it. That's why we study Shakespeare in English classes and Mozart in music-appreciation courses. But who takes courses to understand Madonna? Who needs to? Who takes Soap Opera 101? Who needs Cliff's Notes to understand a Harlequin romance?

These forms require virtually no intellectual discipline or effort. If anything, popular culture strives to *avoid* making the audience work. It's intended to be simple, entertaining, and easy to understand, offering immediate gratification. It grabs our attention with catchy lines, loud intrusive music, and sensational visual effects, all designed to bypass the mind and appeal directly to the senses and emotions. Moreover, popular books and television shows are often written to a formula, with predictable plots and stereotypical characters, so we all know what's going to happen. Readers and viewers glide along without having to think much about where they are going—they just enjoy the scenery along the way. This is cotton candy for the mind.

Now, there's nothing wrong with a little cotton candy in an otherwise balanced diet. But there *is* danger in a steady consumption of junk food. For starters, you may lose your taste for more whole-some food. And with mental cotton candy, that is perilously easy to do. Popular culture easily becomes addictive, destroying our taste for more substantial fare. It may become so handy to let the kids watch cartoons and videos that we no longer discipline ourselves to read classic literature to them. We may get so used to hearing a steady backdrop of popular music on the radio that we no longer put on CDs of Bach and Mozart and learn to appreciate classical music.

Worse, popular culture can break down even our ability to tackle more challenging mental tasks. By focusing on immediate experience, it erodes the skills needed for sustained attention. By offering easy consumption and emotional gratification, it discour-ages us from analyzing what we see and hear. What we must understand is that each form of media encourages a different kind of mental process, as Neil Postman explains in *Amusing Ourselves to Death*. In reading, for example, the printed page unfolds its narrative line by line, training us in a coherent, linear, rational thought process. By contrast, television reduces complex events to fast-moving images, fostering a short attention span, disjointed thinking, and emotional responses.[2] Popular culture is like a nar-cotic: Over time it can actually impair the brain's capacity.

Most troubling, however, is the impact popular culture may have on our spiritual lives. Attention to the spiritual realm requires an entirely different set of skills and sensibilities than do the easy distractions of pop culture. Studying God's Word takes mental concentration and discipline. Prayer and meditation require focused recollection and the ability to shut out the jangle of every-day events. Thus, pop culture (even Christian versions of it) may erode the skills and disciplines needed for a robust spiritual life.

Scripture suggests this principle in the second commandment, when it warns against making graven images. When Postman read the Bible as a young man, he writes, he wondered why God would prohibit his people from representing the deity in visual images. "It is a strange injunction to include as part of an ethical system," he says, "*unless its author assumed a connection between forms of human communication and the quality of a culture.*"[3] Precisely. In the ancient world, each nation had its own tribal deities, represented in statues and images. By contrast, the Bible teaches the existence of a universal deity—a concept so abstract that it simply cannot be expressed in concrete images. "The God of the Jews was to exist in the Word and through the Word, an unprecedented conception requiring the highest order of abstract thinking." This radical conception of God, Postman conjectures, could enter the culture only if concrete representations of God were banned.[4]

In other words, a culture's forms of communication are a major influence in shaping the way people think—even the way they think about God.

What this means is that as long as the content is not immoral, there's no harm in popular culture itself. Watching a good television drama, tapping our feet to the latest Christian pop music, or losing ourselves in a paperback novel for light entertainment can be a pleasant diversion. Many works of popular culture even express genuine moral or spiritual truths, as we shall see later. There *is* harm, however, in making a steady diet of pop culture, because it encourages an unreflective, emotional response to life instead of disciplined thought and analysis—which can lead, in turn, to a simplistic spiritual life. Popular culture fits under the category of things the apostle Paul referred to when he said, "'Everything is permissible'—but not everything is beneficial" (1 Cor. 10:23). We can enjoy cultural "junk food" as long as we have trained ourselves to be selective, as long as we don't fall into habits of escapism and distraction, and as long as we set limits so that the sensibilities of popular culture do not shape our character.

The dangers of modern popular culture were foretold by Aldous Huxley in his classic anti-utopian novel *Brave New World*—which contrasts sharply with another anti-utopian novel, George Orwell's *1984*. Orwell warned of a communist government that would ban books; Huxley warned of a Western government that wouldn't *need* to ban them—because no one would read serious books anymore. Orwell predicted a society deprived of information by government censors; Huxley predicted a society oversaturated by information from electronic media—until people lost the ability to analyze what they saw and heard. Orwell feared a system that concealed the truth under government propaganda and lies; Huxley feared a system where people stopped caring about the truth and cared only about being entertained. Orwell described a world where people were controlled by inflicting pain; Huxley imagined a world where people were controlled by inflicting pleasure.[5] Both novels have proven to be uncannily accurate—Orwell describing the totalitarian plague of our century, Huxley the sickness of affluent free societies.

Huxley goes on to castigate the civil libertarians in the West who are ever on the alert against an externally imposed tyranny but who have failed to realize how easily we can be seduced into a mindless oppression by technology: These guardians of liberty, he says, have "failed to take into account man's almost infinite appetite for distraction."[6] And nowhere is the appetite for distraction more seductively tantalized by the banal, mindless entertainment of pop culture than in America.

How, then, can we protect ourselves and our children against this soft oppression? Only by understanding where popular culture came from, how it developed, what worldview it expresses, and what underlying ideas and trends have led us to this point.

MENTAL JUNK FOOD

The first step in examining the worldview behind popular culture is to find a workable definition of the term. Many people think of pop culture as the contemporary form of folk culture, but that is not accurate. Folk culture consists of the stories and myths, tales and songs that emerge from a particular people's way of life. America's authentic folk culture harks back to colonial days and includes such forms as square dancing, spirituals, banjo tunes like "Oh My Darlin' Clementine," tall tales about Davy Crockett and Paul Bunyan, arts and crafts. Pop culture, on the other hand, is relatively new, without roots in any ethnic or folk tradition; it is mass produced and standardized, shaped more by marketing surveys than by the spontaneous expression of a people's experience.

Kenneth Myers offers a helpful analogy in *All God's Children and Blue Suede Shoes,* comparing cultures to cuisine.[7] Folk culture, with its songs and tales, is like ethnic food—German sausage, Norwegian lutefisk, Russian borscht—arising out of a traditional way of life. But pop culture is like fast food, heavy with salt, sugar, and artificial colors and flavors. It looks attractive, has a strong flavor, but offers little real nutrition. Fast foods like Coke and McDonald's burgers are not rooted in America's distinctive cultural heritage but can be imposed wholesale onto any existing culture—and indeed *have* been transplanted across the globe. By analogy, pop culture belongs to no particular ethnic group but rather invades all cultures. For example, when refugees from southern China were rescued from shark-infested waters by the U.S. Coast Guard, the only English word they knew was *MTV.*

Where did this new, mass-produced, standardized form of popular culture originate? In large measure it is the result of the same theories of art traced in chapter 13. As we explained there, when science was anointed as the only path to truth (scientism), art was demoted to subjective fantasy, and artists were put on the defensive. They responded by crafting a philosophy that eventually cast art as a tool of subversion, a means of thumbing their noses at conventional society. This philosophy of art-as-rebellion migrated from Europe to America, where it infiltrated our own folk traditions. In music, for example, our ethnic culture had produced jazz, blues, folk, and gospel music, but as avant-garde philosophy invaded, the result was rock 'n' roll, Elvis, the Beatles, the Rolling Stones . . . and the rest is history. And as the new philosophy of art gained the upper hand, the relentless attack on mainstream values built to such a fever pitch of profanity and perversity that today we have lyrics that glorify death and violence.

The important point is that the decline in popular culture was not merely a result of declining public taste; it was a direct result of a change in worldview. Art began to champion everything opposed to the Enlightenment and science: It exalted emotion over reason, instinct over rationality, sensation over thinking, primitivism over civilization. Taught first in art colleges, this avant-garde philosophy eventually found its way into recording studios. In fact, a number of influential British rock musicians actually started out as art students, among them Keith Richards, Peter Townshend, Eric Clapton, and John Lennon. As a result, the Beatles, the Rolling Stones, the Who, Cream, and many of the other British bands were deliberately creating music that expressed the philosophy of the artist as a romantic hero who smashes established culture to create a new culture of moral freedom, emotional release, animal energy, and vivid sensation. The sheer energy of rock—the pounding beat, the screams, the spectacle—is intended to bypass the mind and appeal directly to the sensations and feelings.[8]

Thus rock music, by its very form, encourages a mentality that is subjective, emotional, and sensual—no matter what the lyrics may say. This is why Christians must learn to analyze not only the content of pop culture but also the art form itself, the mode of expression.

The danger is that Christian popular culture may mimic the

mainstream culture in style, while changing only the content. The music market is overflowing with Christian rock and rap, Christian blues and jazz, Christian heavy metal. Bookstore shelves are filled with "Christian fiction," from children's adventure stories to almost-steamy romances. Christian theme parks offer an alternative to Disney, and Christian videos for children and exercisers are top sellers. In many ways, this is a healthy development, but we must always ask: Are we creating a genuinely Christian culture, or are we simply creating a parallel culture with a Christian veneer? Are we imposing Christian content onto an already existing form? For the form and style always send a message of their own.

For example, a few years ago Nancy read a startling video review in *Time* magazine: "Provocative images fill the TV screen. Over a driving, syncopated rock beat, a woman's voice—urgent, seductive—tells a story of possession and salvation." No, this was not a new Madonna video. It was a contemporary retelling of the Bible story of Jesus casting out the demons called Legion.[9]

Nancy ordered a copy of the video and discovered that the review was no exaggeration. The almost surrealistic style was so vivid that for all practical purposes it drowned out any biblical teaching. The "message is overwhelmed by the medium," the *Time* review had said, and that was quite true. The producers' goal was admirable—reaching out to young people raised on MTV— but if even a secular reviewer can sense a discrepancy between the biblical message and the style in which it is communicated, then surely we, too, must become more aware.

When we create Christian popular culture, we must take care not simply to insert Christian content into whatever style is currently on the market. Instead, we should cultivate something distinctly Christian in both content and form.[10] We must learn how to identify the worldviews expressed in various art forms in order to critique them and craft an alternative that is soundly biblical.

WHATEVER IS TRUE, WHATEVER IS NOBLE . . .

The way to reverse the degradation of pop culture is once again
to link art to truth. We must challenge the scientism that reduces
truth to what can be known only by the scientific method and
argue for the first plank in the Christian worldview: creation. The
world is the handiwork of a God who is himself Truth, Goodness,
and Beauty. Thus, beauty is as objective and real as the scientists'
particles of matter. The first step in redeeming popular culture,
then, is to craft a biblically based view of the arts (the outlines of
which are suggested in chapter 13).

Second, there are practical steps all of us can take, beginning
with disciplining our personal habits to say no to the worst of
popular culture. It has so infiltrated our homes, our schools, and
our churches that we must start reining it in. Churches that use
mostly contemporary music in their services should consider the
effects of a steady diet of simple choruses and pop-style worship
songs while neglecting the classic hymns of the faith.

In the home, parents need to have the courage of their convictions with their children—to turn off the television, unplug the
earphones, and refuse to let teenagers wear T-shirts bearing airbrushed images of the latest grunge band. I have even "bribed"
my grandchildren, offering them $100 toward their college fund
for each month that they do not watch TV.

Dr. Ben Carson, the world-renowned pediatric neurosurgeon
at Johns Hopkins, was once an angry ghetto kid headed nowhere.
He credits his astonishing turnaround to his encounter with God
and the discipline of his mother, who turned off the television
and made him read the classics and write book reports on them.
"How did your mother manage to do that?" he is often asked. To
which he replies, with irrepressible wit, "Oh, that was back at a
time when parents still controlled families." A family dynamic
that Christian parents need to restore.[11]

Christians can also make a difference in what's offered in the marketplace by voting with our dollars. Refuse to purchase music with obscene or indecent lyrics. Refuse to patronize movies or rent videos that glorify immorality. Refuse to buy romance novels that cheapen the relationship between men and women and even border on soft porn. Boycotts—whether organized or merely individual—may not always get a product taken off the market, but they make an important moral statement.

Currently, for example, several Christian groups, including my own denomination, the Southern Baptists, are boycotting Disney products. I support their decision, for whether or not the boycott has a significant economic effect on Disney, it does serve an important educational function in the church and for the public at large. Until this boycott was publicized, many people—including many Christians—did not know that lurking behind Disney's family-friendly image is a secular, naturalistic philosophy hostile to Christianity. The corporation offers spousal benefits to employees' homosexual partners, and its theme parks hold a special "Gay Day." Disney owns the Miramax film company, which has produced movies like *Priest* and *Sirens,* which viciously attack Christianity. Disney owns ABC, which openly celebrated homosexuality on its program *Ellen* and mocked Christianity in the sitcom *Nothing Sacred.* Parents may still decide to let their children watch Disney films or take their families to Disney World, but at least they should be aware of the anti-Christian worldview their children are being exposed to so they can deal with it appropriately.

But boycotting bad products is only the beginning. The best way to overcome banality is to cultivate something better. We must seek out, as the apostle Paul writes in Philippians, "whatever is true, whatever is noble, whatever is right, whatever is pure, whatever is lovely, whatever is admirable—if anything is excellent or praiseworthy—think about such things" (Phil. 4:8). Notice that Paul doesn't limit that principle to spiritual things; he says if *anything* is excellent. Paul is telling us to train our tastes to love the higher things—things that challenge our mind, deepen our character, and foster a love of excellence—and this includes the music we listen to, the books and magazines we read, the films we watch, the forms of worship we employ.

If we are selective, we can find high-quality popular culture that deals with profound moral dilemmas in ways that teach us new dimensions of good and evil through a gripping story—even if the themes of that story are not overtly Christian. Stephen Spielberg's movie *Saving Private Ryan,* for example, inspires in many viewers a sense of gratitude for the bloody sacrifice made by their parents and grandparents during World War II. Spielberg's *Schindler's List* reminds us of the reality of evil and the need to resist it. *Dead Man Walking* is a powerful portrayal of Christian love and repentance; and my latest favorite, *The Spitfire Grill,* produced by a group of enterprising nuns, is a moving tale of redemption and new life. Mel Gibson, a devout Catholic, has started his own film company, Icon Productions, to create movies that reflect a Christian understanding of good and evil, of honor and courage. One of the company's most successful movies is *Braveheart,* with a script by Randall Wallace, a former Duke Divinity School student who decided he could have a greater impact telling stories than standing in a pulpit.[12]

Among somewhat older films, there is *Chariots of Fire,* based on the inspiring true story of a Scottish athlete willing to put God before an Olympic gold medal. Italian filmmaker Franco Zeffirelli recommitted himself to the Christian faith after a near fatal automobile accident, and since then he has given us films such as *Brother Sun, Sister Moon* (about St. Francis of Assisi), *Jane Eyre* (based on Brontë's classic novel), and his television miniseries *Jesus of Nazareth.* Even a non-Christian filmmaker like Woody Allen sometimes treats moral themes in a serious and thoughtful way, as in his *Crimes and Misdemeanors,* which probes the problem of guilt.[13] (Some of the films listed in these paragraphs have rough language or nudity or violence, so watch them yourself before letting your children see them.)

For family fare, check out the classics section at the video store—films from several decades ago. Many of these will open up a refreshing world to you and your children, for in these films, plot and character were more important than breathtaking special effects. Many of us can never get enough of the well-loved films by Frank Capra, such as *It's a Wonderful Life* and *Mr. Smith Goes to Washington*.[14] Capra successfully portrayed characters who stood for the traditional moral values of honesty, courage, and sacrifice—characters who turned to prayer as naturally as breathing. Capra, who was a practicing Catholic, said, "I deal with the little man's doubts . . . his loss of faith in himself, in his neighbor, in his God." And then, "I show the overcoming of doubts, the courageous renewal of faith."[15]

Ultimately, to be a redemptive force in popular culture, we must encourage Christians to go beyond being critical and start being creative. A surprisingly large number of Christians are seeking to do just that. Martha Williamson was not alone as she faced the trials of working in Hollywood; she was encouraged along the way by a supportive fellowship of believers working there. One such group is Inter-Mission, which is made up of writers, producers, directors, and actors who meet quarterly, with offices in New York and Hollywood; another group is Catholics in Media.[16] The Los Angeles Film Studies Center, a program of the Council for Christian Colleges and Universities, places interns—Christian college students—in the offices of powerful media companies. They work as production assistants and office personnel, learning what it takes to navigate their way through this minefield. And the program is working: Of the Center's two hundred seventy graduates, more than seventy are now working in Hollywood in some capacity, many in strategic positions—an almost incredible percentage.[17]

Some businesspeople are willing to put their own fortunes on the line to make a difference. Norman Miller, who made his mark as the entrepreneurial genius behind Interstate Batteries, has started a fledging film production company to create high-quality, wholesome films subtly interwoven with Christian themes. His first film, *The Joyriders,* is opening in theaters as we write.

One pocket of pop culture that retains a strong religious component, according to Dave Shiflett writing in the *Wall Street Journal,* is country music. "Most of the players of my generation are from church," says mandolin virtuoso Ricky Skaggs, who has been known to do a bit of stage preaching between numbers. "We usually stop our concerts and explain that bluegrass was birthed from church music."[18]

In popular culture, as in every field, the best way to reach a nonbelieving audience is not so much by works that preach Christianity explicitly as by works that express a Christian worldview indirectly. "We can make people attend to the Christian point of view for half an hour or so," said C. S. Lewis, "but the moment they have gone away from our lecture or laid down the article, they are plunged back into a world where the opposite position is taken for granted." Therefore, "what we want is not more little books about Christianity, but more little books by Christians on other subjects—with their Christianity latent."[19]

What would happen if the best popular music on the market were composed by Christian musicians? If the best books in the bookstores were written by Christian authors? If the best television shows implicitly communicated a Christian worldview? Nonbelievers would quickly see that Christianity is not something that can be relegated to a separate part of life labeled "religion" but is a viable worldview that makes better sense of all the things they care about.

Does the devil have all the good music? By our choices, you and I can make sure he doesn't.

He himself is our peace, who has made the two one and has destroyed the barrier, the dividing wall of hostility. . . . His purpose was . . . to reconcile both of them to God through the cross, by which he put to death their hostility.

EPHESIANS 2:14-16

CHAPTER 16

HOW NOW SHALL WE LIVE?

As you read chapter 16, keep the following questions in mind:

- What events led Kim Phuc to become a Christian?
- How is Kim's story an excellent parable of how we should now live?

From Officer Sal in New York to Henryk Górecki in Poland to Martha Williamson in Hollywood, there emerges a common pattern: Christians who understand biblical truth and have the courage to live it out can indeed redeem a culture, or even create one. This is the challenge facing all of us in the new millennium.

As we have sought to demonstrate in these pages, the Christian worldview is more consistent, more rational, and more workable than any other belief system. It beats out all other contenders in giving credible answers to the great questions that any worldview must answer: Where did we come from? *(creation);* What is the human dilemma? *(fall);* and What can we do to solve the dilemma? *(redemption).* And the way we *see* the world guides the way we work to *change* the world *(restoration).*

No worldview is merely a theoretical philosophy. It is intensely practical, affecting the way we live our lives, day in and day out, as well as the way we influence the world around us. If we adopt a false worldview, we will inevitably find ourselves going against the grain of the universe, leading to consequences we cannot live with—as millions of Americans are discovering. If, however, we order our lives in accord with reality, we will not only find meaning and purpose but also discover that our lives are healthier and more fulfilled. Christianity is the only accurate road map of reality, and we must be ready to make the case to those who are growing increasingly aware of the futility of all other worldviews.

But there are five billion people on this planet, you say, and we live amid seemingly endless suffering, conflict, and war. Can we ever hope to help solve the intractable problems that set nation against nation? Our world is fractured by unfathomable chasms between people—by centuries-old enmities, by generations of mistrust and hostility, by all "the sin that so easily entangles" us (Heb. 12:1). Aren't these events shaped by large-scale international forces, far beyond the reach of anything you or I can do?

The answer is that even in these cases God can use acts of faith and faithfulness to heal the ugliest wounds and reconcile the deepest conflicts between people and even between nations.

■   ■   ■

On the mall in Washington, D.C., people can always be seen clustered in front of The Wall that commemorates the soldiers who died in the Vietnam War. Every season of the year, every hour of the day and night, people gather there. Mothers and fathers, now grandparents, trace the names of sons and daughters long dead; children, now adults, search for the names of fathers they barely remember; veterans mourn their buddies; tourists puzzle over the war that never quite made sense. Always people, with their private grief, unanswered questions, and quiet awe in front of the rolls of the dead etched into the polished black marble.

Of course, weather-beaten monuments are scattered across the entire country—memorials to people who died in the Civil War, Spanish American War, World War I, World War II, and the

Korean War. Yet it is the Vietnam War that haunts Americans as no other war ever has.

As a nation, we still can't clearly answer why our young people had to march the Ho Chi Minh trail or why so many had to die. Those of us who are old enough still remember the news photos of black body bags at the Saigon airport, the innumerable troop escalations, the talk of soldiers shooting their commanders, and the ugly confrontations at home between police and antiwar demonstrators. And then that last glimpse of our soldiers fleeing, jumping onto helicopters from the Saigon embassy roof—a sight that filled Americans with shame.

In 1996, in an effort to find some resolution to these questions, several men who had been high-ranking U.S. officials responsible for policy decisions during the war decided to meet with their Vietnamese counterparts. A conference was scheduled in Hanoi, initiated by Robert McNamara, who had served as secretary of defense in the Kennedy and Johnson administrations.[1] Two years earlier, McNamara had published *In Retrospect: The Tragedy and Lessons of Vietnam,* in which he admitted, after a twenty-seven-year silence, that the decisions he and other White House officials had made regarding Vietnam were "wrong, terribly wrong." Yet clearly, he was still struggling to understand *why* U.S. actions had miscarried so disastrously. Perhaps this conference would provide the answers that had eluded everyone for so long.[2]

But it yielded nothing of the sort. From the opening moments the Vietnamese, though smiling politely, lectured the Americans sternly for interfering in what they regarded as a campaign for national reunification. "North Vietnam" had never been a separate country, they insisted; nor had it considered itself to be "intervening" in "South Vietnam's" affairs, any more than the American North considered itself to be intervening in the affairs of the South during our own Civil War. The Americans were stunned and frustrated.

For days, participants went back and forth in heated discussions. McNamara even tried to speak privately with General Vo Nguyen Giap, the general who had defeated both French and U.S. forces in his country. But the general lectured him nonstop on the true history of Vietnam, and McNamara couldn't get in a word.

At the end, former CIA analyst Chester Cooper stepped wearily to the lectern, his necktie loosened, his shoulders slumped, and sarcastically summed up Vietnam's unyielding stance—that "everything we did after the 1954 Geneva agreement was wrong and immoral and everything you [the Vietnamese] did was right and moral." And then he sighed. "I'm tired of saying we were wrong about everything."[3] Later, news photos showed Cooper and McNamara at the Hanoi airport waiting to board their flight home, their suits rumpled in the oppressive heat, their faces exhausted and dejected. Their mission had been an utter failure.

The problem was that McNamara was looking for technical solutions to apply to complex human and spiritual dilemmas. He was the quintessential technocrat: He came to prominence as a supermanager who had produced small miracles at the Ford Motor Company, and later at the Department of Defense, by introducing statistically based planning controls. Better planning and management would solve any problem, he was convinced, especially if it could be rationalized in quantifiable terms and manipulated in formulas.

But the wounds of war are not healed by mathematical analysis and statistics. The real healing must come in a very different way.

.   .   .

I have my own memories of the horror of Vietnam and certainly understand the longing for a solution. As part of the Nixon administration, I listened for years to the briefings of generals and admirals, to then National Security Advisor Henry Kissinger's daily reports, and to many of the president's late-night monologues about Vietnam. At times I helped the president make some of the most agonizing decisions, like the mining and bombing of Hanoi harbor in May 1972, and was involved in the secret negotiations after the election that same year. I was one of the president's men, and I supported his position right down the line. Still, the agony of the war came home to me in various ways. I knew that our decisions were putting my own former marine classmates in harm's way. Yet one image of the war was seared into my memory, and to this day, it remains poignant and painful. . . .

Before sunrise on June 9, 1972, I climbed into my limousine for my daily commute to the White House. En route, I planned to read intelligence and news summaries, as well as briefing memos in preparation for a senior staff meeting that morning. First, though, I flipped open the *Washington Post* to scan the headlines.

Suddenly I felt as if I had received a body blow. On page one, above the fold, was a photo from Vietnam showing the aftermath of a bombing. But something was terribly wrong: the wounded in the picture were not soldiers but children. A weeping boy in dark shorts. Two children running hand in hand. And then the girl. In the center of the photo was a young girl running directly toward the camera, her arms stretched out, her clothes burned off. Her skin was blackened by napalm, and her hands drooped lifelessly, while her mouth screamed in pain, her eyes reflecting the horror of the black exploding sky behind her.

Instinctively, my horrified mind wanted to help this child. I thought involuntarily of my own precious daughter Emily. *What if she had been hurt like this?*

Worse, I couldn't avoid a sinking sense of my own responsibility for this young girl's suffering. Her silent scream made me wince. My own skin burned with guilt and shame.

■   ■   ■

The day the photo was shot, two journalists, Chris Wain from England and Vietnamese photojournalist Nick Ut, were accompanying a ground unit on patrol outside the village of Trang Bang on Highway 1, which ran between Saigon and Cambodia. A North Vietnamese offensive had briefly overrun the village, and then the South Vietnamese had bombed it heavily for three days. The population had taken refuge in a double-spired pagoda in an oasis-like setting of palms, silhouetted against deep-blue mountains. The temple was considered a holy place, and no soldiers, not even the Americans, would ever target it.

Suddenly, the firing grew more intense, and a colored signal fell out of the sky toward the pagoda, designating it as a target. South Vietnamese soldiers on the ground saw the signal and immediately began to hustle the villagers out of the temple, telling them to run for their lives. Chris and Nick looked up to see two planes. One banked and wheeled around, passing in front of the pagoda, right over the fleeing villagers.

As the plane screamed lower and lower, four canisters dropped from its hold. The journalists caught their breath. They knew those tumbling specks in the distance were filled with huge quantities of jellied gasoline. Napalm. In the moment before the canisters hit, everything seemed frozen.

Then, all at once, a tidal wave of fire swept over the road, incinerating everything in its path. The tarmac leading toward the pagoda melted into surging flame. The wind thrown off by the fire was so strong, it snapped the huge palm fronds around the temple.

Then the parade of death began. Out of the flames ran several women and children, strangely silent. An old woman carrying a dying three-year-old boy, his flesh hanging like tattered rags. A brother and sister running hand in hand. Then a young girl appeared, naked, her arms outstretched. The children running at her side began screaming, "Please help! Please help!"

Quickly, instinctively, photojournalist Nick Ut snapped a photograph of the scene. Then the two men caught the girl in their
arms and gave her a drink of water. "So hot," she kept saying. "So
hot." After emptying a canteen of water over the girl's burning
shoulder, they put a rain slicker lightly around her and drove her
to the hospital in their jeep. Somewhere along the way she lapsed
into unconsciousness.

Chris and Nick were both longtime war correspondents, but
neither had ever witnessed anything like this. The next day, Chris
and his video cameraman, Michael Blakey, visited the young girl
in the hospital. She lay facedown, unconscious, suffering from
third-degree burns over her entire back and along her arms,
especially her left arm. Her dark hair had been chopped off, her
wounds bandaged. What looked like a roll of toilet paper was
propped at the side of her mouth. Her mother sat at the end of
the bed, fanning her. They learned that the girl's name was Kim
Phuc, a name that means "Golden Happiness."[4]

Chris asked a male nurse for the girl's prognosis.

"Oh, her?" the nurse said indifferently. "She die, maybe tomorrow, maybe next day."

The callous tone was more than Chris could bear after the
trauma of witnessing the bombing the day before. As it happened,
he carried a bayonet at his back—a macho good-luck charm. He
took it out and pressed the hilt into the male nurse's hand. "Why
don't you just do the kind thing then and kill her now!" he said.
"Take this, and kill her. It's more merciful than what you're doing.
Letting her die a slow death this way!"

The nurse rushed off to find the doctors, and Chris talked to
them fast, loud, and long. Finally they agreed to transfer the girl to
Barsky Hospital in Saigon, a facility founded by an American doctor who first developed surgical techniques to treat Hiroshima victims. The hospital now specialized in plastic surgery for children.

At Barsky, the surgeon of the day, Dr. Mai Lee, took up Kim

Phuc's cause, arguing against her own head nurse, who claimed the hospital lacked the personnel to care for a recent burn victim whose condition might not stabilize. But Dr. Mai Lee insisted, and she prevailed.

.   .   .

After fourteen months in the hospital and seventeen surgeries, Kim Phuc was released and returned home. For years afterward, she was just an anonymous teenage girl who always wore long sleeves to cover her twisted scars and who worried that they were so ugly that no one would ever want to marry her.

But Nick Ut's photo had left a legacy. I wasn't the only one struck by it; it won a Pulitzer prize and became an emblem for an entire nation questioning its reason for being in Vietnam. So in 1980, as the world observed the fifth anniversary of the end of the Vietnam War, journalists began asking what had happened to the young girl in the famous photograph. Vietnamese government officials took note and decided Kim Phuc could be played as a propaganda card, so they tracked her down. By that time, she was studying medicine in Saigon, but officials yanked her out of school and made her work as a secretary in the government offices of her own province, Tei Ling, so she would be on hand to parade before visiting media and dignitaries. Regularly they would ask her to roll up her sleeves and display her scars, making her act as a poster child for the horrors of American aggression.

Kim hated her propaganda role and ran away to Saigon to resume the medical studies she loved. The government retaliated by destroying her academic records. Even then, Kim would sneak away to Saigon at night to study English.

Eventually, she was sought out by journalists interested in telling her story (among them Perry Katz of the German magazine *Stern* and England's William Shawcross). They photographed her in her parents' restaurant and snapped her bowing and praying in the same twin-spired pagoda she had been running from in the famous photo. Her family worshiped in the Cao Dai tradition: a mixture of world religions, with spiritualist practices, including séances where messages were solicited from the dead.

When talking with interviewers, Kim always smiled, but inwardly she desperately wanted to lead her own life. To protect her family, she said nothing, however, for the government could destroy far more than her school records. To prove the point, officials took away all her family's possessions—the restaurant, their large home, everything but their lives. And who knew how long they would spare even these?

. . .

Kim became increasingly depressed. And yet there was one compensation to holding a "show job" with few responsibilities: It allowed her to spend time in a local library, where she read voraciously. And it was there she read the New Testament for the first time. Its portrait of Jesus differed radically from what she had learned about him in Cao Dai, and eventually she began to question her childhood faith. Cao Dai seemed powerless to relieve her depression, even though she prayed more than four times a day at the temple.

Eventually Kim was invited to attend a Baptist church with her sister's brother-in-law, a strong Christian. She was greatly attracted to the Christian faith but reluctant to leave her family's religion. Finally, one Sunday before church she prayed for the first time, asking Jesus Christ for a small but significant favor. "I need one girlfriend I can talk with. If I see a girl sitting alone in the church, that is who will be my girlfriend."

When Kim walked through the church doors, sure enough, she saw one woman sitting alone. She approached her, and they quickly became friends. "I felt very happy," Kim says. "I just tried, and God answered my prayer right away!"

Not long afterward, Kim went forward to the altar and accepted Jesus Christ as her personal Savior. "It was the fire of the bomb that burned my body, and it was the skill of the doctor that mended my skin," she says, "but it took the power of God to heal my heart."[5]

.   .   .

Kim was finally allowed to resume her medical studies in 1986, this time in Vietnam's sister communist state, Cuba. The students lived on the twenty-fourth floor of a high-rise, without running water or a working elevator. This was a problem for Kim, because her burns still required daily washing and medication. A fellow Vietnamese student named Toan offered to carry buckets of water up to her apartment, and it wasn't long before he was touched by the loveliness of Kim's spirit.

Yet Kim remained noncommittal. Toan smoked cigarettes, drank excessively, and still embraced the communist ideology in which he had been raised. She began witnessing to him about Jesus Christ, but his intellectual barriers to faith seemed insurmountable. Gradually, however, Toan did give up both smoking and drinking and eventually asked Kim to marry him. Kim warned him that her injuries made it unlikely that she could ever have children, but he repeatedly reassured her that he truly wanted to marry her anyway. More important, he assured her that he understood and respected her faith. They dated for six years and finally married in 1992.

Kim and Toan honeymooned in Moscow, and on their return flight to Cuba, their Aeroflot jet was scheduled to refuel in Newfoundland. The couple had spoken before about defecting, but Toan was afraid of being caught by communist authorities. He also feared reprisals against their families. As the plane descended into the Gander International Airport in Newfoundland, Kim began praying.

"What are you doing?" Toan asked.

"Toan," she whispered, "if God opens the way, we should stay and live in Canada. I have peace about it."

"Kim, no. We'll never get away with it."

"Toan, I go by faith. If you love me, follow me, because I follow God."

"If they catch us, they'll send us back to Vietnam, and you know what happens then. They'll kill us." He was so worried that he even considered letting her defect without him, if it came to that.

"I know the risk. I love you, Toan, but I love God, too, so I follow him."

When the plane landed, the passengers entered the airport to wait during refueling. Kim had no idea how to go about defecting, and she was frightened. Should she simply hide out in the bathroom? No, when the secret police traveling with them counted the number of passengers, they would see that she was missing and come back for her. "Oh God, how can I stay?" she prayed desperately. "Give me a sign, please. I don't want to go back to Cuba or Vietnam anymore."

When she opened her eyes, her gaze was drawn to a small room off the central waiting room. The door was ajar, and inside she could see a group of people, some of whom she recognized from their community in Cuba. She walked over, put her head inside, and asked them in Spanish, "What are you doing here?"

"We want to stay."

"Me, too. How can I do it?"

"You just give your passport to the officer right up there, at the front of the room."

Providentially, Kim had walked right to the immigration office! Quickly she summoned Toan, and they handed their passports to the officer. "We want to stay in Canada," they said.

"Yes," said the officer. "Okay."

So easy? Kim marveled. *Praise the Lord!*

But then the official said, "Just wait about ten minutes. Another officer will come to interview you."

Ten minutes . . . even that small a delay could mean life or death for the frightened couple. Refueling was almost finished, and time was running out. Kim and Toan stood in the doorway, watching, waiting. Finally, the other officer arrived and asked them to follow him back into the office. Just as they crossed the threshold into freedom, they heard the boarding announcement.

All their belongings were still on the plane; they had nothing but the clothes on their backs. But it didn't matter. "I just say, 'Bye-bye,'" Kim says, "and I feel very happy. I am free!"[6]

Kim and Toan settled into a thriving Vietnamese immigrant community in Toronto, and soon another blessing was in store for them. Kim became pregnant—truly a miracle!—and the couple became the proud parents of a healthy baby boy.

In a recent film about Kim's life, two-year-old Thomas and Kim face each other across a table. Kim touches Thomas's face, first here, then there. "Cheeks," they say together. "Lips. Ears." Then they put their faces right up close and rub noses.[7] A loving mother and son, happy, fulfilled—so far away from that terrible day in 1972, when the sky rained napalm.

Yet Kim Phuc's spiritual healing was eventually to reach out beyond her own home and lead to a much wider healing.

In 1996, Kim agreed to speak at Veterans Day ceremonies held at The Wall in Washington, D.C. She took her place on the rostrum, flanked by U.S. military dignitaries, before a huge crowd of veterans. No one could tell how much it cost her just to stand there and face that sea of uniforms, a sight that brought back terrifying memories of the war.

"As you know, I am the little girl who was running to escape from the napalm fire. I do not want to talk about the war because I cannot change history. I only want you to remember a tragedy of war in order to do things to stop fighting and killing around the world."

Her voice dropped. "I have suffered a lot from both physical and emotional pain. Sometimes I thought I could not live, but God saved my life and gave me faith and hope."

And then she uttered healing words of grace and forgiveness: "Even if I could talk face-to-face with the pilot who dropped the bomb, I could tell him we cannot change history, but we should try to do good things for the present and for the future to promote peace."

When she finished her brief but moving remarks, the veterans rose to their feet and broke into an explosion of applause, many of them in tears. "It's important to us that she's here," one veteran said. "For her to forgive us personally means something."

One man, overcome with emotion, rushed to a patrolman and scribbled out a note, asking him to deliver it to Kim. "*I'm the man you are looking for*," the note read.[8]

Intermediaries asked if she was willing to see him. Yes, she said, if they could arrange a meeting away from the crush of people. Officials brought the man over to her car.

When the reporters cleared away, Kim turned and looked straight into the man's eyes and then held out her arms . . . the same arms she had held out as she ran along the road, in agony from her burning skin. She hugged the man, and he began to sob.

"I am sorry. I am just so sorry!" he said.

"It is okay. I forgive. I forgive," said Kim Phuc, echoing her favorite Bible verse, "Forgive, and you will be forgiven" (Luke 6:37).

■   ■   ■

That day the famous photo of thirty years ago, of the terrified little Vietnamese girl fleeing the napalm flames, was replaced in the national consciousness by a photo of a young mother embracing an ex-GI, silhouetted against the shimmering black memorial.

The words of forgiveness Kim extended that Veterans Day helped heal the consciences of thousands of veterans gathered there; and as news reports carried the story far and wide, her words and the striking photo helped heal the nation's wounds as well. She brought the resurrection power of Christ to a place that serves as a collective memorial for 58,000 Americans, showing how the bitterness of war can be overcome with love.

I can't help but contrast Kim Phuc's message of reconciliation to the ongoing, fruitless efforts by Robert McNamara and so many others, still seeking technocratic solutions to the war. They want so desperately to see, but they remain blind. The only real solution is spiritual: It is forgiveness, repentance, and making restitution, actively pursuing good for our former enemy. Only Christianity provides the power to transform the world.

And so we come full circle, back to the questions with which we began this book. Can Christians really make any difference in the world? Does the Christian worldview give us the map we need for living? Can a culture be rebuilt so all the world can see in its splendor and glory the contours of God's kingdom? Can we really make the world "a new creation"? Kim Phuc, along with all the others we have met in these pages, show us that the answer is emphatically yes.

Every day you and I are making decisions that help construct one kind of world or another. Are we co-opted by the faddish worldviews of our age, or are we helping to create a new world of peace, love, and forgiveness?

How now shall we live?

By embracing God's truth, understanding the physical and moral order he has created, lovingly contending for that truth with our neighbors, then having the courage to live it out in every walk of life.

Boldly and, yes, joyously.

DISCUSSION QUESTIONS

CHAPTER 14

1 Identify Martha's personal vision for ministry. Similarly try to articulate what God is calling you to fulfill as his agent in the world.

2 What did Martha's success require of her?

3 Further discuss the roles of faith and of works in Martha's professional journey. Compare her journey to lessons you've learned about the balance between faith in God and your own faithful effort in carrying out a mission.

CHAPTER 15

4 What are the dangers of a steady diet of cultural "junk food"?

5 How can you protect yourself and your families from the "soft oppression" described in *Brave New World*?

6 Discuss the distinctions between folk culture and pop culture. What are the best regional or folk distinctives of your area, and what can you do to encourage appreciation of them?

7 How did a shift in worldview contribute to a decline in popular culture?

8 Give examples of events or products for which you felt the positive message seemed inappropriately overwhelmed by the medium. Did you nevertheless see any redemptive results?

9 What can you do to "say no to the worst of popular culture"

in your home?

in your church?

in your buying habits?

in your leisure time?

10 What can you do to say yes to truth, goodness, and beauty

in your home?

in your church?

in your buying habits?

in your leisure time?

in your creative ventures?

CHAPTER 16

11 What redemptive elements in Kim's story can you tie to her Christian faith and worldview? How does her story

encourage your spirit?

embolden your witness?

enlarge your vision?

12 Read aloud Ephesians 5:1-16. According to verses 1 and 2, what will be the most obvious indicator that we are imitating God and walking as Christ did?

13 To live consistently in the light of God's truth and love,

what must we avoid?

what should we seek to cultivate?

14 How can you encourage one another to walk in the light, as demonstrated in this chapter?

BOOK OVERVIEW

15 Consider your answer to the seond half of question 3—

identifying God's call on your life. Help one another identify short-range objectives in the following areas:

things I need to study

things I need to change

spiritual disciplines I need to develop

people to whom I should reach out in ministry

people to whom I should reach out for encouragement, feedback, and support

areas in which I can contribute to my church's ministry

CLOSING SUMMARY

What is the most important point you want to remember from this book study?

Complete the following: "More than anything else, I hope and pray that this book study will enable me to _____
_____."

NOTES

INTRODUCTION
1. Read the story of my conversion in *Born Again* (Old Tappan, N.J.: Chosen, 1976).
2. Abraham Kuyper, *Christianity: A Total World and Life System* (Marlborough, N.H.: Plymouth Rock Foundation, 1996), 39–40.
3. Ibid., 41.
4. Cornelius Plantinga Jr., "Fashions and Folly: Sin and Character in the 90s," (presented at the January Lecture Series, Calvin Theological Seminary, Grand Rapids, Michigan, January 15, 1993), 14–15.
5. Ibid.
6. Ibid.
7. Richard M. Weaver, *Ideas Have Consequences* (Chicago: University of Chicago Press, 1984).
8. Samuel Huntington, "The Clash of Civilizations," *Journal of Foreign Affairs* (summer 1993): 22. Huntington identified the major power blocs as the Western, Islamic, Chinese, Hindu, Orthodox, Japanese, and possibly African regions.
9. James Kurth, "The Real Clash of Civilization," *Washington Times*, 4 October 1994.
10. Jacques Toubon, cited in "Living with America," *Calgary Herald*, 6 October 1993.

CHAPTER 1
THE KNOCKOUT PUNCH
1. While Danny Croce's remarkable story is true, some of the secondary characters in this story are composites or fictional. The story is based on interviews with Danny Croce.

CHAPTER 2
SAVED TO WHAT?

1. After a two-week evangelistic crusade through every prison in North Carolina, disciplinary violations dropped precipitously, and most wardens reported reduced tensions and better inmate behavior. Even months later, Bible studies were crowded, and lives continued to be changed. In New York state prisons, recidivism (the rate at which released prisoners return to prison) was dramatically reduced—from an average of 41 percent to 14 percent—among men who participated in at least ten Prison Fellowship programs a year. See B. R. Johnson, D. B. Larson, and T. C. Pitts, "Religious Programs, Institutional Adjustment, and Recidivism among Former Inmates in Prison Fellowship Programs," *Justice Quarterly* 14, no. 1 (March 1997): 145.

2. Critics sometimes contend that Genesis gives two creation accounts, the second one beginning in Genesis 2:4, but this is a misunderstanding of the literary structure. The first chapter of Genesis and the first few verses of chapter 2 function as a prologue, setting the cosmic stage and raising the curtain. The drama itself actually begins in chapter 2 as Adam and Eve, the first husband and wife, begin societal life. Their tasks of tending the Garden and naming the animals mark the beginning of cultural life. True, the author uses a flashback technique to give more details on how Adam and Eve were created, but that does not make this a second creation story. Instead, this passage relates how the cultural mandate begins to be fulfilled in actual history.

3. Al Wolters, *Creation Regained: Biblical Basics for a Reformational Worldview* (Grand Rapids: Eerdmans, 1985), 36. The following discussion relies heavily on Wolters, who in turn popularized Dutch philosopher Herman Dooyeweerd. See Dooyeweerd, *A New Critique of Theoretical Thought* (Lewiston, N.Y.: Edwin Mellen Press, 1997).

4. C. S. Lewis, *The Abolition of Man* (New York: Touchstone, 1975).

5. Dutch theologian and statesman Abraham Kuyper developed this argument of the spheres of authority. See Abraham Kuyper, *Christianity: A Total World and Life System* (Marlborough, N.H.: Plymouth Rock Foundation, 1996). One of the most striking passages in Scripture on the God-given character of the order of creation is Isaiah 28:23-29, where we learn that the Lord teaches the farmer his business. There is a right way to plow, to sow, and to thresh, depending on the kind of grain the farmer is growing. A good farmer knows that, and this knowledge is from the Lord, for the Lord teaches him. This is not a teaching from the Scripture, from

special revelation, but a teaching through the structures of creation, from general revelation. And it comes to us by experience with soil, seeds, and plow.

6. Al Wolters writes, "It is by listening to the voice of God in the work of his hands that the farmer finds the way of agricultural wisdom" (Wolters, *Creation Regained*, 28). The same is true in economics, politics, the arts, medicine, communications, and education—in every area of society. We learn how to take care of God's creation by familiarizing ourselves with the creational structures and living in tune with them, and we formalize that knowledge in a Christian worldview.

7. See Wolters, *Creation Regained*, chapter 4; and Charles Colson with Ellen Santilli Vaughn, *Kingdoms in Conflict* (New York: William Morrow; Grand Rapids: Zondervan, 1987), chapter 7.

8. Tertullian, as quoted in Henry Chadwick, *The Early Church* (New York: Penguin, 1993), 65.

9. Justin Martyr, as quoted in Chadwick, *The Early Church*, 74–83.

10. This dramatic story is told in Christopher Dawson's *Religion and the Rise of Western Culture* (New York: Doubleday, Image Books, 1991) and Thomas Cahill's *How the Irish Saved Civilization: The Untold Story of Ireland's Heroic Role from the Fall of Rome to the Rise of Medieval Europe* (New York: Doubleday, 1995).

11. Saint Patrick, as quoted in Thomas Cahill, *How the Irish Saved Civilization*, 102.

12. Cahill, *How the Irish Saved Civilization*, 105.

13. Kenneth Clark, *Civilisation: A Personal View* (New York: Harper & Row, 1969), 8.

14. John Henry Newman, as quoted in Christopher Dawson, *Religion and the Rise of Western Culture*, 53–54. Newman goes on to explain how the monks accomplished all this: "Silent men were observed about the country, or discovered in the forest, digging, clearing, and building; and other silent men, not seen, were sitting in the cold cloister, tiring their eyes and keeping their attention on the stretch, while they painfully copied and recopied the manuscripts which they had saved."

15. Dawson, *Religion and the Rise of Western Culture*, 126.

16. An eyewitness account describes the transformation of Scandinavian culture in these words: "But after their acceptance of Christianity, they have become imbued with better principles and have now learned to love peace and truth and to be content with their poverty. . . . Of all men they are the most temperate both in food and in their habits,

loving above all things thrift and modesty" (Dawson, *Religion and the Rise of Western Culture*, 98).

17. Pope John Paul II, *Redemptoris Missio*, Encyclical Letter on the Permanent Validity of the Church's Missionary Mandate (December 7, 1990).

18. Timothy George, "Catholics and Evangelicals in the Trenches," *Christianity Today* 38, no. 6 (May 10, 1994): 16.

19. Kuyper, *Christianity*, 69, 110. Kuyper argued strenuously for the kind of cooperation sought in current efforts by Evangelicals and Catholics Together. "Rome is not an antagonist, but stands on our side, in as much as she also recognizes and maintains the Trinity, the Deity of Christ, the Cross as an atoning sacrifice, the Scriptures as the Word of God, and the Ten Commandments as a divinely imposed rule of life" (Kuyper, *Christianity*, 110).

20. Letter from John Calvin to William Farel written from Ratisbon, 11 May 1541. See John Calvin, *Letters of John Calvin*, ed. Jules Bonnet, vol. 1 (Philadelphia: Presbyterian Board of Publication, 1858), 260.

CHAPTER 3
DON'T WORRY, BE RELIGIOUS

1. For example, a 1996 poll showed that 59 percent of Americans were worried about "our country's ethical and moral condition" (James Davison Hunter, *The State of Disunion: 1996 Survey of American Political Culture*, vol. 2 [Ivy, Va.: In Medias Res Educational Foundation, 1996], table 46 F).

2. Berkeley Breathed, "Outland," 17 October 1993.

3. Christopher Jencks, as quoted in William Voegel, "Poverty and the Victim Ploy," *First Things* (November 1991): 37.

4. David Larson, personal interview with Nancy Pearcey (March 1999). We are not denying that government has a role to play in providing a safety net to families in trouble. What is objectionable is the value-free assumption that all family forms are morally equal and that the government's role is to make them equal in all other respects as well.

5. Louis W. Sullivan, "Foundation for Reform," (Washington, D.C.: Department of Health and Human Services, 1991): 15.

6. Judy Mann, "Going Up in Smoke," *Washington Post*, 26 February 1993.

7. See note 3 above.

8. Most of the following studies are based on the objective measure of church attendance (with response options ranging from "daily" to

"never"). Some studies also ask subjects how important religion is to them (with response options ranging from "very important" to "not important at all"). Some studies were limited to Christians, while others included people of all faiths (though given the demographics of the American population, the majority would identify themselves as Christians).

9. D. B. Larson and W. P. Wilson, "Religious Life of Alcoholics," *Southern Medical Journal* 73, no. 6 (June 1980): 723–27.

10. David B. and Susan S. Larson, *The Forgotten Factor in Physical and Mental Health: What Does the Research Show?* (Rockville, Md.: National Institute for Healthcare Research, 1992), 68–69. The Larsons have collected and/or conducted a host of studies on the impact of religion on mental and physical health.

11. Joseph A. Califano Jr., *Behind Bars: Substance Abuse and America's Prison Population* (New York: The National Center on Addiction and Substance Abuse at Columbia University, 1998), 27.

12. Joseph A. Califano Jr., (speech given at the National Press Club, Washington, D.C., January 8, 1998).

13. Richard R. Freeman and Harry J. Holzer, eds., *The Black Youth Employment Crisis* (Chicago: University of Chicago Press, 1986), 353–76.

14. B. R. Johnson, D. B. Larson, and T. C. Pitts, "Religious Programs, Institutional Adjustment, and Recidivism among Former Inmates in Prison Fellowship Programs," *Justice Quarterly* 14, no. 1 (March 1997): 145–66.

15. Larson and Larson, *The Forgotten Factor*, 76–78.

16. George Gallup Jr., "Religion in America," *Public Perspective* (October/November 1995).

17. Armand Nicholi Jr., "Hope in a Secular Age," *Finding God at Harvard: Spiritual Journeys of Thinking Christians*, ed. Kelly K. Monroe (Grand Rapids: Zondervan, 1996), 117.

18. Larson and Larson, *The Forgotten Factor*, 64–65.

19. Ibid., 72.

20. Howard M. Bahr and Bruce A. Chadwick, "Religion and Family in Middletown, USA," *Journal of Marriage and the Family* 47 (May 1985): 407–14.

21. See N. Stinnet, et al., "A Nationwide Study of Families Who Perceive Themselves as Strong"; and Velma McBride Murry, "Incidence of First Pregnancy among Black Adolescent Females over Three Decades." Both studies are quoted in Patrick Fagan, "Why Religion Matters," *The Heritage Foundation Report*, no. 1064 (January 25, 1996):

8. Fagan's excellent report is a collection of studies showing the importance of religion to a healthy society.

22. Both studies are from Larson and Larson, *The Forgotten Factor*, 73.

23. Robert T. Michael, et al., *Sex in America: A Definitive Survey* (New York: Little, Brown & Co., 1994), 127.

24. Larson and Larson, *The Forgotten Factor*, 73–79, 109–23. Bob Condor, "Can Faith Heal?" *Chicago Tribune*, 4 December 1996.

25. Larson and Larson, *The Forgotten Factor*, 110. These findings show a positive association between religious commitment and physical health. This does not appear to be merely a correlation but an actual causal relationship. As Larson and Larson point out, in discussing lower blood pressure among smokers with a high religious commitment: "These findings are striking because the benefits of religion on health are often assumed to be the result of religious motivation for following healthier practices, such as not smoking, avoiding alcohol, and abstaining from harmful dietary practices. In this study, however, it was among the smokers that religious importance made the biggest difference in blood pressure. *Consequently the health benefit of religious commitment was beyond avoiding health-risk behavior*" (116, emphasis in the original). What was the connection then? Larson and Larson quote the authors of the study as saying, "This may reflect a preferentially greater moderating effect for religion on blood pressure among more tense or nervous individuals who may also be more likely to smoke" (116). In short, religious commitment itself appears to be the cause of the health benefits.

26. Patrick Glynn, *God: The Evidence: The Reconciliation of Faith and Reason in a Postsecular World* (Rocklin, Calif.: Prima Publishing, 1997), 67.

27. Guenter Lewy, *Why America Needs Religion: Secular Modernity and Its Discontents* (Grand Rapids: Eerdmans, 1996), 112.

28. Dale A. Matthews with Connie Clark, *The Faith Factor: Proof of the Healing Power of Prayer* (New York: Viking, 1998), 77–80.

29. Herbert Benson, *Timeless Healing* (New York: Scribner, 1996), 197, 208.

30. Larson and Larson, *The Forgotten Factor*, 86.

31. Ibid.

32. David B. Larson, "Physician, Heal Thyself!" *Guideposts* (March 1993): 41–43.

33. Daniel Goleman, "Therapists See Religion As Aid, Not Illusion," *New York Times*, 10 September 1991.

34. Other Christian cost-sharing groups include Samaritan Ministries in

Greenfield, Indiana; the Christian Brotherhood Newsletter in Barberton, Ohio; All Saints in Tyler, Texas; and Helping Hands in Oklahoma City, Oklahoma. See Joe Maxwell, "Medical Cost Sharing," *Philanthropy, Culture and Society* (June 1996).

CHAPTER 4
GOD'S TRAINING GROUND

1. David Blankenhorn, "Where's Dad?" *Atlanta Journal and Constitution*, 19 March 1995; and Barbara Dafoe Whitehead, "Dan Quayle Was Right," *Atlantic Monthly* 271, no. 4 (April 1993): 47. We are not criticizing books that genuinely help children of divorce—only those that treat divorce as morally insignificant.
2. See Norval D. Glenn, *Closed Hearts, Closed Minds: The Textbook Story of Marriage* (New York: The Institute for American Values, 1997).
3. Ibid., 5.
4. Candice Bergen, interviewed in "Candy Is Dandy, but Don't Mess with Murphy," *TV Guide* (September 19, 1992): 8.
5. Ibid.
6. See Robert N. Bellah, *Habits of the Heart: Individualism and Commitment in American Life* (Berkeley, Calif.: University of California, 1985).
7. Barbara Bush, (speech given at the Republican National Convention, August 19, 1992).
8. Pierre Manent, "Modern Individualism," *Crisis* (October 1995): 35.
9. Michael Medved, "Hollywood Chic," *Washington Post*, 4 October 1992.
10. John Stuart Mill, *On Liberty* (Indianapolis: Hackett, 1978), 12.
11. Michael J. Sandel, *Democracy's Discontent: America in Search of a Public Philosophy* (Cambridge, Mass.: Belknop Press, 1996), 113.
12. Stanley Greenspan, as quoted in Don Feder, "Day-Care Study Defies Common Sense," *Boston Herald*, 8 March 1999. For a history of women and the family, see Nancy R. Pearcey, "Is Love Enough?: Recreating the Economic Base of the Family," *The Family in America* 4, no. 1 (January 1990): 1.
13. Steven Mintz and Susan Kellogg, *Domestic Revolutions: A Social History of American Family Life* (New York: Free Press, 1988), 117. For a discussion of these historical trends and a definition of masculinity and fatherhood, see Nancy R. Pearcey, "Rediscovering Parenthood in the Information Age," *The Family in America* 8, no. 3 (March 1994).

14. Cited in Barbara Ehrenreich, *The Hearts of Men: American Dreams and the Flight from Commitment* (New York: Doubleday, 1983), 47. See also Pearcey, "Rediscovering Parenthood in the Information Age."

15. David Blankenhorn, *Fatherless America: Confronting Our Most Urgent Social Problem* (New York: HarperPerennial, 1996).

16. Shere Hite, "The Case against Family Values," *Washington Post*, 10 July 1994.

17. Elayne Bennett, "If She's Facing Adolescent Girls Today," (lecture given at the Heritage Foundation, February 1995).

18. A recent Hawaii Supreme Court decision permitting gay "marriage" is often portrayed as simply opening up traditional marriage to gays. Rather than broaden traditional marriage, however, the decision denies the existence of traditional marriage altogether by redefining "marriage" purely in terms of legally protected economic benefits, leading to the logical conclusion that these benefits ought to be available to any and all people, regardless of gender or sexuality. In the same way, the legal definition of the family has been so watered down that it no longer bears any resemblance to traditional notions, as when a New Jersey judge said that six college kids on summer vacation constituted a family. See Gerard Bradley, "The New Constitutional Covenant," *World & I* (March 1994): 374.

19. Bonnie Angelo and Toni Morrison, "The Pain of Being Black," *Time* (May 22, 1989), 120.

20. As quoted in William R. Mattox, "Split Personality: Why Aren't Conservatives Talking about Divorce?" *Policy Review*, no. 73 (summer 1995): 50.

21. Ibid.

22. Whitehead, "Dan Quayle Was Right," 47.

23. Michael McManus, "Voters Should Care about Divorce Reform," *Detroit News*, 19 September 1996.

24. David Popenoe, *Life without Fathers: Compelling New Evidence That Fatherhood and Marriage Are Indispensable for the Good of Children and Society* (New York: Free Press, 1996), 63.

25. Whitehead, "Dan Quayle Was Right," 47.

26. Judith S. Wallerstein and Sandra Blakeslee, *Second Chances: Men, Women, and Children a Decade after Divorce* (New York: Ticknor & Fields, 1989), 21–31.

27. James J. Lynch, *The Broken Heart: The Medical Consequences of Loneliness in America* (New York: Basic Books, 1977), 69–86, 87–90, 41–50, appendix B.

28. David Larson, as quoted in Mattox, "Split Personality," 50.

29. Allan Carlson is president of the Howard Center for the Family, Religion, and Society, which analyzes the status of the family today and disseminates research that empirically validates marriage as the foundation to a healthy society. These findings are published in *The Family in America,* available from the Howard Center for the Family, Religion, and Society, 934 North Main Street, Rockford, IL 61103, phone: (815) 964-5819.

30. Karl Zinsmeister, "The Humble Generation," *American Enterprise* 9, no. 1 (January/February 1998): 4.

31. Elisabeth D. Dodds, *Marriage to a Difficult Man: The "Uncommon Union" of Jonathan and Sarah Edwards* (Philadelphia: Westminster Press, 1971), chapter 14.

32. See Michael J. McManus, *Marriage Savers: Helping Your Friends and Family Avoid Divorce* (Grand Rapids: Zondervan, 1995).

33. "The National Survey of Family Growth," as cited in McManus, *Marriage Savers,* 93. A number of good programs are available to help churches teach strategies for abstinence. For more information, write or call True Love Waits, 127 Ninth Avenue North, Nashville, TN 37234, phone: (800) LUV-WAIT or (800) 588-9248. See also Josh McDowell, *Why Wait? What You Need to Know about the Teen Sexuality Crisis* (Nashville: Nelson, 1994); and Josh McDowell, *Why Say No to Sex?: The Case for Teaching Sexual Abstinence outside Marriage* (Eastbourne, England: Kingsway, 1995).

34. "The National Survey of Families and Households," as cited in McManus, *Marriage Savers,* 39.

35. PREPARE, P.O. Box 190, Minneapolis, MN 55440-0190.

36. ENRICH, P.O. Box 190, Minneapolis, MN 55440-0190.

37. Retrouvaille, 231 Ballantine, Houston, TX 77015, phone: (713) 455-1656.

38. See http://www.marriagesavers.org/fourchurches.htm, (March 10, 1999).

39. Roger Sider, "Grand Rapids Erects a Civic Tent for Marriage," *Policy Review* (July/August 1998): 6.

40. James Sheridan, as quoted in Michael J. McManus, "Judge Makes Sure Couples Are Prepared for Marriage," *Fresno Bee,* 12 April 1997. In Chattanooga, Tennessee, a broad cross section of civic leaders formed a community-wide organization called First Things First in order to rebuild, renew, and revitalize the city. Chattanooga's divorce rate is 50 percent higher than the national average, so First Things First quickly started working on the problem of divorce. Within just

one year, Hamilton County saw a 14 percent drop in divorce filings. Other initiatives include a Fathering Summit to help teach the importance of fathers, and a program called Reading, Writing, and Responsibility, where community leaders and school personnel teach students nine shared values: respect, responsibility, perseverance, caring, self-discipline, citizenship, honesty, courage, and fairness.

41. Mel Krantzler, *Creative Divorce* (New York: M. Evans, 1973); and Esther Oshiver Fisher, *Divorce: The New Freedom* (New York: Harper & Row, 1974).

42. Diane Medved, *The Case against Divorce* (New York: Ivy Books, 1990); Michele Weiner-Davis, *Divorce Busting: A Revolutionary and Rapid Program for Staying Together* (New York: Simon & Schuster, 1993); and William A. Galston, *Rethinking Divorce* (Minneapolis: Center for the American Experiment, 1996).

CHAPTER 5
STILL AT RISK

1. Third International Math and Science Study, conducted by the National Center for Education Statistics, Michigan State University, Boston College, National Science Foundation, and the International Association for the Evaluation of Educational Achievement (February 24, 1998).

2. Survey conducted by the National Center for Education Statistics (Washington, D.C., 1993). See http://www.nces.ed.gov./timms for further information.

3. Josephson Institute of Ethics, "1998 Report Card on the Ethics of American Youth" (Marina del Rey, Calif.: Josephson Institute of Ethics, 1998).

4. Rita Kramer, "Inside the Teacher's Culture," *Public Interest* (January 1997): 64.

5. John Dewey, *Democracy and Education* (New York: Macmillan, 1992); and John Dewey, *Quest for Certainty* (New York: Putnam, 1929). See also Nancy R. Pearcey, "What is Evolution Doing to Education?" *Bible-Science Newsletter* (January 1986): 6.

6. Catherine T. Fosnot, "Constructivism: A Psychological Theory of Learning," in *Constructivism: Theory, Perspectives, and Practice*, ed. C. Fosnot (New York: Teachers College Press, 1996), 8–13. See also James R. Gavelek and Taffy E. Raphael, "Changing Talk about Text: New Roles for Teachers and Students," *Language Arts* 73, no. 3 (1996): 182.

7. See Sidney B. Simon, *Beginning Values Clarification: A Guidebook for the Use of Values Clarification in the Classroom* (San Diego: Pennant Press, 1975); and Sidney B. Simon, Leland W. Howe, and Howard Kirschenbaum, *Values Clarification: A Handbook of Practical Strategies for Teachers and Students*, rev. ed. (Sunderland, Mass.: Values Press, 1978).

8. William Wordsworth, "Ode: Intimations of Immortality from Recollections of Early Childhood."

9. Friedrich Froebel, *The Education of Man* (New York: Appleton, 1891). The section is based on two articles by Nancy R. Pearcey: "The Evolving Child: John Dewey's Impact on Modern Education, part 1," *Bible-Science Newsletter* (January 1991): 5; and "The Evolving Child: John Dewey's Impact on Modern Education, part 2," *Bible-Science Newsletter* (February 1991): 6.

10. Francis Wayland Parker, as quoted in Richard Hofstadter, *Anti-Intellectualism in American Life* (New York: Random, 1963), 366.

11. Perhaps many children in the 1800s, brought up in an environment permeated by a Christian ethos of hard work and moral excellence, *did* blossom when given some freedom for self-direction. Today, when children are brought up in an environment of self-absorption and moral relativism, of course, the result is quite different.

12. J. Crosby Chapman and George S. Counts, *Principles of Education* (Boston: Houghton Mifflin, 1924), 598; and George S. Counts, *Dare the Schools Build a New Social Order?* no. 11 (New York: John Day Pamphlets, 1932).

13. Frederic T. Sommers, "A Campus Forum on Multiculturalism," *New York Times*, 9 December 1990.

14. For the impact of existentialism on education see George R. Knight, *Philosophy and Education: An Introduction in Christian Perspective* (Berrien Springs, Mich.: Andrews University Press, 1980).

15. William R. Coulson, "We Overcame Their Traditions, We Overcame Their Faith," *Latin Mass* 3, no. 1 (January/February 1991): 14–22. In Carl Rogers's last book, *Freedom to Learn for the Eighties* (Columbus, Ohio: Merrill, 1983), he included a chapter entitled "A Pattern of Failure," in which he describes this and other failures of his educational methods.

16. A. H. Maslow, *The Journal of A. H. Maslow*, ed. Richard J. Lowry, 2 vols. (Monterey, Calif.: Brooks-Cole, 1979).

17. Richard Blum of Stanford University found that students who take drug-education courses actually use alcohol, tobacco, and marijuana in greater amounts and at an earlier age than control groups. See

Richard H. Blum, et al., *Drug Education: Results and Recommendations* (Lexington, Mass.: Lexington Books, 1976); and Richard H. Blum, et al., "Drug Education: Further Results and Recommendations," *Journal of Drug Issues* 8, no. 4 (fall 1978): 379–426. A Lou Harris poll commissioned by Planned Parenthood in 1986 found that teens taking sex-education courses reported higher rates of sexual activity than did their peers who had not taken such courses. See Louis Harris and Associates, "The Planned Parenthood Poll," *American Teens Speak—Sex Myths, TV, and Birth Control* (New York: Louis Harris and Associates, 1986).

18. Story told by William Kilpatrick in *Why Johnny Can't Tell Right from Wrong* (New York: Touchstone, 1993), 81.

19. *Witness,* Paramount Pictures (1985). The use of this scene to illustrate the directive approach to education is from William R. Coulson, "Sex, Drugs, and School Children: What Went Wrong," *Adolescent Counselor* (September 1991): 27–31.

20. John Milton, "Of Education," *Complete Poems and Major Prose,* ed. Merritt Y. Hughes (New York: Macmillan, 1957), 631.

21. For example, in Connecticut in 1996, the Scholastic Assessment Test scores for East Catholic High School were well above the national average: Verbal: East Catholic 545 compared to a national average of 505; Math: East Catholic 517 compared to a national average of 508 ("East Catholic High School's Scholastic Assessment Test Scores," *Hartford Courant,* 6 September 1996). A 1995 study by scholars from the University of Maryland School of Economics revealed that for inner-city children, attending a Catholic high school raises the probability of finishing high school and entering college by 17 percent. Having a Catholic school in the neighborhood is good for public schools, too. Harvard economist Caroline M. Hoxby showed that competition from Catholic schools actually raised the academic performance of surrounding public schools. Both studies cited in Nina Shokraii, "Catholic Schools Hold the Key to the Future for At-Risk Students," *News and Record* (Greensboro, N.C.), 28 September 1997.

22. In 1997, Cornerstone Schools Association students scored far above the national average on the Stanford Achievement Test: Reading: Cornerstone 60 percent compared to the national average of 50 percent; Math: Cornerstone 52 percent compared to the national average of 50 percent; Language: Cornerstone 61 percent compared to the national average of 50 percent.

23. Many of these schools have been inspired by Douglas Wilson's book

Recovering the Lost Tools of Learning: An Approach to Distinctively Christian Education (Wheaton, Ill.: Crossway, 1991), which pays homage to Dorothy Sayers's seminal essay "The Lost Tools of Learning." See also Gene Edward Veith and Andrew Kern, *Classical Education: Toward the Revival of America's Schooling* (Washington, D.C.: Capitol Research Center, 1997).

24. In March 1999, a report was released by Lawrence M. Rudner, professor at the University of Maryland, who conducted the largest nonpartisan study on home-schooled students. Rudner, whose own children attend public schools, tracked the test results of 21,000 students and was shocked to find that the home-schooled students were substantially ahead of their peers in public school. Home schoolers perform an average of one grade level above their counterparts in public and private schools in the elementary grades. By the eighth grade, the gap amounts to four grade levels (Philip Walzer, "Home Schooling Passes Test," *Virginia-Pilot*, [24 March 1999]).

25. David A. Noebel, *Understanding the Times: The Story of the Biblical Christian, Marxist/Leninist and Secular Humanist Worldviews* (Manitou Springs, Colo.: Summit Press, 1991); and Summit Ministries, P.O. Box 207, Manitou Springs, CO 80829, phone: (719) 685-9103; fax: (719) 685-5268.

26. The Character Education Partnership, 918 16th Street NW, Suite 501, Washington, D.C. 20006, phone: (202) 296-7743.

27. Norman Higgins in an interview with Kim Robbins (February 26, 1999); see also Susan Young, "The Right Direction," http://www.bangornews.com/Innovative/day1.html (February 26, 1999).

28. Barbara Moses is now a principal of a Philadelphia inner-city Mennonite high school.

29. Tyce Palmaffy, "No Excuses," *Policy Review* (January/February 1998): 18. Direct Instruction is an alternative to today's popular "constructivist" method of teaching. The constructivist method allows children to be in charge of their learning by experimenting and exploring. The Direct Instruction method puts the teacher in charge of the students' learning. Children are "guided through sequential lessons that provide the foundation for understanding content. Repetition of lessons is frequent to reinforce past learning, and errors are immediately pointed out in verbal recitation." Wesley principal Thaddeus Lott, in commenting on Direct Instruction, says: "We teach them the 'how.' The 'what' and 'why' will come later." He goes on to say that "by giving them the basics, we make it possible for

them to do independent work when we turn them loose" (Lott, "Direct Instruction/Constructivist: Models for Learning," *Daily Report Card* [March 1, 1995]).

30. Margaret Bonilla, "Be Fruitful and Multiply," *Policy Review* (summer 1994): 73–76.
31. See Virgil Gulker, *A World without Welfare,* ed. David M. Wagner (Washington, D.C.: Family Research Council, 1997), 107. See also Amy L. Sherman, *Restorers of Hope: Reaching the Poor in Your Community with Church-Based Ministries That Work* (Wheaton, Ill.: Crossway, 1997), 151–54. This doesn't take a lot of specialized knowledge; mostly it takes the kind of love and initiative that Hannah Hawkins offers children in her low-income Anacostia district in Washington, D.C. There, Hawkins, a retired African-American woman, runs an after-school program for several dozen neighborhood children. Every evening they flock to her home, where she oversees their homework. Though simple and homegrown, such programs are helping grades go up and disciplinary incidents decline.
32. Amity Shales, "A Chance to Equip My Child," *Wall Street Journal,* 23 February 1998.
33. Cal Thomas, "Milwaukee's 'School Choice' Experiment Shows That Competition Works," *Wisconsin State Journal,* 13 November 1998.
34. "In Defense of School Vouchers," *The Hill,* 6 May 1998; and Robert Holland, "Free Markets and Technology Will Transform K–12 Education," *Richmond Times Dispatch,* 2 December 1998. There are eight applicants for every scholarship granted, indicating how much low-income families want for their kids the same break that the rich can get. On January 26, 1999, the Arizona Supreme Court upheld a tax credit for people who donate money for scholarships at private schools ("Can You Spare a Million?" *Washington Times,* 18 January 1998).
35. Pope John Paul II, *Fides et Ratio,* Encyclical Letter to the Bishops of the Catholic Church (October 1998).

CHAPTER 6
ANYTHING CAN HAPPEN HERE

1. The details of Officer Salvatore Bartolomeo's story were gleaned through several interviews and through assistance from Eddie Cordelia and John Stewart. Some of the secondary characters in this story are composites of real people Officer Sal knew on his beat. Additional background information about community policing came

from articles that include James Q. Wilson and George L. Kelling, "Making Neighborhoods Safe," *Atlantic Monthly* (February 1989): 46–52; Myron Magnet, "Saving the Homeless from Some Bad Ideas," *San Diego Union-Tribune*, 18 February 1990; John Leo, "A New Fight against Urban Decay," *Courier Journal*, 2 February 1992; and William D. Eggers and John O'Leary, "The Beat Generation: Community Policing at Its Best," *Policy Review*, no. 74 (fall 1995): 4.

CHAPTER 7
THERE GOES THE NEIGHBORHOOD

1. Ramsey Clark, the attorney general under Lyndon Johnson, wrote, "The crowding of millions of poor people with their cumulative disadvantage into the urban ghettos of our affluent and technologically advanced society not only offers the easy chance for criminal acts—it causes crime" (Clark, *Crime in America: Observations on Its Nature, Causes, Prevention and Control* [New York: Simon & Schuster, 1970], 29). Similarly, when widespread looting occurred in the late 1970s during a blackout in New York City, then President Jimmy Carter explained it as the result of poverty, though later studies showed that most of those looters were employed and stole things they didn't need.

2. These figures from the Federal Bureau of Investigation; the Bureau of Alcohol, Tobacco, and Firearms; and the National Center for Health Statistics were cited in Ted Gest, Gordon Witkin, Katia Hetter, and Andrea Wright, "Violence in America," *U.S. News and World Report* 116, no. 2 (January 17, 1994): 22.

3. George L. Kelling and Catherine M. Coles, *Fixing Broken Windows: Restoring Order and Reducing Crime in Our Communities* (New York: Free Press, 1996), 55–56.

4. Andrew Peyton Thomas, "The Rise and Fall of the Homeless," *Weekly Standard* 1, no. 29 (April 8, 1996): 27. See also Andrew Peyton Thomas, *Crime and the Sacking of America: The Roots of Chaos* (Washington, D.C.: Brussey's, 1994).

5. To read more about this, see Rael Jean Isaac, *Madness in the Streets: How Psychiatry and the Law Abandoned the Mentally Ill* (New York: Free Press, 1990).

6. James Q. Wilson and George L. Kelling, "Broken Windows," *Atlantic Monthly* (March 1982): 29.

7. John Carlin, "How They Cleaned Up Precinct 75," *The Independent*, 7 January 1996.

8. See Kelling and Coles, *Fixing Broken Windows*, chapter 4.

9. Abraham Kuyper, *Lectures on Calvinism* (Grand Rapids: Eerdmans, 1983), 79.

10. Saint Augustine, *The City of God* (New York: Modern Library, 1950), 690. In the Middle Ages, Thomas Aquinas gave Augustine's insight a more positive interpretation, arguing that the state is not only a remedial institution established to curb sin but that it is also a good thing in itself, an expression of our social nature. Living within social institutions is essential to fulfilling our own nature.

11. William Wilberforce , as quoted in Garth Lean, *God's Politician: William Wilberforce's Struggle* (London: Darton, Longman & Todd, 1980), 74.

12. Robert Peel, as quoted in Fred Siegel, *The Future Once Happened Here: New York, D.C., L.A., and the Fate of America's Big Cities* (New York: Free Press, 1997), 192.

13. Eric Monkkonen, *Police in Urban America: 1860–1920* (Cambridge: Cambridge University Press, 1981), as quoted in Siegel, *The Future Once Happened Here*, 192.

14. James Q. Wilson and George L. Kelling, "Beating Criminals to the Punch," *New York Times*, 24 April 1989.

15. Reuben Greenberg, "Less Bang-Bang for the Buck," *Policy Review* (winter 1992): 56.

16. Andrew Heiskell, with Ralph Graves, "Soapbox: Struggling to Save Bryant Park," *New York Times*, 13 September 1998.

17. Robert J. Sampson, "Neighborhoods and Violent Crime: A Multilevel Study of Collective Efficacy," *Science* 277, no. 5328 (August 15, 1997): 918.

18. Delores Kong, "Study Shows Cohesiveness Curbs Neighborhood Violence," *Boston Globe*, 15 August 1997.

19. John J. DiIulio, "Broken Bottles: Liquor, Disorder, and Crime in Wisconsin," Wisconsin Policy Research Institute Report 8, no. 4 (May 1995).

20. Richard R. Freeman and Harry J. Holzer, eds., *The Black Youth Employment Crisis* (Chicago: University of Chicago Press, 1986), 353–76.

21. James Q. Wilson and Richard J. Herrnstein, *Crime and Human Nature* (New York: Simon & Schuster, 1985), 432. In the early 1980s, Wilson sought to discover why crime decreased in the middle of the last century and then, after some fluctuations (up in the 1920s, down in the 1930s), shot up dramatically in the 1960s and has been climbing ever since. He checked all the standard explanations of

criminal behavior but found that none correlated with the historical pattern. Poverty, for example. If poverty causes crime, why was crime so low during the Depression, when more than a quarter of the population had no income at all? And why did it rise during the affluent 1960s and 1970s?

—Then Wilson stumbled on the fact that the decrease in crime in the last century followed the Second Great Awakening. As repentance and renewal spread across the country, church membership rose steeply, Christians formed voluntary associations devoted to education and moral reform, and American society as a whole came to respect the values of sobriety, hard work, and self-restraint—what sociologists call the Protestant ethic. And as the Protestant ethic triumphed, the crime rate plummeted.

—Beginning in the 1920s through the late 1930s, however, the Protestant ethic began to fall out of favor among the educated classes. "Freud's psychological theories came into vogue," explains Wilson, and the educated classes began to view religion and ethics as oppressive. Their cause was no longer freedom for religion—a classic American liberty—but freedom from religion.

—The attitude of these educated classes was restrained by the Depression and two world wars, but in the 1960s it finally percolated through to popular consciousness, resulting in a widespread cultural shift away from an ethic of self-discipline toward an ethic of self-expression. The result was a sudden and dramatic increase in crime. See James Q. Wilson, "Crime and American Culture," *Public Interest* (winter 1983): 22.

22. John Leland, with Claudia Kalb, "Savior of the Street," *Newsweek* (June 1, 1998): 20.

23. Joe Klein, as quoted in Joe Loconte, "The Bully and the Pulpit: A New Model for Church-State Partnership," *Policy Review* (November/December 1998): 28.

24. Leslie Scanlon, "From the PEWS to the Streets: More Churches Are Going beyond Their Walls to Fight Drugs and Crime," *Courier-Journal*, 27 July 1997.

25. Roy Maynard, "Voice of Hope," *Loving Your Neighbor: A Principled Guide to Personal Charity*, ed. Marvin N. Olasky (Washington, D.C.: Capital Research Center, 1995), 57.

26. This story about Chicago and the following stories about Baltimore, Memphis, and Montgomery are told in John Perkins, with Jo Kadlecek, *Resurrecting Hope: Powerful Stories of How God Is Moving to Reach Our Cities* (Ventura, Calif.: Regal Books, 1995).

CHAPTER 8
CREATING THE GOOD SOCIETY

1. From President John Adams's October 11, 1798, address to the military, as quoted in *The Works of John Adams—Second President of the United States,* Charles Francis Adams, ed., vol. 9 (Boston: Little, Brown & Co., 1854), 229.

2. "79 Leaders Unite to Aid Democracy," *New York Times,* 1 June 1940.

3. "To Defend Democracy," *New York Times,* 9 June 1940.

4. Fred W. Beuttler, "For the World at Large: Intergroup Activities at the Jewish Theological Seminary," in *Tradition Renewed: A History of the Jewish Theological Seminary—Beyond the Academy,* vol. 2 (New York: The Seminary, 1997), 667. See also Sidney Hook's address reprinted in the *New Republic,* 2 (October 28, 1940): 684.

5. "Scholars Confess They Are Confused," *New York Times,* 1 September 1942.

6. Beuttler, "For the World at Large," 667. We are indebted to Beuttler, who has performed a great service in studying the history of the conference, and we have drawn extensively on his research. In the course of his study, he discovered a fascinating and revealing historical footnote. In 1956, Nelson Rockefeller launched an ambitious special-studies project to define national goals for America's future. Rockefeller engaged a young Harvard professor, Henry Kissinger, to staff the project. Kissinger shrewdly saw that such an effort would have to have a moral framework for national purpose. Kissinger called in Finkelstein, then heading the Institute of Ethics at the New York Seminary, for advice, specifically in formulating a moral justification for the use of limited nuclear weapons. The question Kissinger put was, What are we "willing to die for in terms of values"? The Institute, under Finkelstein's direction, began extensive discussions, but it soon broke down, just as the conference had earlier. The panelists began to dodge Kissinger's insistent questions as he pushed them to deal more with the role of religion and natural law. Finkelstein's panel eventually gave up trying to reach a consensus, in effect telling Rockefeller and Kissinger that they could only help them clarify their values.

7. Richard John Neuhaus, "The Truth about Freedom," *Wall Street Journal,* 8 October 1993.

8. Dan Shine, "Yale OKs Return of Gift to Billionaire Lee Bass: Clash over $20 Million for Program," *Dallas Morning News,* 15 March 1995.

9. Michael Novak, *Character and Crime: An Inquiry into the Causes of the Virtue of Nations* (Notre Dame, Ind.: Brownson Institute, 1986), 107.

10. Jonathan Friendly, "Public Schools Avoid Teaching Right and Wrong," *New York Times,* 2 December 1985.

11. Michael Novak, "The Conservative Momentum" (speech given at the Center for the American Experiment, March 24, 1993).

12. Michael Novak, "The Causes of Virtue" (speech given in Washington, D.C., January 31, 1994, reprinted by Prison Fellowship in *Sources,* no. 6 [1994]).

13. James Schall, "Personal Sin and Social Sin," *Crisis* (June 1997): 57.

14. Christina Hoff Sommers, "Teaching the Virtues," *Chicago Tribune,* 12 September 1993.

15. Robert P. George, "Why Integrity Matters" (speech given at the National Prayer Breakfast, Washington, D.C., February 7, 1998).

16. Webster's defines *integrate* as "to unite (parts or elements), so as to form a whole; also, to unite (a part or element) with something else, esp. something more inclusive" (*Webster's New International Dictionary,* 2nd ed.).

17. C. S. Lewis, *The Abolition of Man* (New York: Macmillan, 1947), 35.

18. Michael Novak, *Character and Crime,* 38. Novak draws a significant parallel with economics. For centuries people sought the cause of poverty. But the most profound change for the economic betterment of the world came about when the eighteenth-century economist Adam Smith reversed that question, asking instead, What is the cause of *wealth?* See Adam Smith, *The Wealth of Nations: An Inquiry into the Nature and Causes Of* (New York: Modern Library, 1994).

19. Deal W. Hudson, *Happiness and the Limits of Satisfaction* (Lanham, Md.: Rowman & Littlefield, 1996).

20. Ibid.

CHAPTER 9
THE WORK OF OUR HANDS

1. Dorothy L. Sayers, *Creed or Chaos?* (Manchester, N.H.: Sophia Press, 1949), 77.

2. Richard John Neuhaus, *Doing Well and Doing Good: The Challenge to the Christian Capitalist* (New York: Doubleday, 1992).

3. Theologian T. M. Moore in a memo entitled "Economic Aspects of the Biblical Worldview" (August 12, 1998).

4. Robert A. Sirico, "The Enterpreneurial Vocation," available from The Acton Institute for the Study of Religion and Liberty, 1611

Ottawa NW, Suite 301, Grand Rapids, MI 49503, phone: (616) 454-3080. Elsewhere Sirico writes, "By themselves, brilliant ideas do not serve humankind; to be brought into service to man, they must be transformed through complex processes of design and production. The talent to perform this transformation is as rare and as humanly precious as talent in any other field" (See Sirico, *Toward the Future: Catholic Social Thought and the U.S. Economy* [New York: American Catholic Committee, 1984], 28).

5. Theologian T. M. Moore suggests that this balance of private property and social justice can be seen in the description of the godly wife in Proverbs 31. She enters freely into enterprises designed to enrich herself and provide for her family (vv. 13, 16, 19, 24). She is generous to the needy (v. 20), yet she makes certain that the needs of her own household are met (vv. 21, 27). As a result of her labors, she dresses well, and she is not looked down on for this (v. 22). Her industry and productivity reflect well on her husband in the eyes of the city fathers (v. 23). The secret of her success is her fear of God and her determination to live for him (v. 30). And she is deserving of every cent she makes (v. 31)!

6. Mary Hesse, *Science and the Human Imagination: Aspects of the History and Logic of Physical Science* (New York: Philosophical Library, 1955), 263 (emphasis in the original).

7. Eusebius, as quoted in Leland Ryken, *Work and Leisure: In Christian Perspective* (Portland, Ore.: Multnomah, 1987), 66.

8. See Robert A. Sirico, "The Late-Scholastic and Austrian Link to Modern Catholic Economic Thought," *Markets and Morality* 1, no. 2 (October 1988): 122–29.

9. Martin Luther, as quoted in Ryken, *Work and Leisure,* 95, 97. This principle applies to all forms of work, not just paid employment: All our tasks and duties, including those as parents or as citizens, Luther regarded as a call from God.

10. Luther, as quoted in Ryken, 135.

11. Robert A. Sirico, "The Parable of the Talents," *Freeman* 44, no. 7 (July 1994): 354.

12. For further discussion about this issue, see Chuck Colson and Jack Eckerd, *Why America Doesn't Work* (Dallas: Word, 1991).

13. Adam Smith, *The Wealth of Nations* (New York: Modern Library, 1994), 15.

14. Michael Novak, *The Spirit of Democratic Capitalism* (New York: Simon & Schuster, 1982), 79 (emphasis in the original).

15. William Blake, *Milton.*

16. Michael Novak, *Business as a Calling: Work and the Examined Life* (New York: Free Press, 1996).

17. Michael Novak, "Profits with Honor," *Policy Review* (May/June 1996): 50. See also "Sweet Vindication: Award of 1994 Templeton Prize to Michael Novak for Progress in Religion," *National Review* 46, no. 6 (April 4, 1994): 22; and Walter Isaacson, "Exalting the City of Man," *Time* (May 10, 1982): 38.

18. Lance Morrow, "What Is the Point of Working?" *Time* (May 11, 1981): 93.

19. Robert Schrank, as quoted in Morrow, "What Is the Point of Working?" 93.

20. Arlie Hochschild, *The Time Bind: When Work Becomes Home and Home Becomes Work* (New York: Metropolitan Books, 1997), 37. A July 2, 1997, *Wall Street Journal* article asked, Are today's parents neglecting their kids in favor of the "ego high they get from work"?

21. See Maggie Gallagher, "Day Careless," *National Review* (January 26, 1998): 37; Karl Zinsmeister, "The Problem with Day Care," *American Enterprise* 9, no. 3 (May/June 1998): 26; and William Dreskin and Wendy Dreskin, *The Day Care Decision: What's Best for You and Your Child* (New York: M. Evans, 1983).

22. Laura Shapiro, et al., "The Myth of Quality Time," *Newsweek* (May 19, 1997): 42; and Shannon Brownlee, et al., "Lies Parents Tell Themselves about Why They Work," *U.S. News and World Report* (May 12, 1997): 58.

23. Morrow, "What Is the Point of Working?" 93. Even Christians have absorbed secular attitudes toward work. A book-length study surveying attitudes among young people enrolled at Christian colleges and seminaries found that they hold an appallingly secular view of work. James Davison Hunter, who directed the survey, concludes that "work has lost any spiritual and eternal significance and that it is important only insofar as it fosters certain qualities of the personality" (James Davison Hunter, *Evangelicalism: The Coming Generation* [Chicago: University of Chicago Press, 1987], 56).

24. Os Guinness, *The Call: Finding and Fulfilling the Central Purpose of Life* (Nashville: Word, 1998), chapter 4.

25. Many of these ideas are discussed in Chuck Colson and Jack Eckerd, *Why America Doesn't Work* (Dallas: Word, 1991).

26. John Stollenwerk, as quoted in Spencer Abraham and Dan Coats, "Hard-Working Churches," *American Enterprise* 8, no. 4 (July/August 1997): 13.

27. Ronald Marino (in a speech given at the symposium on welfare by

the Family Research Council), *A World without Welfare,* ed. David M. Wagner (Washington, D.C.: Family Research Council, 1997), 86–91.

28. Don Michele (in a speech given at the symposium on welfare by the Family Research Council), *A World without Welfare,* ed. David M. Wagner (Washington, D.C.: Family Research Council, 1997), 91–93.

29. Marvin N. Olasky, ed., *Loving Your Neighbor: A Principled Guide to Personal Charity* (Washington, D.C.: Capital Research Center, 1995), 64.

30. John Perkins, with Jo Kadlecek, *Resurrecting Hope* (Ventura, Calif.: Regal Books, 1995), 95–97.

31. See Virgil Gulker (in a speech given at the symposium on welfare by the Family Research Council), *A World without Welfare,* ed. David M. Wagner (Washington, D.C.: Family Research Council, 1997), 107.

32. The following examples are taken from Amy L. Sherman, "Little Miracles," *American Enterprise* 9, no. 1 (January/February 1998): 64.

33. Alexander Solzhenitsyn, *One Day in the Life of Ivan Denisovich* (New York: Dutton, 1963), 100.

CHAPTER 10
THE ULTIMATE APPEAL

1. The details of King's story are taken largely from Stephen B. Oates, *Let the Trumpet Sound: A Life of Martin Luther King, Jr.* (New York: HarperPerennial, 1994).

2. Martin Luther King Jr., *Why We Can't Wait* (New York: Harper & Row, 1964), 84–85.

3. Ibid., 75.

4. Russell Hittinger, introduction to *Rights and Duties: Reflections on Our Conservative Constitution* by Russell Kirk (Dallas: Spence, 1997), xxvii.

5. The decision was *Dred Scott v. Sandford,* 60 US 393 (1857).

6. Abraham Lincoln, "Proclamation for Appointing a National Fast Day" (March 30, 1863), as quoted in Mark Noll, *One Nation Under God?: Christian Faith and Political Action in America* (San Francisco: Harper San Francisco, 1988), 98.

7. Robert P. George, *A Preserving Grace: Protestants, Catholics, and Natural Law,* ed. Michael Cromartie (Washington, D.C.: Ethics and Public Policy Center; Grand Rapids: Eerdmans, 1997), 94.

8. Marcus Tullius Cicero, *The Great Legal Philosophers: Selected Readings in Jurisprudence*, ed. Clarence Morris (Philadelphia: University of Pennsylvania Press, 1971), 50.

9. See Willmoore Kendall, *The Conservative Affirmation in America* (Chicago: Henry Regnery, 1963), chapter 5. The church played a major role in making this tradition explicit. In the eleventh century, Pope Gregory VII set out to reform the primitive tribal societies of Europe with laws drawn directly from Scripture. The first German law book, written in 1220, stated that "God is Himself law; and therefore law is dear to Him." (H. J. Berman, "Religious Foundations of Law in the West: An Historical Perspective," *Journal of Law and Religion* 1, no. 1 [summer 1983]: 3–43).

10. William Blackstone, *Commentaries on the Laws of England*, vol. 1 (Chicago: University of Chicago Press, 1979), 41.

11. John C. Rager, *The Political Philosophy of St. Robert Bellarmine: An Examination of Saint Cardinal Bellarmine's Defense of Popular Government and the Influence of His Political Theory upon the Declaration of Independence* (Spokane, Wash.: Apostolate of Our Lady of Siluva, 1995).

12. John Whitehead, *The Second American Revolution* (Elgin, Ill.: David C. Cook, 1982), 28–30.

13. John Finnis, *Natural Law and Natural Rights* (New York: Oxford University Press, 1980), 146; Robert P. George, *Making Men Moral* (New York: Oxford University Press, 1993), 47; and Robert A. Sirico, "Subsidiarity, Society, and Entitlements," *Notre Dame Journal of Law, Ethics and Public Policy* 11, no. 2 (1997): 549.

14. Abraham Kuyper, *Christianity: A Total World and Life System* (Marlborough, N.H.: Plymouth Rock Foundation, 1996), 60.

15. Ibid., 46. "Calvin personally preferred a republic," notes Kuyper, in which there would be cooperation between the spheres of society "under mutual control." He also considered it most ideal "where the people themselves choose their own magistrate," and admonished people to take seriously their responsibility to choose their own leaders: "See to it that ye do not forfeit this favor by electing to the positions of highest honor, rascals and enemies of God" (49–50).

16. James Madison, "Federalist No. 10," *New York Packet*, 23 November 1787.

17. Historians are quick to point out that some of the Founders were not Christians but Enlightenment deists, including Jefferson and to some degree Madison. Yet deist and Christian alike agreed that the rule of

law is rooted in a higher law, objectively true and binding—what Jefferson called "the law of nature and nature's God."

—Among the Founders, a minority held the Lockean idea of individuals with natural rights based in their personhood coming together and entering a political contract, by which they consent to be governed. The majority held that a political contract is made within the context of a higher law and that the contract reflects the natural order of things ordained by God.

18. William James, as quoted in R. C. Sproul, *Lifeviews: Understanding the Ideas That Shape Society Today* (Old Tappan, N.J.: Revell, 1986), 89.

19. Phillip E. Johnson, *Reason in the Balance: The Case against Naturalism in Science, Law, and Education* (Downers Grove, Ill.: InterVarsity Press, 1995), chapter 7.

20. Oliver Wendell Holmes, "Natural Law," *Harvard Law Review*, 30–32 (1918): 40.

21. Gene Edward Veith, *Postmodern Times: A Christian Guide to Contemporary Thought and Culture* (Wheaton, Ill.: Crossway, 1994).

22. William Orville Douglas, *Zorach v. Clauson*, 343 US 306 (1952). See also Richard John Neuhaus, *The Naked Public Square* (Grand Rapids: Eerdmans, 1995), introduction and chapter 3.

23. *Edwards v. Aguillard*, 482 US 578 (1987).

24. *Planned Parenthood v. Casey*, 505 US 833 (1992).

25. In making this ruling, the Court could not have been unaware that only once in American history (and that in a contract case) had the Court ever reversed a right protected by the Fourteenth Amendment.

26. The Court followed *Casey* with a series of unusually harsh decisions. It ruled, for example, that pro-lifers may not demonstrate within a bubble zone surrounding an abortion clinic, though pro-choicers remain free to do so (*Madsen v. Women's Health Center, Inc.*, 512 US 753 [1994]).

27. Gerard V. Bradley, "The New Constitutional Covenant," *World & I* (March 1994): 361. In its expansive definition of liberty in *Casey*, the Court was talking about the liberty of whether to define oneself as a mother. But taken to its logical conclusion, this definition of liberty could undercut all law. All laws restrain someone's behavior, and all behavior expresses in some way a worldview, a belief about the meaning of existence and the universe.

28. *Lee v. Weisman*, 505 US 577 (1992).

29. Ibid.

30. *Romer v. Evans*, 517 US 620 (1996).

31. *Compassion in Dying v. Washington,* 79 F 3d 790 (9th Cir 1996).
    What is even more frightening is the argument the justices used
    to reach their decision. *Compassion in Dying v. Washington,* the
    infamous assisted-suicide case of 1997, reached the Supreme Court
    when appellate courts overturned a referendum passed by the voters
    of the State of Washington banning assisted suicide. Since the
    appellate courts had reversed the referendum based on the Supreme
    Court's own decision in *Planned Parenthood v. Casey,* which defined
    liberty as the right to decide for one's self the meaning of life, to be
    consistent the Supreme Court should have affirmed the lower court.
    But even the insulated Supreme Court judges weren't ready to face
    the degree of moral outrage this might have triggered. (Contrary
    to popular opinion, the justices *do* read newspapers and polls.) So
    what did they do? Examine the Constitution or the law? Research
    legislative history? Not at all. Instead, they mused aloud from the
    bench and wrote in their opinion that as a nation we simply haven't
    had enough experience with assisted suicide—or euthanasia—to
    know whether we are ready for it.
        These men and women were not speaking in juridical terms;
    they were using the language of social scientists. This decision was
    not based on principled opposition but on the sociological fact that
    America might not be ready to face it. Their only moral concern was
    reduced to pure pragmatism: Let's see how things work out. Let's
    see indeed.

32. *Boerne v. Flores,* 521 US 507 (1997); *Employment Division v. Smith,*
    494 US 872 (1990). At issue was the expansion of a growing
    Catholic parish in Boerne, Texas, a suburb of San Antonio. City
    authorities objected to the expansion, contending that the church
    was an historic monument and that its quaint charm was important
    to an area being redeveloped for tourism. So a line was drawn in the
    sand: Was the church a museum to draw tourists or a sanctuary for
    worship? The answer the Court handed down was that tourism was
    more important.

33. Though most Americans are unaware of the fact, the power of
    judicial review is nowhere in the Constitution. The Court assumed
    the power in an 1803 case, but only for limited circumstances
    (*Marbury v. Madison).* Not until the *Boerne v. Flores* case in 1997
    did the Court assert unchallengeable authority to interpret the
    Constitution (though something close to this claim was asserted in
    the 1958 case of *Cooper v. Aaron*).
        Furthermore, had the *Boerne* decision been the prevailing law in

the nineteenth century, this country would still have slavery, for it would have held not only that slavery is a constitutional right, as the *Dred Scott* decision held, but also that Congress had no power to restrict slavery even in federal territories. (In fact, Lincoln refused to recognize the *Dred Scott* decision as a binding rule on the legislative and executive branches of the federal government.)

34. Antonin Scalia, "Of Democracy, Morality, and the Majority," *Origins* 26, no. 6 (June 27, 1996). In an unpublished speech at Gregorian Pontifical University in Rome in 1996, Scalia said that while he believes in natural law, it has no place in judicial decision making. In ruling on the Constitution, he said the justices are bound by the literal meaning of the words of the text; they should not take moral truth into account in giving effect to constitutional guarantees. So if the "people want abortion," Scalia concluded, "the state should permit abortion in a democracy."

    —If we substitute *slavery* or *incest* or *anti-Semitism* for *abortion* in Scalia's statement, would the conclusion be different? Logically, no. For in Scalia's view, the majority always rules "and the minority loses, except to the extent that the majority . . . has agreed to accord the minority rights." (Scalia made it plain in his speech that, in his view, the democratic majority should, for the sake of justice, enact legal protections against abortion, but that does not mitigate his judicial positivism.)

35. In the *Casey* case, the Court actually referred to the Constitution as a covenant. See Russell Hittinger, "A Crisis of Legitimacy," *Loyola Law Review* 44 (1998): 83.

36. Bradley, "The New Constitutional Covenant," 374.

37. Russell Kirk, "The 'Original Intent' Controversy," *The Heritage Foundation Report,* no. 138, (October 15, 1987).

38. See C. S. Lewis, *The Abolition of Man* (New York: Touchstone, 1975) and *Mere Christianity* (New York: Touchstone, 1996).

39. Arthur Leff, "Unspeakable Ethics, Unnatural Law," *Duke Law Journal* (speech given at Duke University Law School on April 2, 1979): 1229.

40. Bradley, "The New Constitutional Covenant," 359.

41. Michael Sandel, *Democracy's Discontent: America in Search of a Public Philosophy* (Boston: Harvard University Press, 1996).

42. According to a 1996 Gallup survey of American political culture, 32 percent of Americans have "a great deal of confidence" in the federal government generally, but just 13 percent in the presidency and only 5 percent in the Congress (comparable figures for 1966 were 41

percent for the president, 42 percent for Congress). Eighty percent believe "our country is run by a close network of special interests, public officials and the media." Only one in five Americans is satisfied with the quality of political debate. One-quarter of all Americans believe the nation's government works against the interests of the citizenry; three-quarters believe the government is run by a "few big interests looking out for themselves"; and one in five Americans believes that the people who run our nation's institutions are "involved in a conspiracy!" These figures are based on a study done by James Davison Hunter. See Hunter, *The State of Disunion: 1996 Survey of American Political Culture,* vol. 2 (Ivy, Va.: In Medias Res Educational Foundation, 1996).

43. This is why Pope John Paul II said, "Moral relativism is incompatible with democracy," for rights cannot exist apart from a moral law (in a speech to U.S. Bishops at the Vatican, October 1998).

44. Clarence Page, "On Today's Campus: Consent for a Kiss Is Romance 101," *Orlando Sentinel,* 16 September 1993. See also Martin Gross, *The End of Sanity: Social and Cultural Madness in America* (New York: Avon Books, 1998); and James Hannah, "Applications Up after College Enacts Sex Rules for 'Every Step of the Way,'" *Rocky Mountain News,* 15 January 1995.

45. Meg Greenfield, "Sexual Harasser?" *Washington Post,* 30 September 1996.

46. George F. Will, "The Popcorn Board Lives!" *Newsweek* (October 13, 1997): 88.

47. I have written on this at length in other forums. See *Kingdoms in Conflict* (New York: William Morrow; Grand Rapids: Zondervan, 1987); *Against the Night* (Ann Arbor, Mich.: Servant, 1991); *End of Democracy* (Dallas: Spence, 1997); and *We Hold These Truths* (a pamphlet of "A Statement of Christian Conscience and Citizenship," drafted by forty-four people on July 4, 1997; distributed by Prison Fellowship).

48. Daniel Ritchie, ed., *Edmund Burke: Appraisals and Applications* (New Brunswick, N.J.: Transaction Publishers, 1990), 222.

49. In late 1997, Chinese president Jiang Zemin defended his government's persecution of Christians on the grounds that he could not permit them to incite movements for freedom in China as they did in Eastern Europe. See Diane Knippers, "How to Pressure China," *Christianity Today* (July 14, 1997): 52.

50. See, for example, Robert P. George, "God's Reasons," (speech given at the 1998 American Political Science Association Convention;

published by Prison Fellowship, Reston, Virginia). For example, five colleagues and I, all critics of judicial overreach, wrote on the crisis in the law in a symposium that proved to be enormously controversial. See "The End of Democracy?" *First Things* (November 1996): 18–42. It was reported that this material was read by supreme court justices as they debated the recent assisted-suicide cases.

51. Beckett Fund for Religious Liberty, 2000 Pennsylvania Ave. NW, Suite 3580, Washington, D.C. 20006, phone: (202) 955-0095; American Center for Law and Justice, P.O. Box 64429, Virginia Beach, VA 23467, phone: (757) 226-2489; Center for Law and Religious Freedom (founded by the Christian Legal Society), 4208 Evergreen Lane, Suite 222, Annandale, VA 22003, (703) 642-1070, clrf@clsnet.org; Rutherford Institute, P.O. Box 7482, Charlottesville, VA 22906, phone: (804) 978-3888; Alliance Defense Fund, 7819 East Greenway Rd., Suite 8, Scottsdale, AZ 85260, phone: (602) 953-1200.

52. Alexis de Tocqueville, *Democracy in America* (New Rochelle, N.Y.: Arlington House, 1966), 114. For additional material on the extensive social ministries run by Christians in the nineteenth century, see Gertrude Himmelfarb, *Victorian Minds* (Chicago: I. R. Dee, 1995); and Marvin N. Olasky, *The Tragedy of American Compassion* (Washington, D.C.: Regnery Gateway, 1992).

53. Barbara Vogel, in an interview with Anne Morse, managing editor of *BreakPoint Radio* (January 1999).

54. Institutional separation does not mean that religious truth must never influence public policy, however, which is where the Christian conception of separation of church and state differs from the liberal conception.

55. One of the many examples was Andrew Marshall, "Christians Out to Reclaim GOP Agenda," *Arizona Republic,* 5 July 1998.

56. Sir Thomas More, as quoted in Peter Ackroyd, *The Life of Sir Thomas More* (New York: Doubleday, 1998), 405.

CHAPTER 11
THE BASIS FOR TRUE SCIENCE

1. Daniel Dennett, *Darwin's Dangerous Idea: Evolution and the Meanings of Life* (New York: Simon & Schuster, 1995), 520.

2. David Hume, as quoted in John Herman Randall Jr., *The Making of the Modern Mind* (New York: Columbia University Press, 1940), 273.

3. G. K. Chesterton, *Eugenics and Other Evils* (New York: Dodd, Mead, 1927), 98.

4. Philip H. Phenix, as quoted in Michael D. Aeschliman, *The Restitution of Man: C. S. Lewis and the Case against Scientism* (Grand Rapids: Eerdmans, 1983), 50.

5. Arthur Koestler, as quoted in Aeschliman, *The Restitution of Man,* 55.

6. C. S. Lewis, *The Abolition of Man* (New York: Touchstone, 1975), 83.

7. Christian sociologist Jacques Ellul warned that the contemporary state of mind is so completely dominated by technical values that we are becoming unfamiliar with any other values. See Jacques Ellul, *The Technological Society* (New York: Alfred A. Knopf, 1976).

8. C. S. Lewis, *God in the Dock: Essays on Theology and Ethics* (Grand Rapids: Eerdmans, 1970), 136.

9. The following discussion relies heavily on Nancy R. Pearcey and Charles B. Thaxton, *The Soul of Science: Christian Faith and Natural Philosophy* (Wheaton, Ill.: Crossway, 1994).

10. *Pocahontas,* Walt Disney Productions (1995).

11. Carl Becker, *The Heavenly City of the Eighteenth-Century Philosophers* (New Haven: Yale University Press, 1932), 55.

12. Roger Cotes, preface to the second edition of Newton's *Principia,* in *Newton's Philosophy of Nature: Selections from His Writings,* ed. H. S. Thayer (New York: Hafner, 1953).

13. See Pearcey and Thaxton, *The Soul of Science.*

14. R. G. Collingwood, *An Essay on Metaphysics* (Chicago: Henry Regnery, 1972), 253–57.

15. Newton's theology was not fully Trinitarian, but no historian questions that he was fervent and sincere in his belief or that in most respects his belief was fully Christian.

16. Isaac Newton, as quoted in Pearcey and Thaxton, *The Soul of Science,* 72.

17. Ibid., 91.

18. Cotes, preface to Newton's *Principia,* 134.

19. Becker, *The Heavenly City,* 55.

20. Johnson's books include *Darwin on Trial, Reason in the Balance,* and *Objections Sustained.* Michael J. Behe *(Darwin's Black Box)* and William A. Dembski *(The Design Inference)* demonstrate that design is a rigorously scientific concept. The professional journal *Origins and Design,* edited by Paul Nelson, draws together evidence from a range of scientific fields showing that design is empirically detectable.

21. As we write, the *NOVA* video is still used by the Wheat Ridge High School (Jefferson County) in the Denver, Colorado, area. The only difference in district policy, as a reporter says, is to "ensure that no previously approved materials are removed without board review." See Cate Terwilliger, "Words of Controversy: Changes in Biology Teachers' Platform Rekindles Evolution vs. Creationism Fire," *Denver Post*, 29 January 1998.

22. William B. Provine and Phillip E. Johnson, *Darwinism: Science or Naturalistic Philosophy?* (videotape of debate held at Stanford University, April 30, 1994). To order a videotape, contact Access Research Network, P.O. Box 38069, Colorado Springs, CO 80937, phone: (888) 259-7102.

23. Jessica Mathews, "Creationism Makes a Comeback," *Washington Post*, 8 April 1996.

24. Karen Schmidt, "Creationists Evolve New Strategy," *Science* 273, no. 5274 (July 26, 1996): 420. For a good discussion of the modern design movement, see Nancy R. Pearcey, "The Evolution Backlash: Debunking Darwin," *World* 11, no. 38 (March 1, 1997): 12–15.

25. Johnson, *Biology* (New York: Holt, Rinehart, and Winston, 1994), as quoted in Norris Anderson, *Education or Indoctrination?: Analysis of Textbooks in Alabama* (Colorado Springs, Colo.: Access Research Network, 1995), 6.

26. Miller and Levine, *Biology* (New York: Prentice Hall, 1995), as quoted in Anderson, *Education or Indoctrination?*, 7.

27. Campbell, *Biology* (Reading, Mass.: Addison-Wesley, 1993), as quoted in Anderson, *Education or Indoctrination?*, 12.

28. Arms and Camp, *Biology*, 4th ed. (New York: Holt, Rinehart, and Winston, 1995), as quoted in Anderson, *Education or Indoctrination?*, 22.

29. Norris Anderson, as quoted in Nancy R. Pearcey, "The Evolution Backlash: Debunking Darwin," *World* 11, no. 38 (March 1, 1997): 12.

30. Quoted in the program and abstracts from the annual national meeting of the American Association for the Advancement of Science, held in Boston, February 1993.

CHAPTER 12
BLESSED IS THE MAN

1. The account of Górecki's life and accomplishments is based on sources that include the following: Adrian Thomas, *Górecki* (Oxford:

Clarendon Press, 1997); Joseph McLellan, "Górecki's Symphonies and Sympathies," *Washington Post,* 5 March 1995; John Rockwell, "Górecki: A Trendy Symphony and Beyond," *New York Times,* 30 August 1992; "Top of the Pops: A Symphony?" *Time* (March 8, 1993): 64; and Karen L. Mulder, "Move Over, Madonna: Composer Henryk Górecki Has Found Top 40 Status, but Defers Accolades to God," *Christianity Today* 39, no. 8 (July 17, 1995): 66.

CHAPTER 13
SOLI DEO GLORIA

1. Norman Lebrecht, "The Arts," *Daily Telegraph,* 10 April 1996.
2. See Martha Bayles, *Hole in Our Soul: The Loss of Beauty and Meaning in American Popular Music* (New York: Free Press, 1994), 39.
3. Morley Safer, "Yes . . . But Is It Art?" *60 Minutes* (September 1993).
4. Calvin Seerveld, interview with Nancy R. Pearcey, "Christianity and the Arts," *Perspective* 18, no. 3 (June 1984). See also Calvin Seerveld, *A Christian Critique of Art and Literature* (Toronto: Tuppence Press, 1995).
5. Abbot Suger, *The Book of Suger, Abbot of St. Denis,* as quoted in Elizabeth Gilmore Holt, ed. *A Documentary History of Art,* vol. 1 (Princeton, N.J.: Princeton University Press, 1981), 30.
6. Christ Pasles, "Music/Dance: Hallelujah Appeal of 'Messiah' Is Enduring," *Los Angeles Times,* 26 December 1991; Nan Robertson, "A 'Messiah' Cast of Thousands," *San Diego Union-Tribune,* 14 December 1987; and J. Lee Anderson, " 'Messiah' a Religous Experience," 5 December 1985. In the words of John Hale, Louisville Bach Society education director, Handel "told people after he composed 'Messiah' that he had a vision as he was writing the Hallelujah Chorus. . . . He thought he saw heaven open and God Himself sitting in the middle, with all His angels around Him" ("All Church Music, All the Time?" *Courier-Journal* [Louisville, Ky.], 24 December 1995).
7. Franz Joseph Haydn, as quoted in Patrick Kavanaugh, *Spiritual Lives of the Great Composers* (Grand Rapids: Zondervan, 1996), 39.
8. Derrick Henry, "Arts and Entertainment," *Atlanta Journal and Constitution,* 27 July 1995; and "Columbia Orchestra Takes Up Mozart, Mixes in Mendelssohn," *Baltimore Sun,* 28 January 1999.
9. Antonín Dvořák, as quoted in Kavanaugh, *Spiritual Lives of the Great Composers,* 153.

10. Coleridge became a Christian as he struggled with his addiction. While it is not known whether he was actually freed from addiction, when he was converted, he was certainly freed spiritually. He then underwent years of medical treatment (personal correspondence from Gene Edward Veith, author of *State of the Arts: From Bezalel to Mapplethorpe* [Wheaton, Ill.: Crossway, 1991]).

11. Vigen Guroian, *Tending the Heart of Virtue: How Classic Stories Awaken a Child's Moral Imagination* (New York: Oxford University Press, 1998).

12. Thomas Aquinas, as quoted in Jade A. Hobbs and Robert L. Duncan, *Arts, Ideas, and Civilization* (Englewood Cliffs, N.J.: Prentice Hall, 1989), 274. See also Francis A. Schaeffer, *Escape from Reason* (Downers Grove, Ill.: InterVarsity Press, 1968), 9–13.

13. In the eighth and ninth centuries, in what is called the iconoclast controversy, the church debated the proper use of icons in worship. To the Byzantines (the Eastern branch of the church) the icon was more than a mere picture or mosaic. It was the "window" through which human beings apprehended the divine. As such, an icon itself was often believed to possess a divine presence. The faithful would offer flowers, candles, and incense before their icons; they carried them in processions and kissed them as part of liturgical rites. For some, this was too much like idolatry. In 726, Emperor Leo II declared that all images were idols and ordered their destruction. But theologians such as St. John of Damascus argued that images were made acceptable by the Incarnation, when the Son of God, a spirit, took on a human form, and became the "Living Image of the invisible God" (Carl A. Volz, *The Church of the Middle Ages: Growth and Change from 600 to 1400* [St. Louis, Mo.: Concordia, 1970], 134–35).

14. Kenneth Clark, *Civilisation: A Personal View*, 13 videocassettes (New York: Ambrose Video Publishing, 1969).

15. Gene Edward Veith, *State of the Arts: From Bezalel to Mapplethorpe* (Wheaton, Ill.: Crossway, 1991), 58–63.

16. Martin Luther, as quoted by Donald J. Drew (in a lecture given at L'Abri Conference in Rochester, Minnesota, August 1996), 21. Luther also held literature in high esteem. There should be "as many poets and rhetoricians as possible," he wrote, for by the study of literature "people are fitted for the grasping of sacred truth and for handling it skillfully and happily" (as quoted in Veith, *State of the Arts*, 62).

17. John Calvin, as quoted in Veith, *State of the Arts*, 59.

18. Jacques Barzun, *The Use and Abuse of Art* (Princeton, N.J.: Princeton University Press, 1975), 53.

19. Bayles (quoting the founder of de Stijl), *Hole in Our Soul*, 39.

20. M. H. Abrams, *The Mirror and the Lamp: Romantic Theory and Critical Tradition* (New York: Oxford University Press, 1953), 285. Similarly, art critic Clement Greenberg writes, "the avant-garde poet or artist tries in effect to imitate God by creating something valid solely on its own terms" (Greenberg, *Art and Culture: Critical Essays* [Boston: Beacon Press, 1961], 6).

21. George Bernard Shaw, as quoted in Barzun, *The Use and Abuse of Art*, 46.

22. Abrams, *The Mirror and the Lamp*, 275.

23. Barzun, *The Use and Abuse of Art*, 39.

24. Ibid., 38.

25. Ibid., 51.

26. Luigi Russolo, as quoted in Bayles, *Hole in Our Soul*, 43.

27. Robert Hughes, as quoted in Thomas Ewens, "Rethinking the Question of Quality in Art," *Arts Education Policy Review* (November 1994): 2.

28. Joyce Price, "Art Turns Heads, Stomachs," *Washington Times*, 6 July 1993.

29. John Simon, "Art or Child's Play? A Four-Year-Old Could Do It," *Sunday Telegraph*, 14 February 1993.

30. Os Guinness, "The Purpose of Invitation to the Classics," in *Invitation to the Classics: A Guide to Books You've Always Wanted to Read*, eds. Louise Cowan and Os Guinness (Grand Rapids: Baker, 1998), 14.

31. C. S. Lewis, as quoted in Guinness, *Invitation to the Classics*, 15.

32. Veith, *State of the Arts*, 106–13.

33. "There is more talk about de-funding the National Endowment for the Arts than there is about funding creative work that could be a healthy cultural force," says Ken Myers (personal conversation with Kim Robbins [May 1999]). Myers is the host of *Mars Hill*, a bimonthly audio magazine of contemporary culture and Christian conviction. Mars Hill, P.O. Box 7826, Charlottesville, VA 22906, phone: (800) 331-6407.

34. C. S. Lewis, "Learning in War Time," *The Weight of Glory and Other Addresses* (New York: Macmillan, 1980), 23.

35. Louise Cowan, "The Importance of Classics," in *Invitation to the Classics*, eds. Cowan and Guinness, 19–20.

36. Listen to Soeur Marie Keyrouz, a Lebanese nun who renders ancient

Byzantine chants in a rich, throaty voice—a vivid reminder that the church emerged from Near Eastern culture. Re-create fourth-century sound by listening to the serene Ambrosian chants or the noble sonorities of the liturgy of Saint John Chrysostom, sung by the Greek Byzantine Choir. Several musical groups have also revived medieval music, both Gregorian chant and the lively songs of the visionary twelfth-century Hildegard von Bingen, becoming surprise best-sellers. And there's the astonishing commercial success of Anonymous 4, four women who sing medieval music with transparent tones and ethereal vocal blending.

37. Gerard Manley Hopkins, "God's Grandeur."

38. An account of Irina Ratushinskaya's conversion in a Russian prison camp is told in Charles Colson with Ellen Santilli Vaughn, *The Body: Being Light in Darkness* (Dallas: Word, 1992), chapter 6.

39. Bruno Bettelheim, *The Use of Enchantment: The Meaning and Importance of Fairy Tales* (New York: Alfred A. Knopf, 1976), 10.

CHAPTER 14
TOUCHED BY A MIRACLE

1. The authors are grateful to Martha Williamson for a personal interview in January 1998. Additional details for this story were taken from Martha Williamson and Robin Sheets, *Touched by an Angel: Stories from the Hit Television Series* (Grand Rapids: Zondervan, 1997).

CHAPTER 15
DOES THE DEVIL HAVE ALL THE GOOD MUSIC?

1. Marshall McLuhan, *The Medium Is the Message* (New York: Simon & Schuster, 1967).

2. Neil Postman, *Amusing Ourselves to Death* (New York: Penguin, 1985), 10, 62, 86.

3. Ibid., 9 (emphasis in the original).

4. Ibid., 9.

5. Ibid., see also chapter 11.

6. Aldous Huxley, *Brave New World Revisited* (New York: Harper & Brothers, 1958), 44.

7. Kenneth A. Myers, *All God's Children and Blue Suede Shoes: Christians and Popular Culture* (Westchester, Ill.: Crossway, 1989), 89.

8. Ibid., 134–35.

9. "Short Takes," *Time* (December 7, 1992): 83.

10. Ken Myers describes an attempt by a Christian broadcasting network to produce a Christian soap opera. The program was marked by the same melodramatic music, stock characters, and tear-jerking plots as secular soaps. The only thing that distinguished it from its secular counterparts was that "a few of the characters were Christians, who occasionally spoke of the role their faith played in meeting soap opera crises." The Christian message was a thin veneer, while the real tone was set by the soap opera form—"You'll love our Christian soap opera villain . . . because she gets saved sometime next season. But meanwhile she's just as nasty as her 'secular' counterpart." The soap opera form is inherently contrary to Christian values, Myers concludes, because it depends on "the dramatic equivalent of gossip" (Myers, *All God's Children and Blue Suede Shoes*, 21).

11. You can read more about Ben Carson's dramatic story in his autobiography, *Gifted Hands* (Grand Rapids: Zondervan, 1996).

12. *Saving Private Ryan*, Paramount Pictures (1998); *Schindler's List*, Universal Pictures (1993); *Dead Man Walking*, Gramercy Pictures (1995); *The Spitfire Grill*, Columbia Pictures Corporation (1996); John Meroney, " 'Live' with TAE, Randall Wallace," *American Enterprise*, (May/June 1998): 21.

13. *Chariots of Fire*, 20th Century Fox (1981); *Brother Sun, Sister Moon*, Luciano Perugio, producer (1973); *Jane Eyre*, Miramax Films (1996); *Jesus of Nazareth*, Sir Lew Grade (1977); *Crimes and Misdemeanors*, Orion Pictures (1989).

14. *It's a Wonderful Life*, Liberty Films (1946); *Mr. Smith Goes to Washington*, Columbia Pictures (1939).

15. Frank Capra, *Frank Capra: The Name above the Title: An Autobiography* (New York: Macmillan, 1971). Every Christian family ought to buy a copy of *The Family New Media Guide*, in which authors highlight the films that tell inspiring stories, the audio books that bring the classics alive for children, the computer games that stimulate the imagination while avoiding blood and gore. See William Kilpatrick and Gregory and Suzanne Wolfe, *The Family New Media Guide: A Parents' Guide to the Very Best Choices in Values-Oriented Media, Including Videos, CD-Roms, Audiotapes, Computer Software, and On-Line Services* (New York: Touchstone, 1997). Ted Baehr publishes a newsletter critiquing current films from a Christian perspective. To order the newsletter, contact Movieguide, 6695

Peach Tree Industrial Blvd., Suite 101, Atlanta, GA 30360, phone: (770) 825-0084.

16. Inter-Mission, First Presbyterian Church of Hollywood, 1760 North Gower Street, Hollywood, CA 90028, phone: (323) 462-8460; Catholics in Media Message Line, phone: (818) 907-2734.

17. Los Angeles Film Studies Center, 3800 Barham Blvd., Suite 202, Los Angeles, CA 90068, phone: (323) 882-6224.

18. David Shiflett, "God, What a Hit," *Wall Street Journal,* 21 August 1998.

19. C. S. Lewis, *God in the Dock: Essays on Theology and Ethics* (Grand Rapids: Eerdmans, 1970), 93.

CHAPTER 16
HOW NOW SHALL WE LIVE?

1. The conference, held in June 1996, was called "Missed Opportunities?: Former U.S. and Vietnamese Leaders and Scholars Reexamine the Vietnam War, 1961–1968."

2. Robert S. McNamara with Brian VanDeMark, *In Retrospect: The Tragedy and Lessons of Vietnam* (New York: Vintage Books, 1996).

3. Norman Boucher, "Thinking Like the Enemy," *Brown Alumni Monthly* (November/December 1997): 36–45.

4. Sources for Kim Phuc's story include David Usborne, "Veterans of Vietnam Weep as the Girl Who Became a Symbol of Suffering Comes to Forgive 22 Years Later," *Independent,* 14 November 1996; "Portrait of Forgiveness," *Sarasota Herald-Tribune,* 14 November 1996; Elaine Sciolino, "A Painful Road from Vietnam to Forgiveness," *New York Times,* 12 November 1996; Elaine S. Povich, "A Prayer for Peace," *Newsday,* 12 November 1996. Further background information was provided by Linh D. Vo and Major Ronald N. Timberlake through private telephone conversations and correspondence. These two men were especially helpful in correcting mistaken impressions created by the initial story.

5. Interview conducted by EO (Dutch) Television, 6 December 1998.

6. Ibid.

7. *Kim's Story,* a documentary film produced by Bishari Films Inc. (1997).

8. The man who approached Kim Phuc was John Plummer. Later investigation determined that he was not, in fact, either the pilot who dropped the bomb or the commander who ordered the air strike, as

he claimed. The attack on Kim's village was a South Vietnamese operation with no American involvement. Nevertheless, he symbolically represents all of us who feel directly or indirectly responsible, and his exchange with Kim Phuc that day speaks poignantly of the real solution to war and conflict between nations.

RECOMMENDED READING

WORLDVIEW

Bellah, Robert. *The Good Society.* New York: Alfred A. Knopf, 1991.

Berger, Peter, and Brigitte Berger, and Hansfried Kellner. *The Homeless Mind: Modernization and Consciousness.* New York: Random, 1974.

Blamires, Harry. *The Christian Mind.* Ann Arbor, Mich.: Servant, 1978.

Brown, Harold O. J. *The Sensate Culture.* Dallas: Word, 1996.

Carson, D. A., and John D. Woodbridge, eds. *God and Culture: Essays in Honor of Carl F. H. Henry.* Grand Rapids: Eerdmans, 1993.

Colson, Charles, with Anne Morse. *Burden of Truth: Defending Truth in an Age of Unbelief.* Wheaton, Ill.: Tyndale House, 1997.

Colson, Charles, with Nancy Pearcey. *A Dance with Deception: Revealing the Truth Behind the Headlines.* Dallas: Word, 1993.

Colson, Charles, with Ellen Santilli Vaughn. *The Body.* Dallas: Word, 1992.

Dawson, Christopher. *Religion and the Rise of Western Culture.* New York: Doubleday, 1991.

Dockery, David S., ed. *The Challenge of Postmodernism: An Evangelical Engagement.* Grand Rapids: Baker, 1997.

Dooyeweerd, Hermann. *Roots of Western Culture: Pagan, Secular, and Christian Options.* Toronto: Wedge, 1979.

———. *In the Twilight of Western Thought: Studies in the Pretended Autonomy of Philosophical Thought.* Lewiston, N.Y.: E. Mellen, 1999.

Eliot, T. S. *Christianity and Culture.* New York: Harcourt, Brace and Jovanovich, 1968.

Geisler, Norman L., and Ronald M. Brooks. *When Skeptics Ask: A Handbook of Christian Evidence.* Wheaton, Ill.: Victor, 1998.

Glover, Willis B. *Biblical Origins of Modern Secular Culture: An Essay in the Interpretation of Western History.* Macon, Ga.: Mercer University Press, 1984.

Grisez, Germain G. *The Way of the Lord Jesus.* Vol. 1, *Christian Moral Principles.* Chicago: Franciscan Herald Press, 1983.

———. *The Way of the Lord Jesus.* Vol. 2, *Living a Christian Life.* Quincy, Ill.: Franciscan Press, 1993.

———. *The Way of the Lord Jesus.* Vol. 3, *Difficult Moral Questions.* Quincy, Ill.: Franciscan Press, 1997.

Gunton, Colin. *Enlightenment and Alienation: An Essay Toward a Trinitarian Theology.* Grand Rapids: Eerdmans, 1985.

Halton, Eugene. *Bereft of Reason: On the Decline of Social Thought and Prospects for Its Renewal.* Chicago: University of Chicago Press, 1995.

Henry, Carl F. H. *The Christian Mind-set in a Secular Society: Promoting Evangelical Renewal and National Righteousness.* Portland, Ore.: Multnomah, 1978.

Heslam, Peter S. *Creating a Christian Worldview: Abraham Kuyper's Lectures on Calvinism.* Grand Rapids: Eerdmans, 1998.

Hoffecker, W. Andrew, and Gary Scott Smith, eds. *Building a Christian Worldview.* Vol. 1, *God, Man, and Knowledge.* Phillipsburg, N.J.: Presbyterian and Reformed, 1986.

Holmes, Arthur. *All Truth Is God's Truth.* Grand Rapids: Eerdmans, 1977.

Holmes, Arthur, ed. *The Making of a Christian Mind: A Christian World View & the Academic Enterprise.* Downers Grove, Ill.: InterVarsity Press, 1985.

Kuyper, Abraham. *Christianity: A Total World and Life System.* Marlborough, N.H.: Plymouth Rock Foundation, 1996.

Machen, J. Gresham. *Christianity and Liberalism.* Grand Rapids: Eerdmans, 1990.

Moreland, J. P. *Love Your God with All Your Mind: The Role of Reason in the Life of the Soul.* Colorado Springs: NavPress, 1997.

Noll, Mark. *The Scandal of the Evangelical Mind.* Downers Grove, Ill.: InterVarsity Press, 1994.

Runner, H. Evan. *The Relation of the Bible to Learning.* Toronto: Wedge, 1970.

Schaeffer, Francis. *The Complete Works of Francis A. Schaeffer: A Christian Worldview.* Westchester, Ill.: Crossway, 1982.

———. *25 Basic Bible Studies: Including Two Contents, Two Realities.* Wheaton, Ill.: Crossway, 1996. Also in *The Complete Works of Francis*

A. *Schaeffer: A Christian Worldview.* Vol. 3, *A Christian View of Spirituality.* Westchester, Ill.: Crossway, 1982.

———. *Art and the Bible.* Downers Grove, Ill.: InterVarsity Press, 1973. Also in *The Complete Works of Francis A. Schaeffer: A Christian Worldview.* Vol. 2, *A Christian View of the Bible as Truth.* Westchester, Ill.: Crossway, 1982.

———. *Back to Freedom and Dignity.* In *The Complete Works of Francis A. Schaeffer: A Christian Worldview.* Vol. 1, *A Christian View of Philosophy and Culture.* Westchester, Ill.: Crossway, 1982.

———. *Basic Bible Studies.* In *The Complete Works of Francis A. Schaeffer: A Christian Worldview.* Vol. 2, *A Christian View of the Bible as Truth.* Westchester, Ill.: Crossway, 1982.

———. *A Christian Manifesto.* Wheaton, Ill.: Good News, 1982. Also in *The Complete Works of Francis A. Schaeffer: A Christian Worldview.* Vol. 5, *A Christian View of the West.* Westchester, Ill.: Crossway, 1982.

———. *The Church at the End of the Twentieth Century: Including, the Church Before the Watching World.* Wheaton, Ill.: Crossway, 1994.

———. *Death in the City.* In *The Complete Works of Francis A. Schaeffer: A Christian Worldview.* Vol. 4, *A Christian View of the Church.* Westchester, Ill.: Crossway, 1982.

———. *Genesis in Space and Time.* Downers Grove, Ill.: InterVarsity Press, 1972.

———. *The Great Evangelical Disaster.* Wheaton, Ill.: Good News, 1984.

———. *He Is There and He Is Not Silent.* Wheaton, Ill.: Tyndale House, 1972. Also in *The Complete Works of Francis A. Schaeffer: A Christian Worldview.* Vol. 1, *A Christian View of Philosophy and Culture.* Westchester, Ill.: Crossway, 1982.

———. *How Should We Then Live?* Westchester, Ill.: Crossway, 1983. Also in *The Complete Works of Francis A. Schaeffer: A Christian Worldview.* Vol. 5, *A Christian View of the West.* Westchester, Ill.: Crossway, 1982.

———. *Joshua and the Flow of Biblical History.* In *The Complete Works of Francis A. Schaeffer: A Christian Worldview.* Vol. 2, *A Christian View of the Bible as Truth.* Westchester, Ill.: Crossway, 1982.

———. *The Mark of the Christian.* In *The Complete Works of Francis A. Schaeffer: A Christian Worldview.* Vol. 4, *A Christian View of the Church.* Westchester, Ill.: Crossway, 1982.

————. *The New Super-Spirituality*. In *The Complete Works of Francis A. Schaeffer: A Christian Worldview*. Vol. 3, *A Christian View of Spirituality*. Westchester, Ill.: Crossway, 1982.

————. *No Final Conflict*. In *The Complete Works of Francis A. Schaeffer: A Christian Worldview*. Vol. 2, *A Christian View of the Bible as Truth*. Westchester, Ill.: Crossway, 1982.

————. *No Little People*. In *The Complete Works of Francis A. Schaeffer: A Christian Worldview*. Vol. 3, *A Christian View of Spirituality*. Westchester, Ill.: Crossway, 1982.

————. *True Spirituality*. Wheaton, Ill.: Tyndale House, 1979. Also in *The Complete Works of Francis A. Schaeffer: A Christian Worldview*. Vol. 3, *A Christian View of Spirituality*. Westchester, Ill.: Crossway, 1982.

Schaeffer, Francis A., and C. Everett Koop. *Whatever Happened to the Human Race?* Westchester, Ill.: Crossway, 1983. Also in *The Complete Works of Francis A. Schaeffer: A Christian Worldview*. Vol. 5, *A Christian View of the West*. Westchester, Ill.: Crossway, 1982.

Schaeffer, Francis A., and Udo Middelmann. *Pollution and the Death of Man*. Wheaton, Ill.: Crossway, 1992. Also in *The Complete Works of Francis A. Schaeffer: A Christian Worldview*. Vol. 5, *A Christian View of the West*. Westchester, Ill.: Crossway, 1982.

Sire, James W. *The Universe Next Door: A Basic Worldview Catalog*. 3rd ed. Downers Grove, Ill.: InterVarsity Press, 1997.

Smart, Ninian. *Worldviews: Crosscultural Explorations of Human Beliefs*. 2nd ed. Englewood Cliffs, N.J.: Prentice Hall, 1995.

Sorokin, Pitirim A. *The Crisis of Our Age*. 2nd rev. ed. London: Oneworld, 1992.

Sproul, R. C. *Lifeviews*. Grand Rapids: Baker, 1990.

Vander Goot, Henry. *Life Is Religion: Essays in Honor of H. Evan Runner*. St. Catherines, Ontario: Paideia, 1981.

Veith, Gene Edward. *Postmodern Times: A Christian Guide to Contemporary Thought and Culture*. Wheaton, Ill.: Crossway, 1994.

Walsh, Brian J., and J. Richard Middleton. *The Transforming Vision: Shaping a Christian World View*. Downers Grove, Ill.: InterVarsity Press, 1984.

Wells, David F. *No Place for Truth, or, Whatever Happened to Evangelical Theology?* Grand Rapids: Eerdmans, 1993.

Wolters, Albert M. *Creation Regained: Biblical Basics for a Reformational Worldview*. Grand Rapids: Eerdmans, 1985.

INDIVIDUAL CHOICES

Glynn, Patrick. *God the Evidence: The Reconciliation of Faith and Reason in a Postsecular World.* Rocklin, Calif.: Prima Publishing, 1997.

Larson, David B., and Susan S. Larson. *The Forgotten Factor in Physical and Mental Health: What Does the Research Show?* Rockville, Md.: National Institute of Healthcare Research, 1994.

Lewy, Guenter. *Why America Needs Religion: Secular Modernity and Its Discontent.* Grand Rapids: Eerdmans, 1996.

Matthews, Dale. *The Faith Factor: Proof of the Healing Power of Prayer.* New York: Viking, 1998.

Tournier, Paul. *The Whole Person in a Broken World.* New York: Harper & Row, 1981.

MARRIAGE AND FAMILY

Blankenhorn, David. *Fatherless America: Confronting Our Most Urgent Social Problem.* New York: HarperCollins, 1995.

Carlson, Allan C. *Family Questions: Reflections on the American Social Crisis.* New Brunswick, N.J.: Transaction, 1988.

Christensen, Bryce J. *Utopia Against the Family: The Problems and Politics of the American Family.* San Francisco: Ignatius, 1990.

Dobson, James C. *Coming Home: Timeless Wisdom for Families.* Wheaton, Ill.: Tyndale House, 1998.

———. *Children at Risk: The Battle for the Hearts and Minds of Our Kids.* Dallas: Word, 1994.

Gallagher, Maggie. *The Abolition of Marriage: How We Destroy Lasting Love.* Washington, D.C.: Regnery, 1996.

Horn, Wade. *The Fatherhood Movement: A Call to Action.* Lanham, Md.: Lexington Books, 1999.

Larson, David B. *The Costly Consequences of Divorce: Assessing the Clinical, Economic, and Public Health Impact of Marital Disruption in the United States: A Research-Based Seminar.* Rockville, Md.: National Institute for Healthcare Research, 1995.

Mack, Dana. *The Assault on Parenthood: How Our Culture Undermines the Family.* New York: Simon & Schuster, 1997.

McManus, Michael J. *Marriage Savers: Helping Your Friends and Family Avoid Divorce.* Rev. ed. Grand Rapids: Zondervan, 1995.

Popenoe, David. *Disturbing the Nest: Family Change and Decline in Modern Societies.* New York: A. de Gruyter, 1988.

———. *Life Without Father: Compelling New Evidence That Fatherhood and Marriage Are Indispensable for the Good of Children and Society.* Cambridge, Mass.: Harvard University Press, 1999.

Satinover, Jeffrey. *Homosexuality and the Politics of Truth.* Grand Rapids: Baker, 1996.

Stanton, Glenn T. *Why Marriage Matters: Reasons to Believe in Marriage in Postmodern Society.* Colorado Springs: Pinon Press, 1997.

Wallerstein, Judith S., and Sandra Blakeslee. *Second Chances: Men, Women, and Children a Decade After Divorce.* New York: Ticknor and Fields, 1989.

EDUCATION

Finn, Chester, Diane Ravitch, and Robert Fancher, eds. *Against Mediocrity: The Humanities in America's High Schools.* New York: Holmes and Meier, 1984.

Garber, Steven. *The Fabric of Faithfulness: Weaving Together Belief and Behavior During the University Years.* Downers Grove, Ill.: InterVarsity Press, 1996.

Knight, George R. *Philosophy and Education: An Introduction in Christian Perspective.* Berrien Springs, Mich.: Andrews University Press, 1998.

Kramer, Rita. *Ed School Follies: The Miseducation of America's Teachers.* New York: Free Press, 1991.

Malik, Charles Habib. *A Christian Critique of the University.* 2nd ed. Waterloo, Ont.: North Waterloo Academic Press, 1987.

Marsden, George M. *The Outrageous Idea of Christian Scholarship.* New York: Oxford University Press, 1998.

———. *The Soul of the American University: From Protestant Establishment to Established Nonbelief.* New York: Oxford University Press, 1994.

Nash, Ronald. *The Closing of the American Heart: What's Really Wrong with America's Schools.* Dallas: Word, 1990.

Veith, Gene Edward, and Andrew Kern. *Classical Education: Towards the Revival of American Schooling.* Washington, D.C.: Capital Research Center, 1997.

Wilson, Douglas. *Recovering the Lost Tools of Learning: An Approach to Distinctively Christian Education.* Wheaton, Ill.: Crossway, 1991.

NEIGHBORHOOD

Bennett, William J., John J. DiIulio, and John P. Walters. *Body Count: Moral Poverty—and How to Win America's War against Crime and Drugs.* New York: Simon & Schuster, 1996.

Kelling, George L., and Catherine M. Coles. *Fixing Broken Windows: Restoring Order and Reducing Crime in Our Communities.* New York: Free Press, 1996.

Kunstler, James Howard. *The Geography of Nowhere: The Rise and Decline of America's Man-Made Landscape.* New York: Touchstone, 1993.

Magnet, Myron. *The Dream and the Nightmare: The Sixties' Legacy to the Underclass.* New York: William Morrow, 1993.

Olasky, Marvin, ed. *Loving Your Neighbor: A Principled Guide to Personal Charity.* Washington, D.C.: Capital Research Center, 1995.

Perkins, John, with Jo Kadlecek. *Resurrecting Hope: Powerful Stories of How God Is Moving to Reach Our Cities.* Ventura, Calif.: Regal Books, 1995.

Sherman, Amy L. *Restorers of Hope: Reaching the Poor in Your Community with Church-Based Ministries That Work.* Wheaton, Ill.: Crossway, 1997.

Van Ness, Daniel W. *Crime and Its Victims: What We Can Do.* Leicester, England: InterVarsity Press, 1989.

Van Ness, Daniel W., and Karen H. Strong. *Restoring Justice.* Cincinnati: Anderson Publishing, 1997.

WORK AND ECONOMICS

Bernbaum, John, and Simon Steer. *Why Work? Careers and Employment in Biblical Perspective.* Grand Rapids: Baker, 1987.

Colson, Chuck, and Jack Eckerd. *Why America Doesn't Work.* Dallas: Word, 1991.

Gay, Craig M. *With Liberty and Justice for Whom?: The Recent Evangelical Debate over Capitalism.* Grand Rapids: Eerdmans, 1991.

Goudzwaard, Bob. *Idols of Our Time.* Downers Grove, Ill.: InterVarsity Press, 1984.

Guinness, Os. *Winning Back the Soul of American Business.* Burke, Va.: Hourglass, 1990.

Kuyper, Abraham. *The Problem of Poverty.* Grand Rapids: Baker, 1991.

Middelmann, Udo. *Pro-Existence.* Downers Grove, Ill.: InterVarsity Press, 1974.

Nash, Ronald. *Poverty and Wealth: The Christian Debate over Capitalism.* Westchester, Ill.: Crossway, 1986.

Neuhaus, Richard John. *Doing Well and Doing Good: The Challenge to the Christian Capitalist.* New York: Doubleday, 1992.

Novak, Michael. *Business as a Calling: Work and the Examined Life.* New York: Free Press, 1996.

———. *The Spirit of Democratic Capitalism.* New York: Simon & Schuster, 1982.

———. *Toward a Theology of the Corporation.* Washington, D.C.: American Enterprise Institute, 1981.

Roepke, Wilhelm. *A Humane Economy: The Social Framework of the Free Market.* Wilmington, Del.: Intercollegiate Studies Institute, 1998.

Ryken, Leland. *Redeeming the Time: A Christian Approach to Work and Leisure.* Grand Rapids: Baker, 1995.

Schumacher, E. F. *Economic Development and Poverty.* London: Africa Bureau, 1966.

Sirico, Robert A. *A Moral Basis for Liberty.* London: Institute of Economic Affairs, Health and Welfare Unit, 1994.

LAW AND POLITICS

Alison, Michael. *Christianity and Conservatism.* London: Hodder and Stoughton, 1990.

Arkes, Handley. *First Things: An Inquiry into the First Principles of Morals and Justice.* Princeton, N.J.: Princeton University Press, 1986.

Bloesch, Donald. *Crumbling Foundations.* Grand Rapids: Zondervan, 1984.

Budziszewski, J. *Written on the Heart: The Case for Natural Law.* Downers Grove, Ill.: InterVarsity Press, 1997.

Canavan, Francis. *The Pluralist Game: Pluralism, Liberalism, and the Moral Conscience.* Lanham, Md.: Rowman & Littlefield, 1995.

Colson, Charles, with Ellen Santilli Vaughn. *Kingdoms in Conflict.* New York: William Morrow; Grand Rapids: Zondervan, 1987.

Cromartie, Michael, ed. *A Preserving Grace: Protestants, Catholics, and Natural Law*. Grand Rapids: Eerdmans, 1997.

————. *Caesar's Coin Revisited: Christians and the Limits of Government*. Grand Rapids: Eerdmans, 1996.

Ellul, Jacques. *The New Demons*. New York: Seabury, 1975.

————. *The Political Illusion*. New York: Vintage, 1972.

Finnis, John. *Natural Law and Natural Rights*. New York: Oxford University Press, 1993.

Fitzpatrick, James K. *God, Country, and the Supreme Court*. Washington, D.C.: Regnery, 1985.

George, Robert P. *In Defense of Natural Law*. New York: Oxford University Press, 1999.

————. *Making Men Moral: Civil Liberties and Public Morality*. New York: Oxford University Press, 1996.

Goudzwaard, Bob. *Capitalism and Progress: A Diagnosis of Western Society*. Grand Rapids: Eerdmans, 1979.

Grant, George Parkin. *English-Speaking Justice*. Sackville, New Brunswick: Mount Allison University, 1974.

Hittinger, Russell. *A Critique of the New Natural Law Theory*. Notre Dame, Ind.: University of Notre Dame Press, 1989.

Jouvenel, Bertrand de, *On Power: The Natural History of Its Growth*. Indianapolis: Liberty Fund, 1993.

Kendall, Willmoore. *The Conservative Affirmation in America*. Chicago: Regnery Gateway, 1985.

Kirk, Russell. *Rights and Duties: Reflections on Our Conservative Constitution*. Dallas: Spence, 1997.

Manent, Pierre. *An Intellectual History of Liberalism*. Trans. Rebecca Balinski. Princeton, N.J.: Princeton University Press, 1994.

————. *The City of Man*. Trans. Marc A. LePain. Princeton, N.J.: Princeton University Press, 1998.

Murray, John C., and Walter Burghardt. *We Hold These Truths: Catholic Reflections on the American Proposition*. Kansas City, Mo.: Sheed and Ward, 1985.

Nash, Ronald. *Social Justice and the Christian Church*. Milford, Mich.: Mott Media, 1983.

Neuhaus, Richard John. *A Strange New Regime: The Naked Public Square and the Passing of the American Constitutional Order.* Washington, D.C.: The Heritage Foundation, 1997.

————. *The Naked Public Square: Religion and Democracy in America.* 2nd ed. Grand Rapids: Eerdmans, 1984.

Neuhaus, Richard John, and Michael Cromartie, eds. *Piety and Politics: Evangelicals and Fundamentalists Confront the World.* Washington, D.C.: Ethics and Public Policy Center, 1987.

Nisbet, Robert. *The Quest for Community: A Study in the Ethics of Order and Freedom.* San Francisco: Institute for Contemporary Studies, 1990.

————. *Twilight of Authority.* New York: Oxford University Press, 1975.

Noland, James, Jr. *The Therapeutic State.* New York: New York University Press, 1998.

Noll, Mark. *One Nation Under God? Christian Faith and Political Action in America.* San Francisco: Harper San Francisco, 1988.

O'Donovan, Oliver. *The Desire of Nations: Rediscovering the Roots of Political Theology.* Cambridge: Cambridge University Press, 1999.

Olasky, Marvin. *The Tragedy of American Compassion.* Washington, D.C.: Regnery, 1995.

Sandel, Michael. *Democracy's Discontent: America in Search of a Public Philosophy.* Boston: Harvard University Press, 1996.

Skillen, James W. *The Scattered Voice: Christians at Odds in the Public Square.* Grand Rapids: Zondervan, 1990.

Smith, Gary Scott, ed. *God and Politics: Four Views on the Reformation of Civil Government.* Phillipsburg, N.J.: Presbyterian and Reformed, 1989.

Thielicke, Helmut. *Theological Ethics.* Vol. 2, *Politics.* Philadelphia: Fortress Press, 1969.

Tinder, Glenn. *The Political Meaning of Christianity: An Interpretation.* Baton Rouge, La.: Louisiana State University Press, 1989.

Voegelin, Eric. *From Enlightenment to Revolution.* Ed. John H. Hallowell. Durham, N.C.: Duke University Press, 1975.

THE ARTS

Cowan, Louise, and Os Guinness, eds. *Invitation to the Classics: A Guide to Books You've Always Wanted to Read.* Grand Rapids: Baker, 1998.

Gallagher, Susan V., and Roger Lundin. *Literature through the Eyes of Faith.* San Francisco: Harper San Francisco, 1989.

Guroian, Vigen. *Tending the Heart of Virtue: How Classic Stories Awaken a Child's Moral Imagination.* New York: Oxford University Press, 1998.

Jeffrey, David Lyle. *People of the Book: Christian Identity and Literary Culture.* Grand Rapids: Eerdmans, 1996.

Kavanaugh, Patrick. *Spiritual Lives of the Great Composers.* Grand Rapids: Zondervan, 1996.

———. *A Taste for the Classics.* Nashville: Sparrow Press, 1993.

Lundin, Roger. *The Culture of Interpretation: A Christian Encounter with Postmodern Critical Theory.* Grand Rapids: Eerdmans, 1993.

Lundin, Roger, ed. *Disciplining Hermeneutics: Interpretation in Christian Perspective.* Grand Rapids: Eerdmans, 1997.

Ritchie, Daniel E. *Reconstructing Literature in an Ideological Age: A Biblical Poetics and Literary Studies from Milton to Burke.* Grand Rapids: Eerdmans, 1996.

Rookmaaker, H. R. *The Creative Gift: Essays on Art and the Christian Life.* Westchester, Ill.: Cornerstone Books, 1981.

———. *Modern Art and the Death of a Culture.* Downers Grove, Ill.: InterVarsity Press, 1970.

Ryken, Leland. *The Liberated Imagination: Thinking Christianly about the Arts.* Wheaton, Ill.: Harold Shaw, 1989.

———. *Realms of Gold: The Classics in Christian Perspective.* Wheaton, Ill.: Harold Shaw, 1991.

Sayers, Dorothy. *The Mind of the Maker.* San Francisco: Harper San Francisco, 1987.

Schaeffer, Franky. *Sham Pearls for Real Swine.* Brentwood, Tenn.: Wolgemuth and Hyatt, 1990.

Seerveld, Calvin. *Rainbows for the Fallen World: Aesthetic Life and Artistic Task.* Toronto: Tuppence Press, 1980.

Veith, Gene Edward. *Reading Between the Lines: A Christian Approach to Literature.* Westchester, Ill.: Crossway, 1990.

———. *State of the Arts: From Bezalel to Mapplethorpe.* Wheaton, Ill.: Crossway, 1991.

Walhout, Clarence, and Leland Ryken, eds. *Contemporary Literary Theory: A Christian Appraisal.* Grand Rapids: Eerdmans, 1991.

Wolterstorff, Nicholas. *Art in Action.* Grand Rapids: Eerdmans, 1980.

POP CULTURE

Bayles, Martha. *Hole in Our Soul: The Loss of Beauty and Meaning in American Popular Music*. New York: Free Press, 1994.

Drew, Donald. *Images of Man: A Critique of the Contemporary Cinema*. Downers Grove, Ill.: InterVarsity Press, 1974.

Gelernter, David. *Mirror Worlds: The Day Software Puts the Universe in a Shoebox . . . How Will It Happen and What Will It Mean?* New York: Oxford University Press, 1991.

Jones, E. Michael. *Dionysius Rising: The Birth of Cultural Revolution Out of the Spirit of Music*. San Francisco: Ignatius, 1994.

Kilpatrick, William, Gregory Wolfe, and Suzanne Wolfe. *The Family New Media Guide: A Parents' Guide to the Very Best Choices in Values-Oriented Media, Including Videos, CD-Roms, Audiotapes, Computer Software, and On-Line Services*. New York: Touchstone, 1997.

Myers, Ken. *All God's Children and Blue Suede Shoes: Christians and Popular Culture*. Westchester, Ill.: Crossway, 1989.

Schultz, Quentin J. *Redeeming Television: How TV Changes Christians— How Christians Can Change TV*. Downers Grove, Ill.: InterVarsity Press, 1992.

———. *Dancing in the Dark: Youth, Popular Culture, and the Electronic Media*. Grand Rapids: Eerdmans, 1990.

ABOUT THE AUTHORS

Charles W. Colson graduated with honors from Brown University and received his Juris Doctor from George Washington University. From 1969 to 1973 he served as special counsel to President Richard Nixon. In 1974 he pleaded guilty to charges related to Watergate and served seven months in a federal prison.

Before going to prison, Charles Colson was converted to Christ, as told in *Born Again*. He has also published *Life Sentence, Crime and the Responsible Community, Convicted* (with Dan Van Ness), *How Now Shall We Live?* (with Nancy Pearcey), *The Body* (with Ellen Vaughn), *A Dance with Deception* (with Nancy Pearcey), *A Dangerous Grace* (with Nancy Pearcey), *Gideon's Torch* (with Ellen Vaughn), *Burden of Truth* (with Anne Morse), *The God of Stones and Spiders, Why America Doesn't Work* (with Jack Eckerd), *Answers to Your Kids' Questions* (with Harold Fickett), *Who Speaks for God?, Kingdoms in Conflict, Against the Night,* and *Loving God,* the book many people consider to be a contemporary classic.

Colson founded Prison Fellowship Ministries (PF), an interdenominational outreach, now active in eighty-eight countries. The world's largest prison ministry, PF manages over 50,000 active volunteers in the U.S. and tens of thousands more abroad. The ministry provides Bible studies in more than 1,000 prisons, conducts over 2,000 in-prison seminars per year, does major evangelistic outreaches, and reaches more than 500,000 kids at Christmas with gifts and the love of Christ. The ministry also has two subsidiaries: Justice Fellowship, which works for biblically based criminal justice policies, and Neighbors Who Care, a network of volunteers providing assistance to victims of crime. Also a part of the ministry is the Wilberforce Forum, which provides worldview materials for the Christian community, including Colson's daily radio broadcast, *BreakPoint*, now heard on a thousand outlets.

Colson has received fifteen honorary doctorates and in 1993 was awarded the Templeton Prize, the world's largest cash gift (over $1 million), which is given each year to the one person in the world who has done the most to advance the cause of religion. Colson donated this prize, as he does all speaking fees and royalties, to further the work of PF.

Nancy R. Pearcey studied under Francis Schaeffer at L'Abri Fellowship in Switzerland in 1971 and 1972 and then earned a master's degree from Covenant Theological Seminary and did graduate work at the Institute for Christian Studies in Toronto. She is coauthor with Charles Thaxton of the book *The Soul of Science: Christian Faith and Natural Philosophy* and has contributed chapters to several other books, including *Mere Creation, Of Pandas and People,* and *Pro-Life Feminism.* Her articles have appeared in journals and magazines such as *First Things, Books and Culture, The World & I, The Family in America,* and *The Human Life Review.*

Pearcey is currently a fellow with the Discovery Institute's Center for the Renewal for Science and Culture, in Seattle, and managing editor of the journal *Origins and Design.* She is policy director of the Wilberforce Forum and executive editor of Colson's *BreakPoint,* a daily radio commentary program that analyzes current issues from a Christian worldview perspective. She is also coauthor with Colson of a monthly column in *Christianity Today.*

HOW NOW SHALL WE LIVE?

helps Christians make sense of the competing worldviews that clamor for attention and allegiance in a pluralistic society. Pulling no punches, Colson and Pearcey show that all other worldviews fail to meet the test of rational consistency or practical application in the real world. Only the Christian worldview provides a rationally sustainable way to understand the universe. Only the Christian worldview fits the real world and can be lived out consistently in every area of life.

Weaving together engaging stories with penetrating analysis of ideas, *How Now Shall We Live?* helps Christians defend their faith and live out its full implications in every arena—the home, workplace, classroom, courtroom, and public policy. It is a defining book for Christians in this new millennium.

Resources available from Tyndale House Publishers that support the message and ministry of How Now Shall We Live?

How Now Shall We Live?: cloth

How Now Shall We Live? Study Guide: paper
Two thirteen-week Bible lessons to help Bible study groups absorb and apply the concepts of Colson's magnum opus

How Now Shall We Live? Audio Book: The abridged version on four audiocassettes

Answers to Your Kids' Questions: A guide to help parents know how to talk to their kids about the worldview issues they face every day

Complete adult and youth video curriculum is available from LifeWay Church Resources.

Order by writing to LifeWay Church Resources Customer Service, MSN 113, 127 Ninth Avenue North, Nashville, TN 37211-0113; by calling toll free (800) 458-2772; by faxing (615) 251-5933; or by e-mailing customerservice@lifeway.com.

Look for other books and materials based on *How Now Shall We Live?* from Tyndale House Publishers.

Visit these Web sites for more information:

Charles Colson's books and tapes: chuckcolson.com

Breakpoint: breakpoint.org

Prison Fellowship Ministries: pfm.org

Other books by Tyndale House Publishers: tyndale.com

Addresses for more information:

Terry White
Communications Department
Prison Fellowship Ministries
P.O. Box 17500
Washington, DC 20041-0500

Public Relations
Tyndale House Publishers, Inc.
351 Executive Drive
Carol Stream, IL 60188
phone: (630) 668-8300
fax: (630) 668-3245

The content of this series is drawn from the major sections of *How Now Shall We Live?* Shorter in length, more acessible to readers, and with added questions, these books are ideal for group study. Each book will help readers engage Colson's ideas and learn how to apply them to the world around them.

Developing a Christian Worldview of Science and Evolution: paper

Developing a Christian Worldview of the Problem of Evil: paper

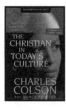
Developing a Christian Worldview of the Christian in Today's Culture: paper